INTRODUCTION TO COMPUTER-INTEGRATED MANUFACTURING

INTRODUCTION TO COMPUTER-INTEGRATED MANUFACTURING

Frank Greenwood
Central Michigan University

HARCOURT BRACE JOVANOVICH, PUBLISHERS
Technology Publications

San Diego   New York   Chicago   Austin   Washington, D.C.
London   Syndey   Tokyo   Toronto

Copyright © 1989 by Harcourt Brace Jovanovich, Inc.

All rights reserved. No part of this publication
may be reproduced or transmitted in any form or by
any means, electronic or mechanical, including
photocopy, recording, or any information storage or
retrieval system, without permission in writing from
the publisher.

Requests for permission to make copies of any part
of this work should be mailed to:
Permissions, Harcourt Brace Jovanovich, Publishers,
Orlando, Florida 32887.

ISBN 0-15-541627-8

Library of Congress Number 89-84378

Printed in the United States of America

To Heman Charles Greenwood

PREFACE

In the past decade, the federal government has outspent the country's gross national product and far exceeded its tax revenues. In so doing, the government delivered booming economic growth and low levels of unemployment, while producing monumental budget and trade deficits and an astronomical debt to foreign nations. Our business leaders must learn to survive and succeed in an increasingly competitive global marketplace. The key to that success is to make our businesses more competitive domestically and to reverse the rising trade deficit. Achieving this will require better decisions based on better information.

While useful information may be scattered, seemingly isolated bits can be integrated into manufacturing processes to reduce costs and time and to improve quality. Such integration of information with business acumen will provide a foundation for solid control and management.

Attaining and maximizing the benefits of these qualities is what computer-integrated manufacturing (CIM) is all about. CIM offers methods for establishing real-time control by a firm, while it supplies the critical information needed for well informed decision-making.

Computers and all the information they can assemble are not a solution in and of themselves. Computers are only as powerful as management is effective. Therefore, this book begins with a consideration of the management needed for a corporation to compete globally. The initial discussion is based on W. Edward Deming's ideas about what is required to create organizations that improve competitively as they raise quality and lower costs.

In order to improve a manufacturing system, we must first understand that system "statistically." We need to develop a precise, quantified image of the system's capabilities that will allow us to predict its performance. Then we must develop methods to control the variables that create that image—Statistical Process Control (SPC).

Having established management skills and their use through SPC, the book turns to Computer-Integrated Manufacturing (CIM) and a consideration of its major components: (1) Computer Assisted Design (CAD), (2) Local Area Networks or Manufacturing Automation Protocol (MAP), and (3) Robots and Artificial Intelligence (AI).

The book concludes with three chapters that bring together the discussions of management, control, and computer capabilities. Each of these chapters is designed to move the reader toward planning, implementing, and finally managing with CIM.

Finally, the author has prepared a number of case studies to augment some chapters. These are real cases about real companies engaged in today's global marketplace. Each case shows managers and organizations grappling with increasing competition, rising costs, and declining quality and productivity. Every case demonstrates some facet of how CIM can bring business challenges under control. The chapters that do not feature cases offer appendices on such topics as database, just-in-time inventory, and manufacturing resource planning. Chapter Eight provides a much-needed introduction to robots and to the potential uses of artificial intelligence. Summaries and review questions conclude each chapter. An instructor's manual will be available for adopters.

ACKNOWLEDGMENTS

Producing and marketing a book depends on many individuals—the purchasers, the retailers, the production people, the editors and all those who contributed to the manuscript. I would like to offer special thanks to The American Productivity and Quality Center, which allowed the case material to be used, and *Modern Machine Shop,* which allowed a reprinting of Charles M. Savage's "Preparing for the Factory of the Future." I also want to thank the reviewers who commented on this project from its conception through the completed manuscript: Professor Lawrence Aft of Southern College of Technology, Jim D. Horton of Central Piedmont Community College, and Professor Helen Webb of Lansing Community College. Their comments and evaluations were valuable contributions to the creation of a better textbook.

We are indebted to the Saginaw Division of General Motors Corporation for the cover photograph. Saginaw has pioneered many CIM procedures and has dedicated its management to quality.

Tally Morgan, of WordCrafters Editorial Services, Inc., production editor, guided the manuscript from printer page to printed page with expertise and rare professionalism. Many others helped create the manuscript and aided in bringing the words into type, but space will not allow them to be listed here. I sincerely thank them for their support and assistance.

CONTENTS

Chapter 1   MANUFACTURING REALLY MATTERS, 1

    Global Competition, 2
    What Can We Do?, 3
    What is CIM?, 4
    Old Stuff, New Technology, 4
    Implementation, 5
    This Book, 6
    Summary, 6
    Review Questions, 7
    References, 7
    Case Study: The Case for Manufacturing in America's Future, 8

Chapter 2   MANAGEMENT, QUALITY, AND COST, 15

    Guaspari on Quality, 16
    Lammi's Commandments, 17
    W. Edwards Deming, 17
    Traditional Management, 18
    Summary, 24
    Review Questions, 24
    References, 25
    Case Study: Integrating JIT, TQC, and EI: Success Through Executive Excellence, 26

Chapter 3   CONTINUOUS IMPROVEMENTS, 43

    Improving Processes, 44
    Planning, 47
    Process Variability, 48
    Inspection, 49
    Maintenance, 49
    A New Ballgame, 49
    Summary, 50
    Review Questions, 50

References, 51
Case Study: National Production Systems—Los Nietos—Implementing Armco's Corporate Quality Strategy at the Plant Level, 52

Chapter 4 STATISTICAL PROCESS CONTROL, 63

Variability, 66
Run Charts, 68
Control Charts, 70
$\overline{X}$ and R Charts, 72
P and nP Charts, 75
Conclusion, 76
Summary, 76
Review Questions, 77
References, 77
Case Study: Cutter Laboratories—Drive for Quality Fuels Participative Technical and Office Protocol, 101

Chapter 5 MANUFACTURING AUTOMATION PROTOCOL, 89

Open Systems Interconnection Model, 90
Local Area Networks, 94
Technical and Office Protocol, 101
Summary, 102
Review Questions, 103
References, 103
Case Study: The Town That Saved Itself, 104

Chapter 6 COMPUTER-AIDED DESIGN, 107

CAD Hardware, 109
CAD Software, 118
Summary, 123
Review Questions, 123
Case Study: Data Base Primer, 124

Chapter 7 NUMERICAL CONTROL, 127

Machine Centers, 130
Coordinates, 131

Programming, 133
NC Developments, 134
Just-In-Time Production, 135
Summary, 136
Review Questions, 136
References, 137
Case Study: Just-In-Time Inventory/Zero Inventory, 138

Chapter 8 ROBOTS AND ARTIFICIAL INTELLIGENCE, 151

Hardware, 154
Programming, 160
Artificial Intelligence, 162
Discussion, 163
Summary, 164
Review Questions, 164

Chapter 9 PROCESS PLANNING, 165

Traditional Process Planning, 166
Computer-Aided Process Planning, 168
Manufacturing Cells, 168
Automated Storage and Retrieval, 170
Automated Transportation, 171
Flexible Manufacturing Systems, 173
Computer-Aided Manufacturing, 174
Material Requirements Planning, 174
Summary, 174
Review Questions, 175
References, 175
Appendix: MRP Systems, 186

Chapter 10 FACTORY MANAGEMENT, 195

Manufacturing Costs, 196
Typical Manufacturing Problems, 198
Manufacturing Technology, 198
Factory Management, 199
Managing Change, 201
Summary, 205

Review Questions, 205
Case Study: Preparing for the Factory of the Future, 207

Chapter 11 COMPUTER-INTEGRATED MANUFACTURING, 235

What to Do, 237
Computer-Integrated Manufacturing, 240
Product Design, 243
Manufacturing, 244
Production Management, 245
Other Business Functions, 245
Summary, 246
Review Questions, 246
References, 247
Appendix: Making CIM Work, 248

Chapter 12 IMPLEMENTING CIM, 255

Stage 1: Introduction, 261
Stage 2: Preparation, 261
Stage 3: Program Plan, 264
Stage 4: Implementation, 265
Summary, 266
Review Questions, 266
References, 267
Appendix: The Impact of Computer Integrated Manufacturing, 268

Index, 281

Chapter One

MANUFACTURING REALLY MATTERS

After you have read this chapter, it will be clear to you that

- Manufacturing matters, and we cannot maintain our standard of living without it.
- Global competition requires that we have a better management philosophy and that we apply computer-integrated manufacturing (CIM).
- CIM is an operating philosophy aiming at greater efficiencies across the whole cycle of product design, manufacture, and marketing, thereby improving quality, productivity, and competitiveness.
- This book first considers the management ideas needed to support global competition (including statistical process control, SPC) and then turns to CIM's components, such as manufacturing automation protocol (MAP) and computer-aided design (CAD).

When America's electronics industry moved TV production offshore, it lost the know-how needed to develop and manufacture the next product, the video cassette recorder (VCR). Therefore, we do not make VCRs in the United States.

When we cannot compete in manufacturing, manufacturing jobs move offshore, as do related jobs such as design, engineering, accounting, and maintenance work. That we have trouble competing is suggested by

- Declining real wages
- Disappointing productivity increases
- Shrinking shares of export markets
- Huge trade deficits in manufactured goods.

The next section presents one scenario illustrating global competition.

GLOBAL COMPETITION

Imagine you are a foreign manufacturer and want to make a place for yourself in American markets. First, identify a high-volume product offering limited options and having firm markets. Be certain its production processes are entrenched. Then, examine the entire production system in detail. You won't find one big problem, rather, there will be weaknesses across all areas of activity. Examples include obsolete machinery, quality subordinated to meeting demand, increasing costs absorbed by raising prices (rather than by improving productivity), and concentration on short-term payback instead of on long-term investment.

Next, create a production system that eliminates these inefficiencies. You can upgrade the entire production process, and you don't need advanced technologies. With these production improvements and investments, ease yourself into US markets. When your success creates the threat of protectionism, move the final assembly to the United States (using American resources to help you get started).

The results of this process are illustrated by the Fremont, California, plant that General Motors (GM) now owns as a joint venture with Toyota. When GM ran the plant, there were about 5000 workers assembling about 240,000 cars a year. Absenteeism was about 20 percent, wildcat strikes occurred, and there were thousands of outstanding grievances.

Japanese managers now use the same plant, labor force, and dated technology to assemble Chevrolet Novas. The same number of cars is built with half the original number of employees. In other words, the plant has the same workers, the same building, the same technology, and the same volume—but different management and a different production system.

US manufacturing emerged from World War II as the heavyweight champ. But we became fat, dumb, and complacent. Our world market share dropped in electronics, automobiles, wide-body jets, and steel. The marketplace reminds us that manufacturing matters and that we cannot maintain our industrial base and our standard of living without it. When we do not run plants using our key technologies, we lose our ability to compete in these technologies.

American wealth and power depend upon manufacturing. Moving offshore to obtain cheap labor gives away the manufacturing advantage. The only workable answer is to use our skilled labor together with our advanced technology to create high-wage, high-productivity, flexible manufacturing. Our standard of living depends on it.

WHAT CAN WE DO?

Customer demands and competitive pressures typify manufacturing. Costs, quality, delivery schedules, and inventory control are traditional problems. Traditional solutions include hiring additional people, building more inventory, and extending lead times.

That was the old environment. Now, delivery times are shorter, market conditions change faster, product modifications are more frequent, and customers expect greater responsiveness. Business survival is in jeopardy, and customary fixes won't do.

American manufacturers have two weapons. First, change the way we do things. Our competitors are committed to thorough training and to participative management. They have few management layers, and they place decision making at as low a level as possible. These ideas are discussed in Chapter 2.

The second weapon is technology. Computer-integrated manufacturing helps factories survive. Computer-aided design creates the product on a video screen, computer-aided engineering analyzes it for performance and producibility, and computer-aided manufacturing automates the shop floor processes. The result is faster, cheaper, and better production.

Computer-integrated manufacturing automates the flow of information through the factory, reducing many costs such as direct and indirect labor and overhead. Robots don't become careless, so quality control is cheaper. Lead time can be slashed. CIM factories thus have lower break-even points (e.g., 30 percent of capacity versus about 65 percent in conventional plants).

We cannot maintain our industrial base and standard of living without an efficient manufacturing industry. Inflation is down, interest rates have dropped, and energy prices have skidded, but many businesses aren't picking up. Many won't until our manufacturing sector becomes more productive.

At the bottom of the recent recession, the chief executive officer (CEO) of an auto manufacturer protested to his financial vice-president (VP) that the finance function had not warned the organization. The VP reminded the CEO of several presentations that had forecasted the recession, and the CEO's reply was, "Yes, but you didn't pound the table!"

Similarly, what we are presenting is more than conversation. We are saying that business survival compels the adoption of a single business system (CIM) upon which the whole organization collectively focuses.

We have to remain competitive across the cycle of product design, manufacturing, and marketing, and we must be productive and responsive throughout head-

4 MANUFACTURING REALLY MATTERS

EXHIBIT 1-1 Some Automation Islands

Computer-assisted design (CAD)
Computer-assisted engineering (CAE)
Computer-assisted manufacturing (CAM)
Manufacturing resource planning (MRP)
Just-in-time (JIT)
Flexible manufacturing system (FMS)
Numerically controlled tools (NC)
Manufacturing automation protocol (MAP)

quarters, factories, and sales branches. The business strategy needed for this is CIM. Focusing collectively on a single system (CIM) benefits the entire organization. For example,

- Office and factory productivity increase.
- Engineering and design costs drop.
- Product quality is better.
- Customer satisfaction improves.
- Employee morale is higher.

WHAT IS CIM?

CIM is a strategic thrust, an operating philosophy. Its objective is to achieve greater efficiencies within the entire business, across the whole cycle of product design, manufacture, and marketing.

Today's typical firm has islands of automation, such as manufacturing resource planning, office automation, computerized market forecasting, and its general ledger system (see Exhibit 1-1). Huge manual efforts and paperwork systems keep the islands from sinking. CIM digitally links these islands, providing fast, accurate, consistent on-line data. CIM thereby cuts costs, raises quality, reduces response times, and improves white-collar productivity.

It takes 4 to 6 years to begin to realize CIM. There is no "one way." A firm with high-priced customized products will proceed in one fashion, and a company manufacturing low-priced standard products will implement it in another way. Again, CIM is a business strategy which refocuses existing and new computerized applications, thereby sharing the combined assets of information networks.

OLD STUFF, NEW TECHNOLOGY

This is, indeed, old stuff. What is new is that the technologies are now cheap and powerful enough and that many organizational cultures are now open to this strategy.

Charles Babbage developed the concept of the modern computer in the early 1800s. But the steam power, pulleys, and levers that characterized his technology could not support its implementation. Similarly, in the early 1960s, the author re-

EXHIBIT 1-2 **Management Cycle for CIM.** [from *Management Guide for CIM* (Dearborn, MI: SME, 1986), p. 11.]

Stage 1: Introduction
    a. Concepts of a CIM business strategy
    b. Managers' roles
    c. Creating interest in CIM
    d. Developing the climate for a CIM initiative

Stage 2: Preparation
    a. Forming a study team for CIM
    b. CIM opportunity candidates
    c. Conceptualizing CIM way of operating

Stage 3: Program plan
    a. Proposal development
    b. Selling proposal
    c. Program commitment

Stage 4: Implementation
    a. Managing the implementation
    b. Measuring and evaluating results
    c. Moving to next opportunity
    d. Sharing experience and expertise

members a management information systems (MIS) director of a large division of an aerospace firm who struggled for several years to implement what we now call CIM. He failed and was fired. Neither the technologies nor the culture were advanced enough to support it. A quarter-century later, the whole thing is finally coming together: hardware, software, communications, costs, and attitudes.

IMPLEMENTATION

Few readers will be surprised by the implementation suggestions for the CIM strategic thrust (see Exhibit 1-2):

- Introduction of the CIM business strategy
- Preparation for developing the necessary expertise
- Development of a specific program plan
- Implementation of CIM.

In sum, CIM improves product quality, productivity, and competitiveness, and there is a real need for these improvements. A revitalized manufacturing company provides stimulating, challenging jobs. By becoming more competitive, such a company needs more services: education, health care, travel, and so on.

Manufacturing and services are mutually dependent. Manufacturers support services such as banking, communication, and software, and services help manufacturers compete. Strengthening our manufacturing sector maintains America's industrial base and our standard of living.

THIS BOOK

This book first considers the management needed to compete globally. W. Edwards Deming's ideas typify what is required to create organizations that raise quality and lower costs as these firms constantly improve.

In order to improve a process, such as a manufacturing system, we need to place it under statistical control so that we know its capabilities and can predict its performance. This is why statistical process control is important.

After discussing management needs and statistical process control, we turn to computer-integrated manufacturing. CIM's components are considered, such as computer-assisted design, local area networks (manufacturing automation protocol), and just-in-time (JIT) shipments of materials.

The reasons manufacturing matters are that it directly accounts for almost 25 percent of our gross national product (GNP) and that it indirectly impacts another 40 to 50 percent. Accordingly, our ability to compete in manufacturing largely determines our standard of living. This remains true notwithstanding frequent observations that America is now a service economy.

CASE STUDY

After reading "The Case for Manufacturing in America's Future," immediately following this chapter, write a brief explanation of why you agree (or do not agree) with its recommendations (i.e., fiscal policy, etc.).

SUMMARY

1. Manufacturing matters, and we cannot maintain our industrial base and our standard of living without it.
2. We now face intense global competition, which means American companies must either meet this challenge or disappear.
3. American manufacturers have two weapons: better management and technology.
4. Computer-integrated manufacturing automates the flow of information through a factory, reducing many costs such as those for direct and indirect labor and overhead. CIM factories have lower break-even points than conventional plants.
5. CIM is an operating philosophy that aims at greater efficiencies across the whole cycle of product design, manufacture, and marketing.
6. Manufacturing technologies are now cheap and powerful enough, and many organizational cultures are open to CIM.
7. This book first considers managing in the intense global competition we now face (discussing the help available from statistical process control) and then turns to CIM (e.g., manufacturing automation protocol and computer-aided design).

REVIEW QUESTIONS

1. What are some probable results when manufacturing jobs move offshore?
2. What evidence can you think of supporting the idea that American manufacturers have problems competing?
3. If you were a foreign manufacturer, how would you make a place for yourself in American markets?
4. What competitive weapons are available to us?
5. Define CIM and explain it.
6. How does one implement CIM?
7. Why is statistical process control important?
8. GM and Toyota jointly own a factory in Fremont, California. What do you infer from its operating results?
9. The American economy is now mostly a service economy, so manufacturing doesn't matter. Comment.
10. Does it matter whether America can compete globally? Why?
11. This chapter refers to "islands of automation." What is this concept and why does it matter?

REFERENCES

1. *Management Guide for CIM* (Dearborn, Mich.: Society of Manufaturing Engineers, 1986), p. 97.
2. "Making the Leap Into the Factory of Tomorrow," *Industry Week,* May 26, 1986, p. 41.
3. "High Tech to the Rescue," *Business Week,* June 16, 1986.
4. S. S. Cohen and J. Zysman, *Manufacturing Matters* (New York: Basic Books, 1987), p. 297.
5. F. Greenwood and M. M. Greenwood, "CIM and You," *Journal of Systems Management,* June 1987, p. 41. Much of this chapter has been taken from this article.

Appendix
THE CASE FOR MANUFACTURING IN AMERICA'S FUTURE*

Rudiger W. Dornbusch
James Poterba
Lawrence H. Summers
with a foreword by
Colby H. Chandler
1988

Manufacturing and the Economy: A Future Intertwined

In the first half of the decade, the United States conducted an experiment in national economic policy which brought both great benefit and great harm to the U.S. economy. Inflation, which seemed out of control in the 1970's, was tamed, and we have experienced the longest peacetime expansion of this century.

These gains, however, were achieved at substantial cost, since we have run the largest budget and trade deficits in our history. These deficits fundamentally altered America's position in the world. Where we were the world's largest creditor, we are now dependent on foreign financing and are its largest debtor.

At the time these policies were being implemented, American manufacturers failed to appreciate how such measures would affect our ability to do business. The toll has been very high. As our competitiveness plummeted, in large measure due to an overvalued dollar, domestic and world markets were ceded to others.

To be sure, there was a silver lining in this difficult period for manufacturers. It forced many of us to make substantial internal adjustments which in many cases had been needed for some time.

As a consequence of our efforts, and a more realistically valued dollar, American manufacturing is doing better. At the same time, this recovery is built on a very fragile base—an economic house of cards.

This report is a summary of an in-depth study commissioned by Eastman Kodak Company to examine economic policy issues from the independent perspective of three leading economists. The study grew out of a concern about the perception that our country is entering a post-industrial, service-based economy, a trend believed by some to be both inevitable and desirable. This report shows it is neither.

*Reprinted courtesy of Eastman Kodak.

The study documents that a strong manufacturing sector is essential to the health of the overall economy and our future standard of living. It also shows that, relative to manufacturing in other industrial countries, U.S. manufacturing is not faring well and could be doing better if appropriate policies were in place.

We need an informed debate in the country about the direction of economic policy over the next several years. We face hard choices and difficult adjustments. This report should add to this essential debate.

Colby H. Chandler

*Chairman and
Chief Executive Officer
Eastman Kodak Company*

MANUFACTURING: SPURRING TECHNICAL PROGRESS

The manufacturing sector is crucial to technical innovation. While manufacturing accounts for about one-fifth of annual gross domestic product, it performs 95 percent of private research development. Manufacturing firms spend an average of nine percent of their revenues on research and development, compared to less than one-tenth of one percent for non-manufacturing firms.

Investment in technology has contributed to higher productivity in manufacturing. The productivity growth rate for manufacturing has averaged 3.5 percent since 1970, while non-manufacturing has managed only a 0.3 percent growth rate.

America's performance in world markets depends upon the technological innovation of manufacturing companies.

The Importance of Manufacturing to Research & Development

	Manufacturing	*Non-Manufacturing*
R&D Expenditures ($ billion, 1984)	69.0	2.6
R&D/Employee ($ thousands, 1984)	3.610	.035

Source: National Science Foundation, Bureau of Labor Statistics.

MANUFACTURING: BETTER WAGES

Men and women in manufacturing consistently earn greater than 20 percent more than those employed in non-manufacturing jobs, and nearly 30 percent more than employees in the service sector.

Manufacturing firms pay employees better for several key reasons. First, the integrated nature of production puts a premium on a stable and motivated workforce—a workforce maintained by top pay and benefits. Second, advanced skills are required in many manufacturing jobs, justifying higher wages. Third, greater productivity in manufacturing may enable firms to pay more.

High-wage jobs and a higher standard of living are more likely to result from expansion of the manufacturing sector than from expansion of other sectors.

Hourly Compensation in Manufacturing and Other Sectors (1986 $ per hour)

	Manufacturing	Services	Trade	Total Non-Manufacturing
1950–86	$12.26	8.47	9.72	8.85
1987 (March)	$14.79	11.73	9.51	12.08

Source: Department of Commerce, Bureau of Labor Statistics.

MANUFACTURING: DRIVING OVERALL GROWTH

Manufacturing is a powerful source of demand for the output of other industries. In 1986, manufacturing directly contributed over one-fifth of America's gross national product, yet shipments by manufacturing companies equalled almost 60 percent of the GNP. The difference, equaling nearly 40 percent of the GNP, reveals the extent of manufacturing's purchases from other sectors of the economy.

Ironically, many services that are featured in "post-industrial economy" scenarios depend on the demand created by manufacturing. Education, banking and communications are among the services for which manufacturing provides a significant portion of the demand.

Unemployment rates offer another striking example of manufacturing's tight bond to the overall economy. A rise in manufacturing unemployment of one percentage point results in unemployment increases of 3.2 percent in construction, 2.4 percent in service and 1.5 percent in retail trade. When manufacturing suffers, so does the rest of the economy.

Spillover Effects of Manufacturing Unemployment

Sector	Increase in Sector Unemployment Rate from One Point of Manufacturing Unemployment
Construction	3.2
Wholesale Trade	1.4
Retail Trade	1.5
Finance, Insurance, Real Estate	0.7
Services	2.4
Professional	−0.1
Government	1.0
Weighted Sum	2.0

Source: Kevin J. Murphy and Robert Topel, "Unemployment in the United States," in *NBER Macroeconomics Manual, 1987.* Stanley Fischer, ed.

MANUFACTURING: DRAMATICALLY IMPACTED BY CHANGES IN THE U.S. ECONOMY

The peaks and troughs of American business cycles are amplified in the manufacturing sector. During expansions, manufacturing output increases about 26 percent, while non-manufacturing output increases just 16 percent. During downturns, manufacturing output typically declines about 7 percent, compared to a 1 percent decline for non-manufacturing.

Manufacturing also bears the brunt of trade imbalances created by economic policies. Manufacturing trade dwarfs trade in services. Thus, the trade deficits in recent years are accounted for almost entirely by a shift in the manufacturing trade balance.

Fluctuations in defense spending also dramatically affect manufacturing. The U.S. defense build-up has greatly helped many manufacturing firms. Nearly 60 percent of all private jobs generated by defense spending are in manufacturing firms. Between 1980 and 1986, when manufacturing jobs shrank by 1.29 million, defense-related jobs actually increased by .74 million. Without this build-up, manufacturing employment in 1987 would have been at its lowest level since 1965. While future levels of defense spending are not established, it seems clear that the major jobs stimulus of increased defense spending has passed. Thus, alternatives for growth in manufacturing jobs will need to be created.

Percentage Change in Output, Manufacturing and Non-Manufacturing

	Manufacturing	*Non-Manufacturing*
Economic Upturns:		
1954 to 1957	12.1%	8.6%
1958 to 1960	11.6%	7.3%
1961 to 1969	58.1%	37.8%
1970 to 1973	22.6%	10.5%
1975 to 1980	21.5%	16.4%
1982 to 1986	28.0%	15.8%
Economic Downturns:		
1953 to 1954	7.3%	0.3%
1957 to 1958	− 8.7%	1.6%
1960 to 1961	0.2%	3.2%
1969 to 1970	− 5.6%	1.2%
1973 to 1975	−11.9%	1.3%
1981 to 1982	− 6.1%	− 1.5%

Source: Commerce Department. Turning point years based on National Bureau of Economic Research dating of business cycle.

MANUFACTURING: HOW DOES THE U.S. COMPARE?

American manufacturers in many industrial sectors have lost market share at home and in export markets. While manufacturing in many other countries has enjoyed substantial growth, the manufacturing contribution to the U.S. economy has been stagnant and U.S. manufacturing jobs have declined.

The loss of markets is clearly seen in the world trade picture. In a recent 15-year period, U.S. exports grew at an annual rate three percent below that of other industrialized nations. Over such an extended period, that difference becomes substantial. Electronic goods offer a typical example of the declines. Between 1979 and 1985, the U.S. share of exports dropped by 6.3 percent in electronic parts, 4.3 percent in automatic processing equipment and 2.8 percent in business electronics, figures the translate into billions of dollars of lost business.

The relative decline of U.S. manufacturing is due in part to a lower rate of manufacturing productivity than other nations. Between 1960 and 1979, U.S. productivity grew at one-third the rate in Japan. Lower productivity growth hampers cost competitiveness and facilitates greater market penetration by foreign producers. A particularly startling example is provided by the capital goods market, where imports today account for nearly 40 percent of the U.S. market, versus 14 percent as recently as 1980.

If the U.S. continues to yield markets abroad and our own markets to foreign suppliers, the country's standard of living will markedly decline. The notion that this decline is inevitable or desirable must be firmly rejected.

Volume of Manufacturer's Exports (Index 1980 = 100)

	1970	1980	1986	*Avg. Growth Rate 1970–86 (%)*
U.S.	49	100	81	3.2
Japan	39	100	142	8.4
Europe	56	100	124	5.0
Developing Countries	30	100	184	12.0
World Exports	51	100	129	6.0

Source: United Nations.

SUMMARY: RECOMMENDATIONS FOR A HEALTHY ECONOMIC FUTURE

The primary reason for the difficulties of American manufacturers is national economic policies that have given rise to huge budget and trade deficits, favored consumption over saving and investment and been insufficiently sensitive to the need for free markets at home and abroad. Following are policy recommendations for each of these areas.

Fiscal Policy

Reduce federal deficits Federal deficit reduction should be the overriding priority of national economic policy. Over two-thirds of private saving in recent years has been absorbed by these deficits. Low national saving reduces the supply and increases the cost of capital, choking off investment needed to increase productivity in manufacturing. Reducing federal deficits will require spending cuts and tax increases. Cuts must be considered in all areas of the budget.

Encourage savings and investment Structural tax policies should be redirected towards the goals of promoting saving and investment rather than consumption. A crucial long-run policy priority is finding ways to raise the anemic American private saving rate.

Structural Trade Policies

Stop the trend toward protectionism U.S. restrictions on trade are increasing faster than those of any other industrialized country—and at a time when such restrictions are most damaging. While an individual firm or industrial sector competing against imports may temporarily benefit from protectionism, manufacturing and the economy in general suffer. For its temporary benefits, protectionism is very expensive, since costs increase for intermediate goods required by manufacturers and for goods sold to consumers. Further, retaliation is likely and foreign markets may close to successful exporters. Even without retaliation, protectionism would strengthen the dollar and hurt exports.

Realize the opportunities of newly industrialized countries (NICs) U.S. manufacturing must realize the opportunities of, rather than seek protection from, the growing role of NICs as competitive production centers. The U.S. must consider bilateral free trade agreements with major NICs like Mexico, Brazil and Korea, where large but mostly protected new markets are emerging. This approach would put the U.S. ahead of Japanese firms who are now entering these markets, offset the increasingly inward focus of the European market, and offer more leeway in convincing the developing countries that trade is a two-way street.

Remain open to direct foreign investment in the U.S. An outward-looking manufacturing sector must hold an open view of foreign investment in the U.S. Foreign investment means competition for managers, but it also means good jobs and increased manufacturing activity. Foreign investment is likely to benefit the economy, even though in some cases it might hurt entrenched American firms.

Exchange Rate Policy

Efforts to stabilize exchange rates at current levels are misguided They run very serious risks of throwing the economy into recession and making an eventual financial collapse more likely. American monetary policy should be directed at insuring continued economic growth as the budget deficit declines, not at arbitrary exchange rate targets. Policy-makers should take a "hands-off" approach, recognizing that a continued dollar decline is both likely and desirable to allow the economy to make a "soft landing."

Rapid growth in the world economy and the expanding markets that it brings about are crucial to the health of the manufacturing sector Easing monetary policy to sustain growth in the face of budget cuts assures that part of the adjustment takes place via dollar depreciation and net exports. Other nations should be encouraged to stimulate their domestic demand, instead of relying on exports to the U.S. for growth.

Chapter Two

MANAGEMENT, QUALITY, AND COST

After you have read this chapter, it will be clear to you that

- ❏ Quality means meeting customers' expectations.
- ❏ Most of us do the best we can most of the time, so telling us to work harder and do better is contraproductive.
- ❏ Quality cannot be inspected into a product but must be built in every step of the way—from design to aftersale relationships.
- ❏ Ray Lammi has a list of quality commandments.
- ❏ A management developed by W. Edwards Deming (which he tested in Japan for 30 years) can help cut costs while raising quality.
- ❏ Traditional management ideas are obsolete.
- ❏ Based on Deming's method we can raise quality and productivity while lowering costs.

As you hand your check to a salesperson, you imagine how a product (or service) will make you feel. From the selling side, the purpose is to help you, the customer, experience good feelings about what you have bought and about yourself.

The customer determines quality by asking, "Does the product do what I expect it to do?" You, the customer, are the expert on quality. You are paying a supplier to determine what you expect and to do whatever is needed to meet your requirements. As far as you are concerned, his or her specifications and tolerances are irrelevant. You decide how you feel about the product. The manufacturer's job is to translate your expectations into specs and tolerances.

So what do you do when your profits and market share fall because of quality problems? How about

- Slogans and targets? Most of us do the best we can most of the time. When we do not, it is usually beyond our control (i.e., in management's hands). Slogans such as Work harder! and Do better! hurt morale and do not deal with the source of the problem (for which only management has the solution).
- More inspections? Adding inspections raises costs and reduces quality. "If it's her job, let her find and fix the defectives. I'm not going to sweat it."

GUASPARI ON QUALITY

If slogans, quotas, and inspection won't work, what will? Here are some ideas from John Guaspari,[1] an authority on quality:

1. *Quality is a matter of survival.* Above all, I'm certain of this. Sometimes people get caught up with all kinds of fuzzy, abstract "Quality is a warm puppy" notions. That's wrong. Quality is profit and productivity and market share. And that's no warm puppy.
2. *Quality may not be free, but it's a lot less expensive than the alternatives.* I never would have believed we could spend so much time and money trying to fix our Quality problems. It would have been a whole lot cheaper had we not had those problems in the first place.
3. *Quality is everyone's job. But it's management's responsibility.* Management's job is to lead. Leadership requires two things: movement and followers. And the movement has to come first.
4. *Most Quality problems are built into The System.* People want to do high-quality work. And they will if The System will let them. That's where management's movement has to go: toward improving The System.
5. *The first step toward improving The System is to get good data about what needs fixing.* Before you can make something good, you have to know what's bad. And the people who are in the best position to have such data are the people with their hands right on the process—the people we used to think of only as inspectors.
6. *The second step toward improving The System is moving from an Inspection mind-set to a Prevention mind-set.* In item 2, I said that Quality is a

lot less expensive than the alternatives. Well, it's sure a lot less expensive to prevent defects from occurring in the first place than to have some people making them, others finding them, and others fixing them.*

LAMMI'S COMMANDMENTS

Ray Lammi is a director of GOAL/QPC, of Methuen, MA, a national leader in making the United States more competitive by improving quality. The quality gospel, according to Lammi, includes these commandments:

1. Thou shalt cease dependence on mass inspection.
2. Thou shalt not award business to vendors on price alone.
3. Thou shalt use statistical methods to improve the system.
4. Thou shalt provide training for all jobs.
5. Thou shalt improve supervision to become responsible for quality.
6. Thou shalt drive out fear and encourage recommendations.
7. Thou shalt work together with other departments.
8. Thou shalt stop demands for higher levels of production through new goals, posters, or slogans without evidence of how to do it.
9. Thou shalt remove barriers that prevent workers from having pride of workmanship.
10. Thou shalt not accept a system of continuing rejects and reworks.

W. EDWARDS DEMING

World War II devastated the major economies—except ours. For years we enjoyed a sellers' market. No more. The Hyundais and Toyotas in the parking lots and the Sonys on our TV stands evidence the new, very competitive world.

W. Edwards Deming helped the Japanese move from the devastation of Hiroshima and Nagasaki to the devastation of our rust bowl. Deming states that the path to wisdom is understanding the difference between a stable system and an unstable one. A stable system has a predictable performance. It is attained by removing special causes of trouble, one at a time (detected by statistical signals).

The responsibility for improving a stable system is management's. Deming says stable systems are not improved by annual appraisals, by management by objective (MBO) or by managing with visible figures alone. They are improved by earning the full cooperation of the workers. The workers are needed not only to get out the product but also to improve the system. They are intelligent people who know how to raise quality while lowering costs.

The bottom line of Deming's approach is that raising quality lowers costs. In other words, the highest-quality producer will have the lowest costs. This concept

---

*Reprinted by permission of the publisher, from I KNOW IT WHEN I SEE IT, pp. 65-66 © John Guaspari. Published by AMACOM, a division of American Management Association, New York. All rights reserved.

> **FIGURE 2-1** A Message from the East: Matsushita on Participation in Management
>
> We are going to win and the industrial west is going to lose out; there's nothing much you can do about it, because the reasons for your failure are within yourselves.
>
> Your firms are built on the Taylor model; even worse, so are your heads. With your bosses doing the thinking while the workers wield the screwdrivers, you're convinced deep down that this is the right way to run a business.
>
> For you, the essence of management is getting the ideas out of the heads of the bosses into the hands of labor.
>
> We are beyond the Taylor model: business, we know, is now so complex and difficult, the survival of firms so hazardous in an environment increasingly unpredictable, competitive and fraught with danger, that their continued existence depends on the day-to-day mobilization of every ounce of intelligence.
>
> For us, the core of management is precisely this art of mobilizing and pulling together the intellectual resources of all employees in the service of the firm. Because we have measured better than you the scope of the new technological and economic challenges, we know that the intelligence of a handful of technocrats, however brilliant and smart they may be, is no longer enough to take them up with a real chance of success.
>
> Only by drawing on the combined brain power of all its employees can a firm face up to the turbulence and constraints of today's environment.
>
> That is why our large companies give their employees three to four times more training than yours, this is why they foster within the firm such intensive exchange and communication; this is why they seek constantly everybody's suggestions and why they demand from the educational system increasing numbers of graduates as well as bright and well-educated generalists, because these people are the lifeblood of industry.
>
> Your "socially-minded bosses," often full of good intentions, believe their duty is to protect the people in their firms. We, on the other hand, are realists and consider it our duty to get our people to defend their firms which will pay them back a hundredfold for their dedication. By doing this, we end up by being more "social" than you.
>
> In 1979 Mr. Konusuke Matsushita of Matsushita Electric Industrial Co., Ltd. spoke to a group of U.S. businessmen about why Japanese companies have taken the world leadership in business. Matsushita Electric is the largest consumer electronics company in the world. In the United States it markets the brandnames Panasonic, Technics, and Quasar.

turns traditional thinking upside down. Nevertheless, Deming demonstrated its accuracy over 30 years in Japan, a country about the size of California with a population half that of the United States. Japanese producers evidenced its accuracy by battering American industries, such as cars, electronics, and machine tools. See Figure 2-1.

TRADITIONAL MANAGEMENT

Deming developed an entirely new concept of how to manage systems of machines and people. Before we explore his ideas, let's review the traditional definition of management.

Humanity has learned much about management over the centuries: Empires rose or fell, armies conquered or were vanquished, and commercial enterprises prospered or failed. Unfortunately, most of this experience was not documented.

About the time of World War I, a French mining engineer, Henri Fayol,[2] published a book defining management. It reflected his experience in taking over an almost bankrupt steel manufacturing company and converting it into a prosperous, integrated firm.

His book was translated into English and became available in the United States. Americans took so well to his management approach that many books are now based on Fayol's theory. The following definition of management is from these books.[3]

Universal concepts in management are equally applicable to commercial, religious, and governmental organizations. (Business management differs from the others mainly in that the profit realized on invested capital is, for many, the most important measure of managerial ability.)

Because of physical and mental limitations, people must cooperate to achieve their goals. The skill of management is basic to this cooperation. The job of management is to get things done through others. In other words, management is the accomplishment of desired objectives by establishing an environment favorable to efficient performance by people operating in organized groups.

Therefore, the subject of management is people, and not technology, facilities, finance, or anything else.

The managerial job is similar at all levels of an organization and in all organizations when the individual is acting as a manager (e.g., when you are selling, you are not managing). The managerial job differs from that of the nonmanager because a manager is responsible for synchronizing the efforts achieved by subordinates.

The manager achieves a coordinated effort reaching toward the goals of the enterprise by planning, organizing, staffing, directing, and controlling the activities of others. The essence of management is coordinating the activities of people, and it is achieved by means of the five functions defined here.

> *Planning* is the function of selecting the objectives of the enterprise and the policies, programs, and procedures for achieving them.
>
> *Organizing* is the function of determining and enumerating the activities required to achieve the objectives of the enterprise, grouping these activities, assigning such groups of activities to a department headed by a manager, and delegating authority to carry them out.
>
> *Staffing* is the function comprising activities that are essential in manning, and in keeping manned, the positions provided for by the organization's structure.
>
> *Directing* is the executive function embracing activities related to guiding and supervising subordinates.
>
> *Controlling* is measuring and correcting the performance of subordinates in order to make sure that the objectives of the enterprise and the plans devised for attaining them are accomplished.

As a manger you are responsible for the performance turned in by your part of the organization. You must therefore have the authority to require that subordinates conform to decisions. Authority makes your position real. But it must be used very carefully, only as a last resort, in fact. Selling and persuading are the first choices.

Although this is a somewhat sketchy but reasonably usable definition of management, we must keep in mind that management will always be primarily an art, because the subject of management is people. There is no substitute for managerial experience.

The person who understands that management is this distinct kind of work will, however, probably understand his or her job better and improve his or her performance.

Management is getting things done through other people. Its essence is coordination, which is achieved by planning, organizing, staffing, directing, and controlling the activities of people. Coordination is accomplished with information: information about what is planned, who is supposed to do which job, how actual performance compares to the budget, and so on. The core of management is coordination, which is realized by means of information.

The Traditional Manager[4]

Consider a trucking firm managed by a man educated according to current management methods taught in our schools of business management. He will consider his job to be to run the company as profitably as he can and to expand its business. To do so he may call on the best consultants he can get to help him design the best possible system. He may set up work standards for the drivers and institute computer-based procedures to keep track of the performance of the drivers, trucks, and dispatchers. He will study his markets and their opportunities. And he will keep extensive records of income and expenses, ever on the alert for opportunities to profit.

Of course, he will not be able to do these things alone, and as his organization grows, he will institute methods to see that his desires for efficiency and performance are carried out. Perhaps he will adopt management by objectives and teach it to his subordinates. He may assign as much as 5 percent of his work force to data gathering and performance monitoring, ever searching for possible profit opportunities.

In short, his idea of a good manager is one who sets up a system, directs the work through subordinates, and by making crisp and unambiguous assignments develops a basis to set standards of performance for his employees. He sets goals and production targets for his people. He rates the employees as objectively as he can, sometimes even calling on consultants to help him do so. He identifies poor performers and gives them further education to meet the work standards, or he replaces them. He hopes thereby to create the most efficient system possible.

What Is Deming's Way?

Contrast this with the behavior of a manager who follows Deming's way. This manager sees his job as requiring him to provide a consistency and continuity of purpose for his organization and to seek ever more efficient ways to meet its purpose. For him, making a profit is necessary for survival but is by no means the main purpose of his organization. His view of the purpose of his organization is to provide the best and least-cost transportation system for his customers and continuity of employment for his workers. He does not view the concepts of "best" and "least-cost" as contradictory.

He will consider that he and the workers have a natural divsion of labor. They are responsible for doing the work within the system, and he is responsible for improving the system. However, he realizes that the potentials for improving the system are never ending so he does not call on consultants to teach him how to redesign the "best" system for he knows that it doesn't exist. Any system can be continuously improved on. He knows that the only people who really know where the potentials for improvement lie are the workers themselves. He knows that the system is subject to great variability. Traffic conditions change, trucks break down, shipping docks are not always ready to discharge or receive goods, mistakes are made in routing or addressing. There are countless ways for the system to go wrong and out of control, decreasing quality and increasing cost. He knows that these ways occur randomly. To make it possible for him and the workers to work together, he knows they must regard the system in the same way and speak a common language. Therefore he learns elementary statistics and teaches it to the workers, engaging an expert consultant in statistics if necessary to help him and the workers when they come to a problem beyond elementary statistics. All of his employees learn to keep their own statistics. Truck drivers keep track of how long they have to wait at docks and study the circumstances at each event. They develop their own control charts and look for trends, for correlations with other events, usually events beyond their control. The drivers meet with each other and sometimes with the dispatcher and compare notes. They keep data on the performance of their trucks and discuss their statistical charts with the purchasing agent and each other. Based on these data the manager, who is responsible for the system, makes the changes, and the workers, based on their statistical information, help him to learn how effective the changes have been. When the manager instructs the purchasing agent to buy on "quality," not just on first cost, the purchasing agent has the information from the drivers with which to do just that, and to demonstrate that he has done so. Everyone spends about 5 percent of their time in this pursuit. No one spends 100 percent of the time, except the company statisticians. The employees will see the setting of work standards as a dumb idea since it inhibits their ability to improve the system. They will not need to "manage by objectives" because they will be engaged in consistently redefining their objectives themselves and recording the performance of the system.

The workers and the manager will be aware of the results reported by Juran—that in most systems 80 to 85 percent of the problems are with the system and 15 to 20 percent are with the worker. This is an important understanding, for it can free the workers to speak out without fear, a quality of the work place that the manager assiduously cultivates.

Under Deming's way, the manager understands that he needs the workers not only to do the work but to help him to improve the system. Thus he will not regard them simply as robots made of flesh and bone, but he will rather consider them as thinking, creative human beings. No one will have to teach him to be nice to people. He will not try to motivate them with empty slogans, such as "Zero Defects!" Because they will be measuring and counting the defects themselves and helping him to remove them, there will be no need for the slogans. He will not ask them to sign pledges to be polite to customers. Nor will he select the "Polite Trucker of the Week." Instead, he and they will have been studying the records of repeat orders and asking what they can do to improve the statistics.

From time to time he asks for volunteers from his work force to take time out to interview customers and vendors, to understand what they want or can supply to provide better service. They report back to him and the rest of the work force on what they have found, statistically analyzed.

In short, the Deming-trained manager will have a natural basis for building a team and will not have introduced adversarial relations.

Under currently taught methods of management it is presumed that the relation between boss and worker is inherently adversarial. The result is that bosses who wish to fit the understood image must be careful not to develop too intimate a relationship to the worker, lest they lose their objectivity in judging and rewarding performance. (Recall the restrictions on officers in the military against mixing socially with the enlisted men. This is probably a good idea for a system in which no one is supposed to propose improvements!) Under Deming's way the boss and worker work together naturally and can even afford to like each other!

Deming's way is therefore more than just attention to quality control. It is a managerial philosophy for achieving lower cost and higher quality. And it works not only in the factory, but in hospitals, in service industries, and even in the office.

It is in seeing how a changed managerial self-image could lead to such phenomenal successes that Deming had one of those brilliant flashes of insight that few of us are privileged to have. As Newton with the apple, Einstein with relativity, Freud with the subconscious, Deming saw a new way for management.

The basic idea that Deming had is this: If management is to be responsible for improving something as complicated as a modern assembly of machines and people (whether in the factory, the hospital, the office, or anywhere else), managers must have a way of learning (1) which parts of the problems are due to the workers and (2) which parts are due to the system. Deming understood that this can happen only if the two circumstances are fulfilled:

The worker and the management can speak the same language.

The management uses the workers as essential "instruments" in understanding what is happening at the place where the work gets done.

Given the complexity of modern systems, there is no way the managers can begin to understand what is happening without the full cooperation of the workers. And even given a cooperative spirit, there is no way they can work together if they do not have a language suitable for discussing the inherent randomness in such systems.

And what is that language? It is the language of statistics. Deming, an established and esteemed statistician, understood this immediately. We all use statistics every day. It dominates the reporting of the sports announcers. We gamble. We handicap the horses. We listen to Jimmy the Greek. But for some reason or other, among "educated" people, there is a tendency to shun statistics and to avoid even the simplest taking of averages, the calculation of how much variation to expect, or when to decide that something is "unusual." Among "educated people" (for example, hosts on TV talk shows) as soon as something in elementary mathematics is introduced, one hears, "Oh, I was never very good with numbers," spoken as a badge of honor, as though the ability to do so marked one as a drudge. Among the "common folk" there may be "mathaphobia" but no one is proud of it!

Uncontrolled variations in a factory or other place of work lead to low productivity, poor quality, and increased need for capital equipment to obtain high rates of production. If the management is to control the variation, there is no escape from learning how to use statistics. Furthermore, if the cooperation of the workers is to be obtained, they, too, must learn the language of statistics.

Most American managers today tend to take the system as given and to try to get the most out of it as is. Thus they believe the problems of the factory are to be found in better understanding of morale, the work ethic, work standards, job definitions, more communications, slogans, exhortations, personnel selection, better record keeping, better union bargaining, and so on. They equate increased productivity only with increased capital spending (e.g., on automation) and have an easy out in blaming the tax laws, interest rates, and labor rates. It never occurs to them that people do not have to work harder, just smarter. And they do not comprehend that they must provide the leadership in working smarter. "Overmanaged and Underled" is the way Don Alstadt, CEO of the Lord Corporation, describes American industry.

In a typical corporate environment, the conventional system often works in a self-defeating way. How often is someone promoted because he or she knows how to get things done "in spite of the system"? And how often is someone passed over because he or she spent too much time developing corporate relations in a setting in which departmental infighting was the order of the day? How many managers make exorbitant demands on their workers as a way of "keeping them on their toes" rather than taking the time to discuss with them how to change the system so that the workers can do their jobs better?

If the workers and the bosses both speak the language of statistics, they will have something to discuss at their quality circle meetings. If they do not, quality circles can be an invitation to controversy and misunderstanding.

If managers adopt Deming's way, they will understand that they need the workers—not just as arms and legs to do what they are bid, but as intelligent human beings who can provide insights into how to improve the output and efficiency of the place. And we know that the improvement in management-labor relations can come from such an attitude, honestly felt and experienced.

Conclusion

From the experiences at Ford, Nashua Corporation, and several Japanese-managed companies in the United States, we now have substantial evidence that Deming's methods work wherever they have been seriously tried.

We may say with confidence that the poor showing of American industry in competition with the Japanese is entirely due to the management. The attitude of the government plays a role, of course, but in many cases this is also the result of management's approaches in the past. It is the culture of the managers that must change, and quickly.

There are some who say that ultimately Dr. Deming will be recognized as the Father of the Second Industrial Revolution. Be that as it may, he has this to say about future competition: "There will be no room for managers who do not know how to work with their people to produce high quality goods at low cost. High reliability cannot be secured without worker cooperation. Complex systems cannot be understood without statistics. In the competitive world of the future, companies which have not mastered these ideas will simply disappear. There will be no excuses."

CASE STUDY

Read the case at the end of this chapter, "Integrating JIT, TQC, and EI: Success Through Execution Excellence." Then,

1. Define JIT, TQC, and EI.
2. Explain PFM
3. Explain each of the four figures.

SUMMARY

1. Quality does not come from slogans and targets. Most of us do the best we can most of the time, so slogans and targets are harmful.
2. Inspection adds costs, not quality. Prevention, not inspection, is the answer.
3. John Guaspari's six points on quality (e.g., quality is a matter of survival) contain tested truths.
4. Ray Lammi's commandments (e.g., cease dependence on mass inspection) are also tested axioms.
5. W. Edwards Deming's ideas were tested in Japan for 30 years, so, when he tells how to improve quality while cutting costs, it is not a theoretical presentation.
6. The traditional American theory of management says managers get things done through others via the management functions (e.g., planning). This chapter considers how a traditional manager would operate a trucking firm.
7. Then, Deming's way of running the trucking business is presented to illustrate the contrast (traditional versus Deming). American companies are overmanaged and underled.
8. Managers who cannot work with their people to produce goods of high quality and low cost won't survive.
9. These benefits (e.g., high reliability) cannot occur without worker participation.
10. Complex systems of people and machinery cannot be understood without statistics.

REVIEW QUESTIONS

1. What is quality? What are blueprint specifications? Who decides what is quality?
2. Slogans, targets, and inspection guarantee quality. Comment.
3. Compare and contrast Guaspari's ideas with Lammi's.
4. What does Deming mean when he refers to a "stable system"? What is its importance?
5. It is impossible for the producer of highest quality to have the lowest costs. Do you agree? Why or why not?

6. Briefly summarize the traditional American approach to management. Illustrate it.
7. What is Deming's way?
8. The management-labor relationship is inherently adversarial. Comment.
9. Why does variation matter? How much of it can workers usually control? How much can management typically control?
10. Who needs statistics anyway?
11. Increased productivity can come only from increased capital spending (e.g., on automation). Do you agree? Why or why not?
12. The Japanese advantage is cultural, so forget it. Comment.

REFERENCES

1. See John Guaspari, *I Know It When I See It* (New York: AMACOM, 1985), pp. 65–66.
2. Henri Fayol, *General and Industrial Management* (London: Pitman, 1949).
3. See, for example, H. Koontz and C. O'Donnell, *Management* (New York: McGraw-Hill, 1976).
4. From Myron Tribus, "Deming's Way" (Cambridge, Mass.: MIT Center for Advanced Engineering, 1982), pp. 4–7.

Case Study
INTEGRATING JIT, TQC, AND EI: SUCCESS THROUGH EXECUTION EXCELLENCE*

Paul Boulian
Leo Everitt, Jr.
Tom Kent

INTRODUCTION

The feeling is growing among production executives and managers that something is frightfully wrong with the way change is occurring in the production environment. One element creating this fright is the number and scope of demands for organizational and system change being placed on the production organization. Regretfully, many of the so called "solutions" for production ills are creating problems. These programmatic "solutions" include: JIT, TQC, EI, QWL, CIM, etc. Achieving excellence in execution can most effectively be achieved through an integrated approach, developed and led by production.

Scene: Typical production plant conference room next to the plant manager's office.

Occasion: Monthly project review of ongoing efforts to "improve the plant's effectiveness."

Participants: The plant manager, production manager, quality manager, materials manager, controller, personnel manager, total quality control (TQC) project coordinator, Just-in-Time (JIT) task force leader, Manufacturing Resources Planning (MRP) project leader, Employee Involvement (EI) effort leader, cost reduction project manager, maintenance manager, product engineering liaison, and production engineering manager.

The controller starts the meeting with a review of plant-wide performance measures for the previous week, month, and year-to-date. Noteworthy items: shipments for the week and month are running 5 percent above schedule, but shipments for the year are still down 2 percent; labor hours assigned to meetings and training are up, violating corporate direction to reduce labor hours diverted from production; overhead is up; days inventory is improving but not approaching the corporate goal of 10 days per year (the corporate goal is to drop from 55 days to 15 days in four years at 10 days per year); warranty claims attributable to production from six

---

*Originally published as "Integrating JIT, TQC, and EI: Success Through Execution Excellence," by Paul Boulian, Leo Everitt, and Tom Kent. Productivity Brief 49, American Productivity & Quality Center, December 1985.

months ago are up; exempt headcount is down two people and non-exempt down four people one-half percent) from the previous month.

No comments are made regarding the meaning or cause of these results. A lone cynic comments on the requirement for EI, TQC, JIT training in tandem with corporate edict to decrease labor diverted from production.

The production manager states his position, "If we did not have so many projects going on, I would be making better progress against my goals. If we didn't have so many meetings for all the programs and training going on, my diverted labor would be improving; and I'd have more people doing real work. Lastly, I am not hitting inventory goals because they are unrealistic given the delivery schedule set by marketing and because the MRP task force and JIT project team can't agree on the approach. I am tired of everybody telling me how to run my shop!"

The JIT project leader objects: "If manufacturing would only put its full faith behind JIT, things would really improve. But production is uncooperative. Corporate has mandated implementation of JIT in 12 months and we've already lost four of those to lack of cooperation. We can't schedule JIT training in Department 999, one of the most important in the plant, because they have an 8-week backlog. If they would just let us do the JIT training and support the JIT philosophy, things would improve there."

The production manager responds, "We're not seeing drastic improvements in other departments where the three days of training have occurred so far! So, why will it be any different in Department 999?"

The plant manager interrupts: "Okay guys, I know there's a lot of frustration and difficulty getting everything done. Let's listen to all the project reports and then discuss everybody's concerns."

The TQC project coordinator announces that final statistical process control (SPC) training has been completed for all production management including foremen and that the three-day program has been a "success." He also states that all hourly employees have now been scheduled for the half-day SPC training that will take place over the next four months. He notes that 14 quality circles have been formed and are now choosing circle names and identifying symbols and that in the next month or so they'll begin identifying team projects.

The MRP project leader states that the last software module for MRP implementation will be on-line in two months—only 6 months behind schedule—and that training for key people involved with this is beginning. He also states that if things go as projected, there's a good chance the plant will accomplish "class A" MRP certification in 10 months.

The EI effort leader suggests that the involvement of employees is not progressing at the rate required by corporate and that there seems to be a real lack of understanding among shop supervisors about what EI really means. He says he overheard some foreman saying that the EI effort is an attempt by the company to "give the place over" to the hourly employees. Turning to the production manager, he asks that "something" be done about the poor attitude of first line supervision.

He says he is concerned that management is falling behind in its efforts to increase cooperation with the unions and that if something does not happen soon to build an understanding of EI, the window prior to negotiations will close.

The cost reduction project leader states that for the fourth month in a row, the cost reduction target has been hit but that the committee has concluded that the "easy apples have been picked" and the next months look "pretty bad." He also notes that the number of hourly employee suggestions for cost reduction has dropped to near zero since the decision not to include cost reduction ideas in the employee suggestion program.

At this point, the production manager angrily exclaims, "It seems that month after month, the focus of all this attention is on my organization; yet, I don't control or have much say about anything anymore. My plate is overflowing and all I hear is more, more, more. Each new project or task force creates a new set of objectives for my organization and they all use my resources. My organization is undermanned, overworked, and overwhelmed."

The plant manager says, "You know, Bill, I agree with you. Your guys are getting swamped and pushed around. We need to find a way to help. We're all in this together. But I would also say that we have to improve the way this place operates. We have no choice. Business out there is getting rougher and tougher. We're performing better than ever, but the competition is beating us. We just have to figure out how to make all of this work and still ship product. The demands on us are not going to abate. I propose that we appoint a plant-wide project coordinator who'll keep track of all the projects going on and help resolve issues when they come up. What do you think about this idea?"

After a short discussion the role of plant-wide project coordinator, reporting directly to the plant manager, is set up. Leaving the meeting, the production manager takes the quality manager aside. "Bob, we've just managed to push the disaster out another few months. We still refuse to deal with the real issue here."

WHAT IS THE REAL ISSUE HERE?

As competitive and marketplace dynamics have become rougher and tougher, pressures on production to contribute more and differently to the business enterprise have mounted. Unfortunately, numerous panaceas touted as "solving" the productivity problems of American corporations have been "discovered" over the last five years to ten years. Implementing these "panaceas" in the strongly functional production and business environment results in a total lack of integration of approach to production improvement.

For example, in one large Northeast manufacturing concern operating units must undertake 60 major projects in the area of production improvement, all with their own task forces, training requirements, principles, costs, etc. Synergy, where it exists at all, develops only because of individual initiative or luck.

In another company, the operating staff could not understand why they spent 8 to 10 hours per day in meetings and then did "day-to-day" work at home. After two days of analysis and discussion, the group discovered it had over 100 improve-

Mass Production Tenets

- People are dedicated to or limited to a few tasks.
- Machines are dedicated to or limited to a few operations.
- Material is thought of as being in large lots or batches or in noncontinuous repetitive cycles.
- Quality is based on allowable or acceptable quality limits.
- Management decides on and creates action through commands and control.
- Executives and managers tend to be functionally trained and promoted and tend to have an action orientation.

Execution Excellence Tenets

- People are expected to perform in any role they are capable of toward achieving business success.
- Machines are grouped to produce unique products with similar processes.
- Material is thought of as being in a continuous flow.
- Quality is based on aggressive striving for zero defects and continuous improvement.
- Management leads by and toward values and principles—continuous improvement and problem solving.
- Executives and managers have a broad base of skills and experience and tend to have a thoughtful understanding of and ability to execute the system that leads to effective action.

FIGURE 1 Some key tenets of "mass production" culture versus those of "execution excellence."

ment projects ongoing in the plant in the areas of materials, quality, maintenance, computer aided manufacturing, flexible machining, and employee involvement. This did not include capital projects, safety, labor relations, introduction of new office automation, and an upgrade of the computer system.

In a third company, production managers worried about the president going off to another conference to learn about new ideas to solve their problems. Frequently after these forays into the public domain, new "efforts" and "directions" would flow from corporate staff.

There are historical and cultural reasons for this. As a country, we created an industrial base founded on the tenets of mass production (see Figure 1). These tenets are different from those espoused by the new philosophies of production excellence embodied in such approaches as JIT and TQC. The culture of mass production and the thinking inherent in it contribute significantly to functionalism and specialization among production managers. Therefore, solutions to production problems flow from these functional disciplines, rather than from a total organization perspective. As the demand for production performance has escalated, so too has the fragmentation of approaches.

As managers have cried for a coherent, integrated approach, functional experts have responded by proclaiming their favorite approach as the "umbrella" under which all other approaches will exist. Thus, managers frequently hear, "If you elevate my project (i.e., JIT) to top status, everything else will fall under that philosophy and approach. It will guide everything you have to do." Unfortunately, this is incorrect and misleading. It fails to take into account the integrated nature of production organizations and attempts to give a simple solution to complicated production problems. Managers are receptive to these solutions because they are under such intense pressure for results, but managers lack the capability to think through and lead changes of this magnitude at their plant sites.

There is a profound misunderstanding in the corporate and production environments about how change occurs in large organizations. Few managers appreciate the complexity that has developed in our production systems.

Few appreciate how much leadership and thinking is required of managers at all levels in the implementation of production system changes.

Organizations are not a patchwork of disparate, unrelated pieces. What affects one piece affects all others. This is not a new idea, but one that is frequently misunderstood or forgotten. Our challenge is not to decide how one part of the system fits with or into another, but rather: 1) How do we create mental frameworks that will cause people to deal with things in an integrated way? and 2) How is the leadership provided to bring that integration about?

Addressing these tough challenges requires a major change in the way we think about and do things.

In the past, when life was "simpler" (and competition seemed less threatening and less global) the piecemeal approach worked to some extent. If there was a problem, a project team was set up to study it, devise and force a solution. Minimal attempts were made to disrupt the organization. Maintaining the "steady state" was of paramount importance.

Today, however, managers are finding the competitive world very different, the demands on performance extremely tough, and "solutions" to produce problems flowing from every corner. No longer is it possible to integrate improvement projects into the organization without disruption. In fact, today it has become difficult to distinguish the projects from the organization and know what gets integrated into or with what.

Instead, we must recognize the need for significant behavioral changes among our employees and significant conceptual changes in our organizations. We cannot continue to dream we can improve without changing.

The issue for us is how to bring about a significant shift in thinking about what we need to change and how to make that change.

PRESENT POPULAR APPROACHES TO IMPROVEMENT IN PRODUCTION

Before describing an integrated approach to achieving excellence in production, let us focus on the basic philosphies behind TQC, JIT, and EI. These three approaches are getting a great deal of "play" today and have the same conceptual set of beliefs.

TQC   Total quality control, or TQC, is a *philosophy* of managing that espouses: 1) a total commitment at *all* organization levels to perfect quality in every endeavor; and, 2) the need to ensure that products and/or services satisfy the customer's requirements.

The philosophy is put in place by ensuring that the total process, from engineering through production through marketing, is understood and controlled to meet business requirements. (We might note here that most people associate TQC principally with production processes, not the entire corporate process.) TQC requires each functional area to create a quality plan that sets out the customer's requirements and the means by which those requirements will be met to achieve conformance between business requirements and the results of internal operations. For example, production might work with engineering to design the product and tooling to assure satisfaction of the customer's requirement for foolproof assembly or engineering would develop a plan to insure that drawings have zero defects. TQC can drive many organization sub-systems including materials, preventive maintenance, job design, pay and advancement. Many proponents of TQC have said that this philosophy is all one needs to operate an excellent operation.

JIT   Just-In-Time, or JIT, is a *philosophy* of managing that espouses: 1) continuous improvement of everything done; and, 2) elimination of all waste (i.e., only do work which adds value to the product).

Some writers have noted up to 14 major elements of JIT. These include: a) having a place for everything and having everything in its place; b) shorter set-up times; and c) pull production. JIT is often confused with "inventory reduction programs." JIT can drive many organization sub-systems including quality, job design, pay and advancement, and preventive maintenance. Many proponents of JIT have said that it is all one needs to run an excellent operation.

EI/participative management   Employee Involvement, or EI, is a *philosophy* of managing that espouses: 1) harnessing the untapped innovative potential and energy of the workforce through involvement; and, 2) continuously improving plant-wide performance through increased employee capability.

EI approaches range from suggestion programs to development of "high performance" and/or "technician" work sytems. At times EI efforts have flowed from JIT or TQC concepts, including the tidal wave of "quality circle" programs that developed in the late 1970's and 1980's. EI can drive many organization sub-systems including quality, materials, job design, pay and advancement, and preventive maintenance. Many proponents of EI have said that this philosophy is all one needs to run an excellent operation.

CONCEPTUALIZATION OF AN INTEGRATED APPROACH

The development of an integrated approach to JIT, TQC, and EI requires a new way of thinking about these approaches and a new way of thinking about the integration of business strategy, strategy implementation, and material flow concepts. JIT, TQC, and EI represent production philosophies and to be effective they require philosophical changes in the organization. Today, many of the JIT, TQC, and EI approaches and training programs highlight these philosophical changes, but most implementation time is spent building skills or providing techniques. When philosophy itself is discussed, it is usually through examples of what "successful" others have done. Implementation is often discussed as a list of things "to watch out for" or "to do" (for example, "make sure top management is actively supportive and onboard"). But this does not help the organization and plant site grapple with the implications of systemic changes. On the contrary, it makes things appear deceptively simple!

Cultural change requires a comprehensive approach that takes into account the uniqueness of each organization in which changes are intended. Therefore, the approach to implementation in production organization "A" *must* be different from the approach taken in production organization "B."

Changing the philosophy and managing processes of an organization is difficult. "Managing processes" include all those interactions among people at any level of the organization through which desired outcomes are established, planning and problem solving occur, behavior is reinforced or changed, performance and performance standards are upgraded, and motivation is enhanced. Managing processes can be usefully categorized into three types: strategic processes, leadership processes, and operational processes (see Figure 2).

The purpose of these processes must be the ongoing perfection of the operation, maintenance, and improvement of the organization's material and information flows.

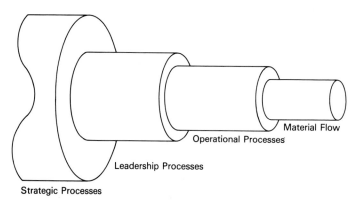

FIGURE 2 The relationship of managing processes and material flow.

Material flow refers to the transformation process (inputs, throughputs, and outputs) that convert a product from one form to another in a way that increases the "value" of that product—brings it closer to a point where it can be consumed. Ideally this flow consumes the least energy and material necessary for creating the distinctive value required by the user.

Strategic processes include those interactions necessary for establishing overall business direction and functional targets or goals, creating organizational values and principles, and defining the kind and scope of improvement needed to achieve the direction, targets, and principles.

Leadership processes include those interactions required to develop the thinking and behavior of people to ensure total organization alignment with the direction and principles (i.e., development of a supportive culture).

Operational processes include those interactions necessary for 1) ensuring execution of the material flow to principles and standards; 2) ensuring processes, systems, and structures are in place and used to achieve the direction and targets; 3) examining current practices and testing them against the organization's values and principles; and 4) bringing about personal changes that reflect organizational values and principles.

INTEGRATION AND APPLICATION OF EACH MANAGING PROCESS

Each managing process has a unique focus. Different activities develop within each which lead to the integration of production systems. But each process is also devoted to achievement of the overall purpose: high business performance.

At the strategic level, work by the production site staff needs to focus on: 1) development of the strategic role of production in the overall business; and, 2) the development of principles of execution excellence.

As a foundation for this work at a production site, involvement of production staff in the development of strategic direction at a corporate or division level is important, since plant staff should understand the overall direction of the corporation (and of the division of which it is a part). This implies that the staff understand what the corporation (and division) is trying to achieve in the marketplace; the strategic position in the marketplace of the products produced by the production site; the strategic requirements and interfaces among engineering, marketing and production; and the philosophy and principles by which the corporation will be managed and led.

At the production site the strategic positioning of production as a competitive weapon requires broadbased understanding of the position of the production site's products, technology, and customers in the marketplace and the relationship of these to marketing strategy. This includes determining what combination of cost, quality, and delivery is required to insure competitive advantage and determining the degree of symbiosis with the customer in terms of customer technology, production and marketing. This approach helps ensure that production opens opportunities for competitive advantage for the corporation. This work is best done by production site staff and key representatives from marketing and engineering in multi-day meetings over several months. This is infrequently done but essential to the development of an integrated approach in which the emphasis on improvement is focused on business or competitive advantage and on internal functioning.

The development of principles of execution excellence is critical to the integration of the myriad "solutions" operating managers are considering and trying today. Principles serve as the guiding beacon or standard of excellence for our day-to-day performance and define the boundaries within which we operate. Furthermore, we align the thinking of employees at all levels with these principles. This ensures that all employees can audit performance against standards without individual opinion being a major factor.

In the creation of what we might call high performance organizations, all employees must understand and have a stake in principles of "execution excellence." These principles relate to both operations and organization. The development of an integrated set of principles requires extensive thought. More often than not, organizations have some principles that drive thinking in one direction and other principles that totally contradict these. A principle might be, "All employees are accountable for ensuring that all work leaving their work station is of highest quality." A simultaneously held but contradictory principle might be, "Management makes all decisions regarding the interruption or termination of the material or information flow." This internal contradiction sends confusing messages to employees. What is the thinking we want to establish in employees?

Principles provide the basis for the scope, form, and direction of the cultural change required to implement changes in the execution of work. Principles are the major tool used in leadership processes to change thinking, behavior and ultimately performance results. For operational processes they provide the integration of material flow (the work itself), technology (the tools), and capability (people and skills). Thus, failure to agree on a congruent set of principles of execution excellence ensures increased randomness of thinking, increased variances to acceptable behavior, and decreased overall performance of individuals and the organization. Figure 3 provides a few examples of principles of execution excellence that have been developed at a number of production sites.

A full set of these principles would integrate JIT, TQC, and EI and serve to create the thinking foundation for achievement of high organizational performance.

Much of the struggle that managers have in developing an agreed to set of integrated principles of execution excellence stems from the fact that few organizations currently operate in accordance with these principles, so the experience of most managers is foreign to this thinking. Thus, managers often must operate at a high level of personal faith. They must believe that operating in accordance with principles they do not fully understand will achieve the results they require.

The work of the production manager with respect to principles of execution excellence is to: 1) develop the principles; 2) commit to them; 3) begin to behave in ways consistent with them; and, 4) audit his own and others' behavior against them.

Operational Principles

- The product must be so designed as to insure the lowest cost for its production, the highest level of perfection in its production execution, and the greatest ease in its delivery.
- Every employee will be held accountable for insuring that only products of the right quality will move beyond his or her scope of responsibility.
- Products and technology will be innovated at a rate that ensures continuous competitive advantage in cost, quality, delivery, and fitness for use.
- Everything throughout the organization will be viewed as being under the care of all employees—no individual employee will "own" anything.
- Everything will have a place and everything will be in its place.
- Competitive effectiveness cannot be achieved in an environment that is unsafe and untidy.

Organizational Principles

- Every level of the organization hierarchy must add value to material flow in a distinctive way free from redundancy.
- Each person must be provided the flexibility to do whatever is required within his or her ability to meet his or her customers' needs.
- Every individual will have the information necessary to understand the business, including current and future competitive and customer dynamics, and all necessary information to function effectively in specific task assignments.
- Planning and information flows must unify the organization toward competing to improve competitive position and in challenging creative capabilities.
- Operating systems must increase operational capability to improve the value adding process, increase control over the operational process, and eliminate waste from the process.
- Interactions must be dedicated to ensuring absolute control and order over material flow.
- Interactions must continuously stretch, develop, and challenge the thinking and skills of organization members while eliminating barriers to each person's increased contribution to business excellence.

FIGURE 3 Examples of principles of execution excellence.

A most effective process for creating principles of execution excellence involves a "diagonal slice" group of employees going off site for two-day periods over three to four months. During these sessions, principles are "pounded out" and agreed to. Between sessions, members of the group share the thinking to date with employees throughout the organization for upgrade and reflection. The diagonal slice group facilitates this because it is composed of employees at multiple levels across all functions. For organizations where this approach requires too much initial change, a number of production sites have developed a top-down process, starting with principle development by the plant staff in multiple meetings and in-between meetings testing thinking down through the hierarchy. Both of these processes serve to build commitment to principles as they are developed. This is in contrast to many processes where the principles are announced and employees are expected to understand and commit to them.

LEADERSHIP LEVEL PROCESSES

Strategic process has to do with creating overall direction. The second category of processes, leadership processes, has to do with developing the thinking and behavior of people so it is aligned with principles and targets set at the strategic level.

During most major projects or change efforts, we hear statements such as: "This needs to be supported at the very top" or "We need top management backing." These statements are generally true, yet too simple to describe what is actually required from the top. Nor do they provide any sense of the difficulty top level people have in meeting the expectations of such requirements. How would we describe support or backing? Giving public pronouncements or speeches is not adequate to motivate employees. Assessing progress and taking appropriate reinforcing action is impossible when several projects must be backed and when each of these is championed by a portion of the organization. So what is required in terms of leadership?

We begin with the assumption that direction and principles have been established as described at the strategic level. Leadership process must bring about a change in thinking and action in employees at all levels to align with that direction, so leadership must be evident at multiple organization levels. We are not speaking here about leadership in terms of roles or certain people, i.e., as in "the top leaders." We are describing the kinds of processes and interactions leaders in the organization might bring about or manage in order to shift people's thinking and, therefore, the organization's culture.

For example, interactions would be required to ensure and/or develop the deep understanding of the direction and principles created by the strategic process. All levels of the hierarchy would meet repeatedly in both functional and cross-functional groups to develop implications, goals, and standards for achieving and exceeding the strategic demands. The leadership for these processes would come from multiple people at multiple organization levels, including non-exempt employees.

Interactions among employees are required to design organization structures, systems, and processes that continue to support the organization in moving to higher and higher levels of performance. For example, employees at all levels would be involved in planning plant expansions or the installation of new equipment so that commitment and understanding is achieved. Leadership processes would develop people's ability to envision new possibilities for systems and structures that would be more aligned with strategic direction. Production staff, process engineers, operators, and supervisors would meet regularly, before the actual design and installation of hardware, to create ideas and resolve differences.

Interactions would be required to look at those elements which are maintaining the "status quo," and to develop ways to shift those elements. The production staff, for example, would conduct an ongoing cultural analysis and would test its findings through working with groups at all levels in the plant. A key to excellence in leadership process is understanding the relationship among production site culture, individual thinking, and achieving competitive advantage. Aligning these three factors speeds up the implementation process and decreases the chances that "false starts" will occur.

One tool that the production staff can use for understanding cultural dynamics comes from anthropology. Among other things, the study of ancient cultures teaches that cultures are developed through mutual reinforcement of: 1) ideas, things or positions to which the culture gives relative importance; 2) rewards and how they are used to maintain certain behaviors; 3) rites and rituals and what they maintain in terms of beliefs and behaviors; and, 4) taboos or unacceptable ideas or behavior and their purpose. Leadership process serves to help the production staff and other employees to consciously change the culture of the organization to support performance requirements by: 1) changing what is important and will be reinforced; 2) providing rewards for desired thinking and behavior; 3) putting repetitive events and requirements in place and building "stake" among employees; and, 4) being clear about unacceptable thinking and behavior.

OPERATIONAL LEVEL

An integrated approach to TQC, JIT, and EI at the operational level creates a material flow that adheres to the principles of execution excellence. It embodies the philosophy and principles inherent in TQC, JIT, and EI without invoking a particular approach. A true umbrella is created. The umbrella at the operational process level is called process flow mapping (PFM). Process flow mapping is a visualization of:

- The ideal support activities, which ensure the flow operates as intended, including preventive maintenance, materials staging, and plant site maintenance;
- The ideal flow of material based on the principles of execution excellence;
- The ideal material input, throughput and output steps required to support the flow, including feeds and speeds, tolerances, and other activities.
- The ideal capability to ensure that the people who are engaged in the flow have the necessary skills and thinking;
- The ideal information and control procedures to ensure flow measurement and quality, including measurement of inputs, throughputs, and outputs of each transform that comprises the flow;

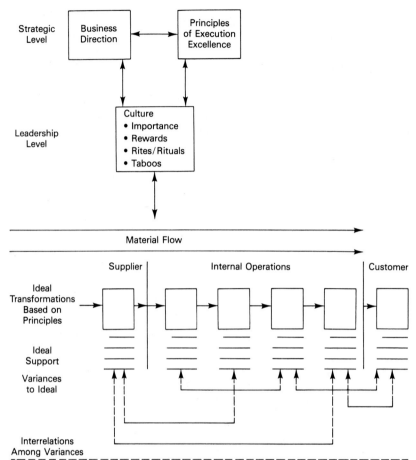

FIGURE 4 Process flow mapping relationship to strategic and leadership levels.

- The variances (deviations from ideal) and interrelations among variances at each level of the "ideal." These variances are differentiated on the basis of the business demands outlined in the strategic level work and laid out in "pareto" fashion.

An overview of PFM and its relationship to the strategic and leadership levels is presented in Figure 4.

Process flow mapping is developed through active engagement of technical resource people, functional experts, and employees directly engaging the material flow. PFM can therefore serve as the foundation from which employee involvement efforts are launched and can be the focus of shop floor team development. The activity and thinking developed in creating ideal states and variances to these serves not only to set the foundation for an improvement process but also to create improvements while the PFM is being developed. Thus PFM gives meaningful content to an involvement effort and takes the effort out of the realm of "it would be nice to involve employees." PFM makes involvement a necessary part or aspect of doing business to ensure production excellence. Additionally, PFM gives focus to the interactions among technical staff and those actually engaging the material on a day-to-day basis.

PFM removes the narrow focus so often found when TQC and JIT concepts are developed and championed by functional experts. So, for example, statistical process control applies to the entire transformation process, not just process control variances. Process flow mapping provides the database from which to drive the *overall* improvement process.

Job design efforts may be driven from the process flow mapping. "High quality" jobs are immediately apparent because the full scope of the work associated with a particular transform is developed.

For example, "self-managed work teams" can be developed with the use of PFM by noting the areas where the interrelations among variances are concentrated or come together and defining teams within these boundaries. These natural boundaries within the material flow provide the area within which teams would focus their improvement efforts.

PFM also integrates at the material flow level the interface among us, our suppliers, and our customers. When the PFM process is defined for the entire material flow, it defines the type of symbiotic relationship that is required with customers and suppliers.

PFM defines the capabilities required to carry out the transformation process. Therefore, it serves as the basis for employee orientation, training, and skill development. Because people are teamed around the material flow, differentiation of skills and capabilities can be more easily defined. This alleviates a persistent problem encountered by many organizations endeavoring to improve performance through the use of JIT, TQC, and EI. Today, for example, employees will often receive separate and time consuming training in JIT, TQC, and EI. Each program will have its supporting functional group developing and leading training, which includes philosophy, do's and don'ts, implementation hints, and a bag of skills.

Building capability under the concepts presented here would occur quite differently. First the principles and philosophy of execution excellence would be provided uniformly and consistently throughout all training and would be viewed as critical to developing the appropriate mind set of employees throughout the organization. Second, when particular skills would be required to maintain and improve the material flow, these would be provided without reference to their source. For example, statistical process control would be taught as a tool or technique to achieve execution excellence, not to achieve TQC. This requires trainers and functional specialists to integrate their approach so employees experience an integrated whole.

SUMMARY

Process flow mapping in conjunction with the leadership and strategic level processes builds a sound foundation from which constant improvement can be achieved. This overall approach enables changes to occur throughout the production site in a high quality way with the appropriate emphasis on orderliness and control. Driven by principles of execution excellence, all employees can contribute to overall performance in a consistent manner. Keeping the overall approach presented here in mind, let's return to the production managers meeting a year after the initial meeting.

A NEW VIEW ON THE PLANT MANAGER'S MEETING

Scene: the typical production plant conference room next to the plant manager's office.

Occasion: the weekly planning meeting of the plant staff with the division manager present on an informal basis.

Participants: the plant manager, the production manager, the materials manager, product engineering manager, personnel manager, controller, quality manager, representatives from non-exempt production team 14, and the division manager.

The plant manager opens the meeting by reviewing the agenda for the session: review of business situation and implications for plant functioning, review of the integration efforts in the training area; key issues facing the plant in terms of a total business approach to change, and a report from production team 14 regarding their efforts at improving execution.

The production manager describes the current increase in demand for the production site's products. Marketing attributes this increase in demand directly to an increase in quality and a decrease in lead times. Competitive pressure is mounting for significant price reductions. Marketing is wondering how fast production costs can be brought down. Engineering, for the first time, is responding to competitive pressures by organizing a value engineering process using plant resources, including shop employees.

A discussion ensues regarding the implication of this for the plant. Several conclusions are reached which are best summarized by the production manager: "We need to continue building an understanding of our principles of execution excellence so we have more people leading the effort and fewer following. We need to involve engineering in a stronger fashion, looking at all products from a design and producibility perspective. We need to speed up the training of all employees in statistical analysis tools. And we need to continue the process mapping of the next bunch of production processes."

(Note: During the last year numerous changes have occurred in the responsibilities and thinking of people and in the way the plant operates. For example, the staff spent a considerable amount of time participating in the development of the plant business strategy. They reached the conclusion that they could be a significant "competitive weapon" by increasing quality and decreasing lead-times to customers. They changed the roles of a number of managers, including the materials manager, who now has responsibility for transportation and purchasing so that materials movement to and from the plant is integrated under one function. In addition, the materials manager and quality manager have technical accountability to the production manager. All of the project leaders have had their roles changed. They are now technical resources working for the production manager, not project heads. As part of the staff's work to integrate all of the old programs, major cultural changes are beginning. Greater importance is now given to staff support of the line at the operator level and to people agreeing on solutions prior to implementation. In fact, some managers laugh about being "cultural changers.")

The plant manager asks the production manager to talk about the integration of training programs. "Well, it has not been easy, but the response has been good. We use the principles of execution excellence as the philosophical base that guides all training. For those employees who understand and have committed to the philosophy and principles, we are now providing technique and skills programs that fit the particular improvement needs of each area. This has forced us to prioritize where to spend our time and energy. It has also caused us to reschedule many of the old tasks we had and to eliminate some extraneous ones. And I might add that in all of the training, we are trying to have intact work groups of exempt and non-exempt employees attend together."

The quality manager says to the production manager, "Bill, you might say something about some of the problems we've encountered."

"Well, the biggest one is that the champions of the original projects and training programs feel somewhat betrayed. While the strategy and direction we have set makes sense to them and they understand the urgency for becoming more competitive, they feel stripped of their badge of identification. I have been working with them, but they are uncomfortable. They don't know that all of this means."

The product engineer adds, "I've had the chance to sit in on the philosophy sessions and some of the skills and techniques sessions, and what I see is a lot less confusion about what we are doing. People are no longer asking how does this fit with that and why does this contradict that. Being new to the plant and having been in a lot of other plants, I can see us really beginning to function in a non-functional way."

The plant manager introduces representatives from team 14. Team 14 members describe their process flow mapping work and the improvements they have achieved. They display numerous diagrams, drawings, and sheets of butcher paper that describe the total production process in their work area. They request the assignment of an engineer part time to help them re-balance the line and develop a new work layout. They project a net 15 percent decrease in cost over the next year with this layout change.

The plant manager comments, "I knew sooner or later we'd have to assign resource people directly to the teams. I think we need to 'belly up' and decide how we're going to do this. Let's meet next week to decide. Bill and I will put together a proposal and we'll get it out prior to the meeting. I am really glad team 14 brought this to us. It shows the power of a disciplined way of improving how we do work."

Just before the meeting breaks up, the division manager says, "I am impressed! When I first saw your strategic work, I thought that you were just creating more of the same. I thought the principles you laid out for execution excellence were just words on paper. It appears to be that you've managed to get a good deal of understanding about improvement down to the production worker. And the quality of work done by team 14 is amazing. When I see work like theirs, I can see that there's no limit to what people can achieve. You've also broken down the barrier against talking about trying to change culture. In most of the rest of the company, the word "culture" is meaningless. But I can see that dealing with changes in culture is critical to your success. I also appreciate the forthrightness of your staff members. Facing up to problems is a major step in sustaining improvement. Thanks for inviting me."

Chapter Three

CONTINUOUS IMPROVEMENTS[1]

After you have read this chapter, it will be clear to you that

- ❏ Global competition has replaced domestic competition, bringing tougher standards.
- ❏ Management's job now is continually to work on improving factory and office processes.
- ❏ Planning is necessary because uncoordinated changes in processes cause chaos.
- ❏ Reducing variability is critical to process improvement.
- ❏ Inspection and maintenance should usually be handled by the production department.
- ❏ Today's high-quality producer is usually the one with the lowest costs.

Henry Ford founded the Ford Motor Company in 1903. Using mass-production methods and a moving assembly line, he sold 15 million Model T's between 1908 and 1926. This approach got a new lease on life after World War II, when almost all economies were destroyed. Unscathed, we could sell virtually anything we manufactured.

Times have changed. We have giant federal deficits, huge foreign debts, and an eroding standard of living, to mention just three symptoms of our competitiveness difficulties. The environment of the 1990s is much different from that of the early 1900s of Henry Ford.

Our legacy is that the cultures of many manufacturers can be typified as follows: Since employees don't care about their work, management has to drive them with slogans, quotas, and performance appraisals. This engenders defensiveness, causing divisiveness, which creates barriers between people and departments.

Competition is becoming even tougher, and survival hinges on accepting the need for continuous improvement. This is achieved by every employee continually striving to reduce variability. This, in turn, requires new approaches to training and motivation, plus enlightened policies governing relationships with employees, suppliers, and customers. The plant's cultural legacy is usually an impediment.

Global competition has replaced domestic American competition. Foreign companies consistently produce for one-third less total cost. They are down to almost zero rejects (versus our 1 to 3 percent). Deliveries and product services are a lot tighter. Our experience competing with American rivals is of little help. Applying our traditional approaches—developed to compete with other American firms—won't work in the new global competition.

The global manufacturing culture now means that many U.S. firms have cost of sales that are one-third too high, plus quality, delivery and service that are uncompetitive. Reasons often include:

- Twice as many management levels;
- Ten times the inventories; and,
- Five times the cost of keeping the records.

IMPROVING PROCESSES[2]

Management's job now is continually to work on improving factory and office processes. The choice is to learn how to increase quality while lowering costs or sell out to those who do know how. The general approach is discussed next.

Quality means meeting customer expectations. Thus, quality is the basis of the management of a business, and every employee is part of the quality system. It is only by meeting their customers' expectations that a firm can reach its own goals. This implies the following.

> *The customer comes first.* This means learning about both internal and external customers' ever-changing needs and meeting their expectations on an ongoing, continually improving basis.

IMPROVING PROCESSES   45

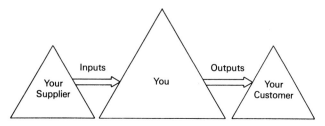

FIGURE 3-1   You add value in the process.

All work is part of a process. This reflects the way we must think about and perform job assignments, whether large or small. Every process has customers who receive your work, suppliers who provide input to your work, and you, who adds value to the input and therefore to the product.

A customer is any person that receives your output. You are a customer when you receive input from someone. You then perform a series of value-added tasks that transform it into output.

A supplier is any person that provides you with input. You become a supplier when you give the result of your work to someone else: your customer.

A process is a series of value-added tasks that you perform on a specific input that results in specific output. The value you add transforms the input into an output (see Figure 3-1). The overall quality of any process depends on the effectiveness of these internal customer-supplier relationships. An organization consists of a series of internal customer-supplier relationships as illustrated in Figure 3-2.

The customer-supplier relationship has requirements and feedback.

Requirements

Requirements are the most critical characteristics of your output as defined by your customer. Requirements should be

Specific: Identify exactly what is needed.

Comprehensive: Make sure all dimensions (who, what, where, etc.) are considered.

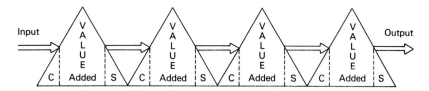

FIGURE 3-2   The process is a series of value-added tasks.

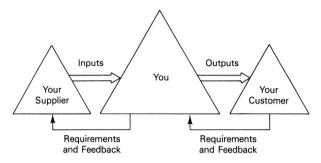

FIGURE 3-3 Requirements and feedback.

Understandable: Terminology should be clear to you and to your customer or supplier.

Measurable: Define what is supposed to be done in quantitative and qualitative terms.

Feedback

Feedback from your customer is the degree to which your output conforms to the requirements negotiated with your customer (see Figure 3-3).

In summary, the customer-supplier relationship involves four key steps:

1. Define the process or task that needs to be improved.
2. Define your value-added contribution to that process or task.
3. Have your customer define his or her expectations; i.e., negotiate specific requirements and define appropriate feedback, or measurements, with your customer.
4. Based on your customer's expectations, go back to your supplier and negotiate your requirements and feedback mechanisms, just as you did with your customer.

Taking these simple steps will significantly improve the quality of your work as it is defined by the most important person in the process—your customer. A departmental analysis is illustrated in Figure 3-4.

Prevention through planning. Prevent problems by anticipating them. This avoids the time and costs associated with "inspecting them out" and rework.

Quality happens through people. People make your business successful. Within an environment that stimulates their self-motivation and creativity, they take ownership of the processes that make your business and others succeed.

Quality improvement never ends. Every process can be improved, no matter how good we think it is today. Through continuous improvements, we foster the creativity and breakthroughs required to survive.

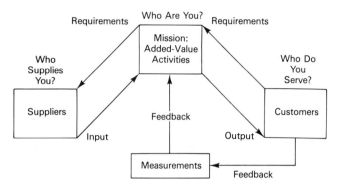

FIGURE 3-4 Department analysis.

PLANNING

The quality of our processes matters, and we have to improve. In the 1950s, real hourly compensation in the United States grew 3.7 percent per year, and incomes doubled in 19 years. In the 1980s, real compensation grew at 0.1 percent per year, a rate that will double incomes in 720 years. This suggests why we must improve our processes.

Most American companies will have to involve all employees every day in improving their processes (hence quality, yields, costs, and so on). This massive transformation takes 5 to 10 years and requires long-range planning. If employees undertook uncoordinated changes in systems and processes, chaos would result.

The heart of the plan is the company's mission: why it is in business, where it is going, and how it plans to get there. Employees need to know these things and to understand their roles. The new focus is on systems—the weaknesses of current systems and new systems that are needed. (See Figure 3-5 for Ford's mission statement.)

Planning needs to recognize the necessity for most managers and technical workers to understand the Deming philosophy (see Chapter 2), and this means training. Then, everyone must become involved in improving the processes: first, in the critical manufacturing areas, then, in all other manufacturing areas, and last, in the nonmanufacturing functions. Ultimately, all employees will be involved in continual improvements. The key interfaces between departments are crucial. Eventually, ex-

FIGURE 3-5 Ford Motor Company statement of mission.

Ford Motor Company is a worldwide leader in automotive and automotive-related products and services as well as in newer industries such as aerospace, communications, and financial services. Our mission is to improve continually our products and services to meet our customers' needs, allowing us to prosper as a business and to provide a reasonable return for our stockholders, the owners of our business.

ternal suppliers will be included, usually by evaluating the suppliers' systems (e.g., their statistical process control, see Chapter 4). Implicit in all this is that we are replacing the traditional quality systems based on inspection with quality systems which control the process itself. We discuss process (system) variability next.

PROCESS VARIABILITY

Variability in a system's outputs is normal. There are two sources:

Common causes, a natural part of any process, account for about 85 percent of all variation

Special causes, which are sporadic and unpredictable, are responsible for about 15 percent of all variation.

Any system has natural variations (the common causes) producing relatively constant results. Your first job is to establish such a *predictable process.* You can achieve predictability by removing the special causes of variation, leaving only the natural variations within the process (i.e., only the common causes of variation).

Now, you have a *controlled* process which is predictable. You cannot improve a system's outputs until it is in control, which is why establishing a predictable system is your first step.

The responsibility for improving a stable system is management's. Deming says stable systems are not improved by annual appraisals, by management by objectives, or by managing with visible figures alone. They are improved by earning the full cooperation of the workers. The workers are needed not only to get out the product but also to improve the system. They are intelligent people who know how to raise quality while lowering costs.

Workers do their jobs within the system, and management has authority over the system. In most systems, 80 to 85 percent of the problems are with the system and only 15 to 20 percent are with the workers.

Recognizing the difference between a stable system and an unstable one is crucial. A stable system is one that has a predictable performance. A *stable system* is achieved by removing special causes of problems (detected by statistical signals as discussed in Chapter 4) one by one. The responsibility for improving a stable system is management's.

In a high-quality system everything works right the first time. The work goes smoothly, and productivity improves. The productivity of labor, of capital, and of management all rise, while costs drop. By working on processes (systems) this way, you simultaneously cut costs and raise quality. You thereby work smarter, not harder.

The last two aspects of continuous improvement we will consider are inspection and maintenance, both of which impact directly on the process.

INSPECTION

Traditionally, inspection has been the job of the quality control department, often performed by taking samples to determine whether to accept a particular product lot. Sampling plans, such as Dodge-Roemig and Military Standard 105D, give the size and frequency of samples (based on lot size, trend, and number of defectives). Such inspection after the fact is expensive in time, rework, and scrap.

Sampling inspection was developed when lower levels of quality were customary, for example, when defectives were stated in parts per thousand. Now, the same industry probably measures defectives in parts per million.

The new emphasis on process control and on continuous improvement implicitly suggests that new inspection systems be set up and administered by production workers. One reason is that there is now a much shorter time interval between finding a problem and correcting it. Such inspection procedures often involve a mixture of self-inspection (checking your own work), sequential inspection (inspecting the work of the preceding operation), and source inspection (e.g., inspecting the supplier or the design activity). There are no full-time inspectors. Inspection is handled by production workers, and they should be responsible for light maintenance, as discussed next.

MAINTENANCE

Like it or not, most manufacturers have to become more automated. This means increasing dependence on automated machinery. Therefore, we need to ensure that the equipment stops only as planned and scheduled.

Maintenance has to become everybody's job. Production workers need to be trained to do routine checks and to perform light maintenance, and their training should include how to avoid hazards. There may be some union contract issues to negotiate. It helps everyone when people work together to keep the machines running efficiently.

A NEW BALLGAME

Many American manufacturers are compelled to compete globally. It is a new ballgame with tougher standards which require new approaches.

New management attitudes are indispensable. Deming's ideas, discussed in Chapter 2 and listed in Chapter 4, are recommended. A key assumption is that most of us do the best we can most of the time.

Also, we need constantly to improve the processes in our factories and offices. There is no other choice, because our competitors don't stand still. Chapter 4 discusses the tools for process improvement (statistical process control). Process improvement depends heavily on blue-collar people, and whether their potentials are tapped depends directly on how they are managed.

Manufacturing is now characterized by a new principle: The producer with the highest quality tends to be the producer with the lowest costs. Getting there hinges on continuous improvement. Constantly bettering processes depends on employees' attitudes. Whether they contribute is critically influenced by how they are managed. In other words, good management encourages employee involvement, which yields continuous improvement, making the plant a supplier of high-quality, low-cost goods, which means survival.

CASE STUDY

After reading about Armco's Los Nietos plant at the end of this chapter, write out

1. An explanation of the Q+ process.
2. A description of what MIS, office automation, and CAE/CAM have to do with Q+.

SUMMARY

1. In the new global environment earlier standards are not competitive.
2. Management's job now is to work continually on improving factory and office processes.
3. Every process has customers who receive the work (output) and suppliers who provide the input. The process adds value to the input.
4. If process improvements aren't planned, the lack of coordination can result in chaos.
5. Reducing process variability is a crucial source of improvement.
6. Inspection and maintenance systems can often be improved if they are established and administered by production workers.
7. A cardinal principle now is that the low-cost producer tends to be the producer with the highest quality.
8. The recipe for continuous improvement is that good management encourages employee involvement, which yields continuous improvement, making the plant a supplier of high-quality, low-cost goods, which means survival.

REVIEW QUESTIONS

1. Contrast the manufacturing environment of the early 1900s of Henry Ford with that of today.
2. Characterize the cultures of many American plants.
3. What sort of traditions stand in the way of our competing globally?
4. Explain some of the considerations in process improvement.
5. Explain Figure 3-4.
6. What is the role of planning in process improvement?
7. We are replacing quality systems based on inspection with quality systems which control the process itself. Comment.

8. Variability in a system's outputs is normal, and there are two sources. Explain.
9. How can you work smarter, not harder?
10. Inspection should continue to be the job of quality control. Comment.
11. Maintenance systems should be devised and administered by production workers. Why?
12. Why are manufacturers involved in a new ballgame?
13. Explain why, in today's environment, the producer of highest quality tends to be the producer of lowest costs.
14. Briefly list the recommendations you would make to a traditional American plant manager about how to survive the new global competition.
15. What does manufacturing technology have to do with continuous improvements?

REFERENCES

1. This chapter draws heavily on the material in the Instructor's Guide to Quality Literacy, a course developed and offered by GOAL/QPC of Methuen, Massachusetts.
2. This material is from AT&T's workshop, "Quality Improvement Process."

Case Study
NATIONAL PRODUCTION SYSTEMS—LOS NIETOS: IMPLEMENTING ARMCO'S CORPORATE QUALITY STRATEGY AT THE PLANT LEVEL*

Armco is a large, multi-national company employing over 50,000 people. Now in its 84th year, Armco has six separate lines of business, including oil field equipment and production; aerospace and strategic materials; specialty steels; financial services; fabricated products and services; and carbon steel. It is a diversified and decentralized company; each operating unit functions in a highly autonomous manner.

BACKGROUND

During the last decade American steel producers entered a very difficult economic period. Foreign competitors captured an increasing market share, unhampered by high labor costs and lagging quality and productivity levels. These last few years have been characterized by layoffs and struggles to survive for most large American steel manufacturers. Armco has experienced similar difficulties in its steel-producing divisions. In addition, the severe downturn of the American energy business has created a stressful period for companies such as Armco, involved in oil field equipment and production.

Like many in "smokestack America," Armco faced the necessity of taking a new look at the way its businesses were managed. In identifying ways to better manage the company, Armco management began to analyze methods for improving quality and productivity. Currently, the organization has instituted a long-term, comprehensive process to meet those goals. As stated by Harry Holiday, Jr., chief executive officer, on the cover of the 1982 annual report, "We are managing in these adverse times so as to create a stronger company for the years to come."

PLANNING FOR IMPROVED QUALITY

In early 1981, Armco officially began developing a process to improve quality and productivity throughout the organization. Top management, including the chief executive officer and chief operating officer, were involved and committed to the project from the beginning. In May of 1981, Robert Boni, the chief operating officer, attended a quality improvement training session sponsored by the Crosby

---

*Originally published as "National Production Systems—Los Nietos: Implementing Armco's Corporate Quality Strategy at the Plant Level," Case Study 33, American Productivity & Quality Center, 1984.

Quality College. Subsequently, several key people in the Armco management team also attended that training. In June of 1981 management allocated resources and personnel to form the group that would bear the responsibility of developing a corporate-wide quality and productivity improvement process.

The person chairing the original planning group was Pete Trepanier, now vice president, productivity, quality and information resource management. Planning the process was a long and exhaustive process. In addition to utilizing consultants and attending seminars, workshops and training sessions, the group scheduled visits with firms that were farther along in their quality/productivity efforts. According to Trepanier, "Any company that doesn't take several months and go outside the company to gather information is missing a lot. We consulted with approximately 100 'excellence' companies. We learned a great deal about what other companies are doing and still maintain those relationships."

ARMCO'S "Q+" SYSTEM

Through the efforts of the planning group, Armco has developed a comprehensive improvement process, entitled "Q+" (quality + productivity + participative involvement). The process is designed to involve every level of employee, from top management to shop floor workers in any Armco company that wants to use the Q+ system. Top management makes up a steering committee responsible for administration and direction of the efforts that follow. Middle management is the primary focus of Q+ and actually forms the "Q+ team" in each operating unit. The Q+ team is responsible for training operating unit employees and coordinating the entire quality improvement process. Supervisors and the work force participate in CATs (corrective action teams) or quality circles. The Q+ structure is outlined fully on page 61.

Basic to Q+ is Armco's belief that quality improvement comes from a positive corporate culture, with involvement and participation on every level being the primary ingredient. They believe that trust, respect, listening and involvement breed perceptions of justice, dignity, cooperation and ownership in the work force. And, perhaps the most important feature of the Q+ process is Armco's practical application of their firmly believed philosophy that real and lasting improvement is a direct result of participative involvement. All employees in locations utilizing the Q+ system are given the opportunity to participate and be involved in the quality improvement process.

When asked why Armco has put such emphasis on quality improvement, management is quick to answer, "It's exciting, unifying and mobilizing!" Trepanier states in an awareness presentation he gives to groups both inside and outside of Armco, "My job is working for our 50,000 employees, supporting them with tools, skills and a process to change the parts of the system that keep them from being fully effective, being satisfied with their work and feeling good about themselves. No one is against quality; we all want to produce quality. And, the interesting thing is that when you improve quality, you also lower costs in the long run and, thus, improve productivity. At Armco, we have really focused on quality as opposed to productivity. I view the difference in the two much like I view the difference in theology and religion. Theology is open to debate, somewhat academic. Whereas, religion is a gut issue with people. I tend to see productivity as defined in many ways and debated by executives, whereas quality is the responsibility and the goal of workers and managers."

The first phase of the quality improvement process is aimed at building a "positive corporate culture" through introduction of participative involvement and error cause removal. The second phase is intended to implement systems and strategies for quality improvement, such as computer-aided engineering, computer-aided design, computer-aided manufacturing or statistical process control.

Although designed by a corporate team, the Q+ system is not a mandatory program. Each operating unit that utilizes the system must ask for the help of the Q+ committee. "It's not a directive," said Trepanier. "We act as a support team for the operating units." Typically managers have decided to introduce the system after hearing, by word of mouth, of the successes of other users.

Before introducing the Q+ system at a given operating unit or plant, that unit's top management typically meets with the corporate Q+ team and attends a week-long quality improvement training session. The training session was developed in-house by the corporate Q+ group. Based in large part on materials from Phil Crosby, W. Edwards Deming, Joseph Juran and other quality experts, the training was customized and tailored for the Armco culture.

Armco's belief is that the commitment and direction of middle management is crucial to the success of the system. Thus, selected middle managers from all functional areas receive the week-long training. After the training program, these middle managers go back to their operating units as a "Q+ team." At this point, the Q+ team is asked to "carry the ball." The team is responsible for introducing the process throughout their work place, training employees in communication and problem solving and planning for implementation. Essentially, the team manages the resulting quality improvement process, including culture building and system introduction, throughout the operating unit or plant. The process has been introduced at 56 locations to date.

NATIONAL PRODUCTION SYSTEMS—LOS NIETOS (SANTA FE SPRINGS)

One of the plants that has successfully instituted the Q+ process is the Los Nietos location of National Production Systems, one of four major divisions of Armco's National Supply Company. It is involved in the production segment of the energy market, with its primary mission to develop, manufacture, market and service equipment and technology for producing crude petroleum and energy related products.

The Los Nietos plant encompasses 13 acres in Santa Fe Springs, California. It was originated in 1924. Not a modern plant, it is comprised of a series of buildings with a total of approximately 200,000 square feet. Approximately 310 people are employed at Los Nietos.

Primary functions include machining, abrasive metal removal (grinding and honing), assembly, testing and inspection of oilfield production equipment. Because Armco decentralizes staff functions, Los Nietos also contains departments for product design engineering, manufacturing engineering, accounting, personnel and industrial relations, quality assurance and materials management. An on-site product management function, which is part of the division's marketing group, brings marketing needs and requirements to the Los Nietos plant.

The products of National Production Systems include sucker rod pump systems, hydraulic pump systems, fluid control systems, fabricating services and machine repair services. Approximately 14,000 items are produced from such materials as stainless, nitronic alloy and carbon steels, carbides and cobalt and brass alloy—all of which require close tolerances and matched fits and, often times, require outside processes such as coating and plating.

The current effort at Los Nietos had its origins in a plant survey conducted in the late 1970s. It was designed to gauge employee perceptions and attitudes. All hourly and salaried employees, including managers, participated. The survey was administered to and measured on the basis of work groups—a minimum of three employees with similar or interdependent responsibilities—to guarantee uninhibited responses. The questions focused on such issues as organizational climate, management leadership support, work group performance and career development, work environment and inter/intradepartment communication. Respondents selected answers from a Likert scale (i.e., To what extent is management receptive to employee suggestions? a. to a great extent, b. to some extent, c. to a minor extent, d. not at all).

Results of the survey were very helpful to Los Nietos management, according to plant manager, Pete Jacoby. "We learned a lot about our shortcomings. For example, the responses indicated a good deal of frustration with the office environment—a number of employees made comments about the 'gunmetal grey' furnishings and inadequate lighting. Within the next few years, we refurbished virtually all offices. A number of the hourly workers indicated some concern about tool and gauge inventory; the company has spent several hundred thousand dollars to date in building that inventory.

"We also discovered that we were doing some things right," said Jacoby. "We found a strong commitment on the part of our first-line supervisors throughout the plant. It was really helpful to know what areas needed new direction and which were going well."

Armed with the information gleaned from that survey, management began considering ways to improve the corporate culture of the plant. Although not a direct result of the survey, a quality circle program was introduced about the same time by an outside consultant. The quality circles, now in their fourth year have helped build a positive, participative culture at Los Nietos.

QUALITY IMPROVEMENT AT LOS NIETOS

Those improvements in the corporate culture led to a growing awareness of quality issues at Los Nietos. As understood by Jacoby, "There are the traditional values associated with quality, such as: 1) customer satisfaction, 2) acceptable quality level and 3) inspection and appraisal. We see these as the traditional values. But, customer satisfaction can only be judged after the fact, an acceptable quality level may not be good enough and we all know that quality cannot be inspected into parts after they have already been produced."

Now, Armco's Los Nietos employees are looking at new values. They believe that what an individual expects, in terms of a quality level, in his or her personal life should carry over into professional life. "You don't expect or tolerate mistakes in your paycheck. You wouldn't go to a surgeon fully expecting that you will be the one mistake he makes that day. You don't want to fly an airline that allows pilots to make errors. And, if your toaster doesn't work, chances are you won't buy that brand again. The bottom line is that you should expect the same quality standards in your work place. There cannot be a double standard," Jacoby noted.

The important strategy, according to Los Nietos management, is instilling the "do it right the first time" norm throughout the plant. "With that, you close the loop on productivity because you don't have to do it over," stated Jacoby.

INTRODUCING THE Q+ SYSTEM

To reach the *long-term* goals of quality and productivity improvement, Los Nietos management realized it would need more than the "do it right the first time" strategy; it would need a more comprehensive process. The Q+ system that the Armco corporate team offered appeared to be an excellent tool. Although Los Nietos personnel had attended the Crosby Quality College about the same time as Armco's COO and had already begun to improve the corporate culture of the plant, the Q+ system helped bring a focus to the efforts at Los Nietos.

As stated by Jacoby, "The Q+ system is in Armco's blood. It is not a program, but a system—a philosophy. It has top management support and involvement as evidenced by the widely used video presentation featuring our CEO, Harry Holiday." But, to really instill a productivity/quality improvement process, Los Nietos management understood the need for middle management support. The Q+ process at that plant started with and evolved from middle management.

THE QUALITY IMPROVEMENT TEAM

Several essential elements make up the Los Nietos quality process. The Q+ system provides the umbrella within which the middle management level quality improvement team (QIT), acting as a steering/policy making group, helps to lay in place the proper culture for participative management that involves all employees in problem solving efforts. Additionally, office automation and MIS (management information systems), as well as CAE/CAM (computer-aided engineering/computer-aided manufacturing) enhance quality and productivity in white collar areas.

The QIT was appointed early in the process by Jacoby. It is comprised of the managers of each functional area. This group became the foundation and beginning of all further efforts. The initial step in the formation of the team was training.

In the fourth quarter of 1981, the selected group of managers from the Los Nietos plant attended a week-long quality improvement training session. After completing the training, that QIT began to meet regularly. They were recognized as the steering committee for the process and responsible for all policy decisions, as well as planning and communication.

In the fall of 1982, the QIT developed and administered a "train the trainers" program for all quality circle facilitators. When that was completed, all first-line supervisors attended that training program. Within the next eight to ten weeks, the facilitators and supervisors who had been trained were asked to train all other plant employees. Members of the QIT acted as "advisors" to those trainer groups.

COST OF QUALITY

According to David Beranek, local union president and original QIT member, Los Nietos management defines quality as "conformance to customer requirements." They believe to appropriately measure results of the efforts, management must look at the cost of quality. The key to the system is prevention and the performance standard for all employees is "do it right the first time." To address the measurement issue, the QIT instituted a "cost of quality" subcommittee to advise functional area management. The group was chosen primarily from the financial management and cost accounting functions because of their previous experience in appraising costs of quality failures. A "rogues' gallery" of bad parts and the cost of each failure has been prominently placed on permanent display in the plant.

Another Q+ subcommittee has worked on quality awareness through posters located throughout the plant and a Q+ newsletter, distributed to all employees involved in the Q+ process. In addition, all Q+ members currently wear a special pin on their name badges.

ERROR CAUSE REMOVAL

The QIT set up two vehicles for plant-wide employee involvement in the quality improvement process. The CARE system (Committee for Action for Removal of Errors) is a system for employees to define those problems that keep them from doing their job right the first time. Five boxes are located throughout the Los Nietos facility to allow employees to submit standardized CARE forms describing their suggestions for improvement or identified barriers to quality. Six bulletin boards keep employees informed about CARE activities.

The CARE committee, made up of employees from each of the functional areas, meets weekly to review the submissions. The committee's membership changes constantly, with one member rotating about every two months. The only exception is the chairperson, a member of the QIT, who does not leave the committee unless "burnout" occurs or a new QIT takes over.

In addressing an employee submission, the CARE committee asks a number of questions before any action is taken:

- "Do we understand the problem/solution?"
- "Has the employee talked to his or her supervisor prior to submitting the problem/solution?"
- "Does the problem keep employees from doing the job right the first time?"

If each of those questions can be answered satisfactorily, the committee then determines what kind of action to take. In 1983, 96 suggestions were received, accepted and acted upon. For example, an employee submitted a problem—a large number of incoming calls requesting information on products not produced at Los Nietos. The suggestion was sent, through the CARE committee, to the plant manager. Within a period of weeks, a comprehensive directory listing products available from each location was prepared and later accompanied by a toll free phone line which corporate had been establishing.

Only about 15 submissions were sent back to employees with no action taken. In each case it was because the forms did not answer all three questions appropriately.

The quality circle program begun four years ago remains an important employee involvement, problem solving strategy. There are now 17 active circles at Los Nietos, led by a full-time facilitator. Of the 310 blue and white collar employees of the plant, 110 are circle members. In the nearly four years of active circles, only three have disbanded; in each case it was because key members left the plant due to layoffs.

Each circle is comprised of eight to 12 employees, generally from the same work group. All members are trained through an eight-week process consisting of video presentations followed by a practice exercise for each concept covered.

Circles meet once a week on company time and work on problems of their own choosing. The solutions they find are formally delivered in quality circle management presentations, attended by QIT members. To date, 21 presentations have been made—and all 21 suggestions have been implemented.

The circles have received wide acceptance from employees at Los Nietos. All have names that reflect the individual pesonalities of the groups. A recent contest solicited entries for a plant-wide quality circle logo. The large number of entries received clearly demonstrated the enthusiasm of plant employees.

When asked how much money the circles have saved the plant, Jacoby answered, "I have problems with that question—all presentations document cost reductions. But, how many dollars is it worth to see people committed, to see people use their lunch hours or work at night to figure out solutions to our problems? A couple of years ago, we had a major layoff on a Friday and could not, for obvious reasons, tell those involved. A circle presentation was scheduled for the following Monday evening at a monthly mangement club meeting. The laid-off employees, to a man and woman, showed up on that Monday to give the presentation. That's where the benefit is. Dollar savings just come along as a by-product."

MANAGEMENT INFORMATION SYSTEMS

The Management Information System (MIS) is another source of pride for Los Nietos Q+ members. A total transition—from a manual cardex system to a fully integrated computer system—was planned and implemented over the last three years.

In attempting to simplify the MIS system, a seven-member group was appointed, from various functional areas to identify needs, research available hardware and software and plan for implementation.

The group felt that it was necessary to work in close proximity to each other and to actual plant operations. Thus, a trailer was installed at Los Nietos to house the team.

The group also believed careful, meticulous planning would be critical to the success of the project. They documented each step in the planning process, from examining each task to determining needs. Representatives from each functional area within the plant were asked to participate in the process. Those representatives explained the tasks, needs and desired benefits of such a system.

With that information, the team set out to find an appropriate system and plan for its implementation. The group visited several manufacturers to learn what was being done in the area. In addition, they went to software facilities in search of the best possible program. The entire process was carefully tracked by the use of a large flow chart. The chart allowed the group to cluster the planning, acquisition and installation steps into 19 phases. Also, through the use of the flow chart, the group was able to keep top management informed through each step of the process.

A great deal of training was required to implement the new MIS system. Prior to the actual installation, a training course was developed by the group to acquaint all users with the equipment and its capabilities. Users now receive training in system operation through that course; it utilizes a purchased video program and hands-on training. A second trailer had to be added to accommodate the training process. In all, the team estimates over 10,000 hours of training on the system has been completed to date.

One lesson that the group learned was that for such a system to work, routing and inventory record accuracy at the facility should be approximately 95 percent. When looking into those records at Los Nietos, the group found only 64 percent record accuracy. A plan was developed and implemented by the group to improve that figure; it consisted of limiting access to specific areas of the plant, improving inventory storage so that particular parts are stored in a one place instead of several places and instituting a "sign-off" process for shipping and receiving all parts. The record accuracy has now reached 96 percent in all warehouse locations.

Other improvements have been documented as a result of the switch to MIS, most notably reductions in inventory. The team has been able to demonstrate a 12 percent reduction in finished goods, a 19 percent reduction in work-in-process, a 36 percent reduction in "blanks" (semi-finished goods) and a 40 percent reduction in raw materials. This reduction has not hampered the production process. With more accurate records, limited access, orderly storage and the new system control, the amount of inventory needed at any given time has been reduced and is timed very closely to actual production.

OFFICE AUTOMATION

In addition to the MIS functions, Los Nietos has implemented office automation tools designed to provide a wide range of aides for improved quality of management. The goal, according to David Nu, supervisor, systems, is to increase management effectiveness. "A manager's work is events-driven, characterized by a variety of tasks and reliant on effective communication. It typically entails geographical independence and is essentially comprised of decision-making responsibilities."

At Armco's Los Nietos plant, managers have access to an electronic mail system, electronic calendaring and reminder systems, word processing and a sophisticated telephone system. To provide decision support, the system allows managers to generate business graphics (such as pie or bar charts), compose and edit reports and do "what if" analysis, ad hoc inquiries and financial modeling. An electronic filing system enables managers to maintain and archive personal files and gives them access to community files.

The entire system utilizes "fourth generation" language, which is user friendly and allows quick, easy programming. The benefits of such a system—flexibility and rapid response—allow the user to design a program on the system in a matter of a few hours.

COMPUTER-AIDED ENGINEERING/ COMPUTER-AIDED MANUFACTURING

As stated earlier, the second phase of the Q+ process is the implementation of quality/productivity improvement systems. As the MIS and office automation efforts have aided management in this improvement, the CAE/CAM systems are aiding the design and manufacturing processes. The CAE process encompasses computer-aided design and frees engineers and designers from the time-consuming, manual task of detail drawing. It also allows them to look at interference fits, simulate flows of products downwell or size products for a customer proposal. With CAE, a field service engineer can call the computer over a dial-up line, run the required programs and return to the customer with products properly sized for the required application.

Computer-aided manufacturing allows numerical control programmers to call up parts geometry from the data base, develop tool paths, plot for verification and generate an NC tape which tightly controls the actual production process. Additionally, CAM provides for layering of design drawings and family of parts programming. It is a system that makes mass production with small variance possible.

RESULTS

In addition to the documented results of tracking the cost of quality and reductions in inventory, National Production System's Los Nietos plant management feels certain that overall improvements have been made. With pride, managers will tell a visitor to look around—and see smiles. "If you want to know how well the Q+ system works, go to a plant and ask the workers," Trepanier concluded.

While no attempts have been made to measure attitudinal improvements, workers do express pride in their work and their company. A great deal of commitment and dedication is evident in employees at all levels. According to local union president, Beranek, "There were some misgivings on the part of union people at the beginning. But now attitudes are good. People understand that quality is important and that we need to improve quality and productivity to be competitive. It's really an exciting time for labor and management."

The future quality improvement efforts at Los Nietos look equally promising. Within the next few months, Los Nietos will enter a new phase of the Q+ process. After intensive culture building (phase one) and installation of systems for improvement (phase two), the original QIT will step down and turn the responsibility of future efforts over to the second level of management. According to Jacoby, the QIT has four goals yet to reach before the turnover:

1. Vendor orientation—the QIT wants to "take their show on the road" to all of Los Nietos' major vendors. The team believes that vendors are an integral part of the quality improvement process and, as such, need to become aware of the process and of the role they play.
2. Cost of quality—six of eight functional areas of the plant have not yet developed a cost of quality program. The team would like to make sure there is plant-wide involvement in cost of quality.
3. Selection of next QIT—the group has not yet determined criteria for the selection of the next generation QIT. The basic questions yet to be answered by the team are "who" and "why."
4. Q+ Day—the culmination of all efforts to date is to be recognized at a "Q+ Day." The original team is still in the planning stage for that event.

Jacoby estimates that the turnover, originally scheduled for June of 1984 will actually occur in the late summer.

ORGANIZATIONAL MODEL OF THE Q+ PROCESS

Improvement is supported by integrated activity in the three major layers of the organization.

Strategy Productivity and quality are added to the list of critical success factors which include marketing, organization development, research & development and financial performance. When setting objectives, key elements in each of these factors are considered. Achievement of objectives is a major element in performance appraisal and compensation. Renewed emphasis is placed on quality as part of Armco policy which is supported with a participative culture.

Labor-management steering (L/M) Leaders from both labor and management come together at the beginning of the process for training. They develop a knowledge of tools and choices available to them. A steering group made of labor and management then decides on the appropriate strategy for their organization to follow in implementing the Q+ process.

Quality plus (Q+) Q+ (quality + productivity + participative involvement) consists of a quality management system, training programs, measurements, participative involvement and group problem solving. Q+ is injected at the middle management level where ownership and direction resides in a multi-function Q+ Team. The Q+ Team members manage the process in their organizations and provide training for everyone. They tailor the process to fit their local culture. The Cost of Quality is a local measurement tool used by the Q+ Teams. Corporate-wide controls are avoided.

Corrective action teams (CAT) The habit of improvement must be part of a business culture in order to remain competitive; and improvement is made project by project through Correction Action Teams. CAT's provide a strong framework to carry the Q+ process to the work force. The development of employees is accomplished by training modules in effective team development, CAT leader training methods, quality management, problem solving techniques, effective meetings and management presentation methods. This process creates employee involvement throughout the organization. This is a critical step toward making the cultural change to a more participative style and improving the level of trust and cooperation within the organization.

Performance Strategy will have the greatest impact on long-term performance. Decisions at this level impact the *effectiveness* of the organization (doing *the right things*). Perhaps 80 percent of the productivity improvements will be determined by upper level decisions.

Q+ and CAT have a heavy impact on the *efficiency* of the organization (*doing things right*). These processes have the potential to reduce operating costs 10 to 25 percent by improving quality and correcting problems.

Management commitment and involvement is needed to ensure interaction between organization layers. Labor-management cooperation and joint participation provide the energy for never-ending improvement.

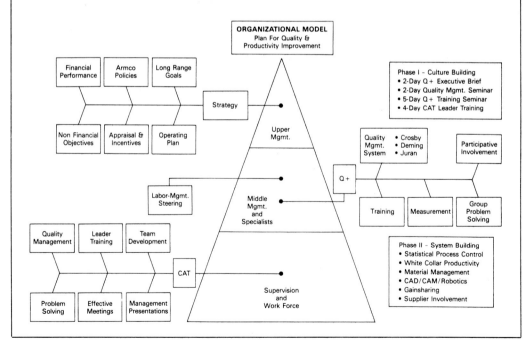

Chapter Four

STATISTICAL PROCESS CONTROL

After you have read this chapter, it will be clear to you that

- ❏ W. Edwards Deming's 14 points and his 7 deadly diseases tell how to become a producer of low cost, high quality, and high productivity simultaneously.
- ❏ An understanding of process variability is critical to Deming's approach.
- ❏ Plant and office processes are subject to two kinds of variation: special causes (about 15 percent of all variability and usually correctable by workers) and common causes (about 85 percent of all variability and correctable only by management).
- ❏ When the special causes of variation are removed, the system is in statistical control and the real work of improvement begins. Control charts help tell whether a process is in statistical control.
- ❏ $\overline{X}$ and R charts apply when the data come from measurements, such as length or weight.
- ❏ P and nP charts are for data based on counts, such as the number of defectives.
- ❏ Management, statistics, and systems analysis are a single integrated entity (and not three largely unrelated areas).

Global competition has created the imperative that American managers either learn to reduce costs through increasing quality or sell out to those who already know how.

Fortunately, W. Edwards Deming has documented what can be done in his 14 points (Figure 4-1) and in his 7 deadly diseases (Figure 4-2). Together they constitute a recipe for becoming a producer of low cost, high quality, and high productivity simultaneously.

FIGURE 4-1 Deming's 14 Points for Management. [From W. Edwards Deming, *Quality, Productivity and Competitive Position* (Cambridge, Mass.: MIT, 1982), pp. 16-50.]

1. *Create constancy of purpose to improve the product and service.* Plan for long-term business growth by investing in resources, research and development, maintenance of equipment, and aids to production.
2. *Adopt the new philosophy.* The American industry can no longer live with mistakes, defects, and delays. The statistical portion of the new philosophy is simple and accurate.
3. *Cease dependence on inspection to achieve quality.* Quality cannot be inspected into products. Processes must be brought under control statistically and inspected continually by all personnel.
4. *Stop awarding business on price alone.* The initial cost of a product may be only a fraction of its total cost if it lacks quality. Aim to work with one chosen supplier and build your relationship based on trust and statistical process control (SPC).
5. *Improve constantly and forever every process for planning, production, and service.* Use statistics to identify the problems and work to eliminate them. Remember though, once management chooses to begin statistical process control, they must not choose to ignore the results.
6. *Institute training on the job.* The work force is generally your single largest investment and greatest resource. Invest in education to improve all employees' abilities.
7. *Adopt and institute leadership.* The aim of management should be to help people and machines do a better job. Train your supervisors to act on reports of defect, maintenance requirements, poor tools, or other conditions undermining quality.
8. *Drive out fear.* The failure to communicate is a staggering problem today in America's major corporations. An environment must be created where employees feel secure to ask questions, make suggestions, report problems with material affecting quality, poor working conditions, etc.
9. *Break down interdepartmental barriers.* Eliminate problems encountered in manufacturing, encourage communication between gorups. A good idea might be to compose teams made up of representatives from each of these areas, to monitor quality problems.
10. *Eliminate goals and slogans urging productivity.* Goals and slogans cannot change defects if the process is incapable of producing anything else. Most employees do try to do their best. Motivational requests for quality are useless without the necessary tools required to improve the process.
11. *Eliminate numerical quotas for the work force and numerical goals for management.*

Work standards that establish numerical quotas don't help anyone do a better job, and they don't make considerations for defective raw materials.

12. *Remove barriers that rob people of pride of workmanship. Eliminate the annual rating or merit system.* Remove barriers that deny employees the right to pride of their workmanship. Fear and confusion, failure to communicate, ignoring defects, and hiding problems all rob employees of the right to do a good job and be proud of it.
13. *Institute a vigorous program of education and self-improvement for everyone.* To improve quality, everyone in the organization needs to be educated in statistical process control (SPC) techniques, benefits, and applications, establishing constancy of purpose.
14. *Put everybody in the company to work to accomplish the transformation.* Top management must demonstrate their permanent commitment to quality and their obligation to implement this new philosophy.

FIGURE 4-2 The Deadly Diseases. [From W. Edwards Deming, *Out of the Crisis* (Cambridge, Mass.: MIT, 1986), Ch. 3.]

1. Lack of constancy of purpose to plan product and service that will have a market and keep the company in business, and provide jobs.
2. Emphasis on short-term profits: short-term thinking (just the opposite from constancy of purpose to stay in business), fed by fear of unfriendly takeover, and by push from bankers and owners for dividends.
3. Evaluation of performance, merit rating, or annual review. Deming believes that employee reviews are demoralizing and tend to cause more variability rather than reduce it. Employee reviews do not recognize the individual, encourage communication, or help people to do a better job.
4. Mobility of management; job hopping. Executives that move in and out of positions in only a few years can never absorb enough knowledge about the company or become committed to its policies. It takes time to establish relationships and learn how to work together.
5. Management by use only of visible figures, with little or no consideration of figures that are unknown or unknowable. Quoting reports on productivity or the number of defects produced does nothing to remedy the situation—these numbers are referring to defect detection, rather than prevention.

Peculiar to industry in the U.S.:

6. Excessive medical costs. As William E. Hoglund, manager of the Pontiac Motor Division, put it to me one day, "Blue Cross is our second largest supplier." The direct cost of medical care is $400 per automobile ("Sick Call," *Forbes,* 24 October 1983, p. 116). Six months later he told me that Blue Cross had overtaken steel. This is not all. Additional medical costs are embedded in the steel that goes into an automobile. There are also direct costs of health and care, as from beneficial days (payment of wages and salaries to people under treatment for injury on the job); also for counseling of people depressed from low rating on annual performance, plus counsel and treatment of employees whose performance is impaired by alcohol or drugs.
7. Excessive costs of liability, swelled by lawyers that work on contingency fees.

Essentially, Deming is saying that people work in a system and that the manager's job is to improve that system with their help. Managers are thus responsible for improving the quality of the performance of people, machines, processes, and procedures. Continuous improvement becomes everybody's focus. Note that if a manager tries to use numerical quotas to improve a system, the system will usually beat him (and in unexpected ways).[1]

The quality of a product depends (among other things) on:[2]

- The quality of the design
- The quality of the materials
- The quality of the manufacturing process.

Therefore, everyone must participate in the improvement process.

Since improvement is everybody's business, managers and other employees all need to develop three sets of abilities:[3]

- The ability to check on the performance of a system.
  To know how to describe a system so other people will understand what is being talked about
  To know how to gather data
  To know how to analyze data
  To know how to communicate results.
- The ability to cooperate with other people in generating methods for improving systems.
  To participate in group problem definition
  To participate in group problem solving.
- The ability to deal with statistical variation. This requires the mastery of simple methods of analysis needing no more than grade-school-level capabilities in mathematics.

Literacy in statistics is needed for all of the above, so we begin with a discussion of variability.

VARIABILITY

Variability embraces these ideas:[4]

- Variation is part of any process.
- Planning requires prediction of how things and people will perform. Tests and experiments on past performance can be useful but not definitive.
- Workers work within a system that—try as they might—is beyond their control. It is the system, not their individual skills, that determines how they perform.
- Only management can change the system.
- Some workers will always be above average, some below.

Manufacturing commercial clothes dryers is a process, preparing invoices to send to customers is a process, and collecting accounts receivable is also a process.

Each process is subject to normal variability: the number of dryers that cannot pass final inspection, the number of errors in today's invoices, or the number of days to collect payment.

Such plant and office processes contain two types of variation:

- *Special causes* occur on an unpredictable basis and are easily identified, such as a faulty control device or a specific error in a chemical mix. Special causes account for approximately 15 percent of all sources of variation. Because they are the easiest to identify, the first step in controlling a process is to eliminate them.
- *Common causes* are natural variations within a process, such as environmental or human differences, and account for approximately 85 percent of all sources of variation. The effect of one common cause on a process is insignificant, but the total effect of all common causes can have a major impact.

When the special causes of variation have been removed from a process, it is stable and *in statistical control*. (Note that calculations of the mean, standard deviation, t test, chi-square, and the like, are useless for process improvement unless the process is in statistical control.) When all special causes found so far have been removed, the remaining variability is from common causes such as[5]

- Poor design of a product or service.
- Failure to remove the barriers that rob the hourly worker of the right to do a good job and to take pride in his or her work.
- Poor instruction and poor supervision (almost synonymous with unfortunate working relationships between foremen and production workers).
- Failure to measure the effects of common causes and to reduce them.
- Failure to provide production workers with information in statistical form that shows them where they can improve their performance and the uniformity of the product.
- Failure of incoming materials to meet the requirements.

Special causes are usually traceable to a certain group, a specific person, a local condition (e.g., temperature), or a particular machine. Experience suggests that such special causes are responsible for about 15 percent of all sources of variation. Employees, who work within the process or system, can usually correct these special causes; that is, only about 15 percent of the problem is in the workers' hands. Eighty-five percent of the problem involves the system, which management controls. Workers can do nothing about causes of variability common to everybody in the system; that's up to management.

When the system is in statistical control, there are advantages:[6]

- The process has an identity; its performance is predictable. It has a measurable, communicable capability. Production and dimensions and other quality characteristics, including the number of defects, if any, remain nearly constant hour after hour, day after day.

- Costs are predictable.
- Productivity is at a maximum (and costs at a minimum) for this system.
- Relationships with the vendor who delivers material that is in statistical control are greatly simplified. Costs diminish or quality improves.
- The effects of changes in the system (management's responsibility) can be measured with greater speed and reliability. Without statistical control it is difficult to measure the effect of a change in the system. More accurately, only catastrophic effects are identifiable.

Statistical control implies that a process is stable and that variability is predictable. This random variability may still produce defective items even though the process is in statistical control. Once statistical control is achieved, the real effort to cut costs and to raise quality can begin. Again, a process in statistical control is stable and shows no indication of special causes of variation. It is predictable in the near term and has a definite capability so that you know the specifications it can meet.

Control charts tell whether a process is in statistical control. As noted, when a process is in statistical control, the remaining variation is from common causes (the special causes of variability having been removed), and the real work of improving the process can begin.

As suggested by Deming's 14 points (Figure 4-1), people are part of the process (i.e., system). This means that how people feel, their attitudes, their fears, and all their other complex facets are part of the system, too. Fortunately, most of us do the best we can most of the time, which makes our imperfect systems function. Experience shows that people working in a system control only about 15 percent of the sources of variation (the special causes). People directing the system (i.e., managers, who work on the system) control about 85 percent of the variability (the common causes).

RUN CHARTS[7]

Run charts are graphs that show process performance over time, for example,

- Invoice errors
- Rework costs
- Absenteeism
- Defects per shift.

Figure 4-3 is a run chart for the number of days it takes to collect amounts charged on invoices, and the *median* number of days to collection is 47 (i.e., the observation that has an equal number of items above and below it). Assuming this manufacturer's policy is "30 days due," there is a problem. A typical invoice is paid in 47 days (versus 30), and tying up working capital this way can create the extra cost of interest on money borrowed for, say, material and payroll.

RUN CHARTS

Invoice No.	Days to Pay	Invoice No.	Days to Pay
300	18	315	57
1	23	6	76
2	80	7	45
3	14	8	3
4	44	9	25
305	81	320	73
6	38	1	9
7	62	2	46
8	67	3	21
9	77	4	49
310	60	5	79
1	33		
2	61		
3	71		
4	22		

(a)

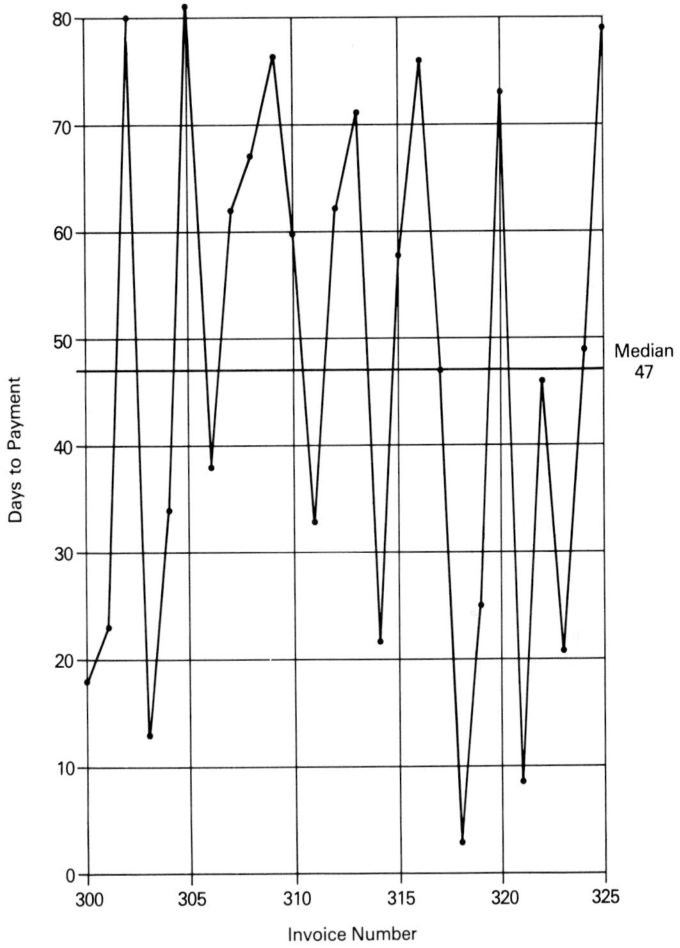

FIGURE 4-3 (a) Data. (b) Run chart.

Presumably, the information from this run chart triggers improvements in collection procedures. These improvements can be tracked by new run charts which can begin to distinguish between common and special causes of variation. The process is predictable when the causes of variation that are not a natural part of the system (i.e., the special causes) have been identified and eliminated. Control charts help to reveal the special causes of variation and are discussed next.

CONTROL CHARTS[8]

A *control chart* is simply a run chart with statistically determined upper (Upper Control Limit) and lower (Lower Control Limit) lines drawn on either side of the process average. See Figure 4-4.

These limits are calculated by running a process untouched, taking samples, and plugging the sample averages into the appropriate formula. You can now plot the sample averages onto a chart to determine whether any of the points fall between or outside of the limits or form "unnatural" patterns. If either of these happens, the process is said to be "out of control." The fluctuation of the points within the limits results from variation built into the process. These result from common causes within the system (e.g., design, choice of machine, preventive maintenance, etc.) and can only be affected by changing that system. However, points outside of the limits come from a special cause (e.g., people errors, accidents, etc.) that is not part of the way that the process normally operates. These special causes must be eliminated before the control chart can be used as a monitoring tool. Once this is done, the process would be "in control" and samples can be taken at regular intervals to make sure that the process doesn't fundamentally change.

"*Control*" doesn't necessarily mean that the product or service will meet your needs. It only means that the process is consistent (maybe consistently bad). For example, see Figure 4-5.

In this case, the process is in control but it is not capable of meeting the specification. Either you improve the process or you change the specifications. Just remember that *specifications* are what you think you need (man made) and *control limits* are what the process can do consistently (data made). It should be noted that a control chart typically shows only the control limits (not the specification limits). The example in Figure 4-5 is for illustrative purposes only.

Variability is part of the working environment. For example, when variability is reduced, parts fit better after assembly, and the finished product performs better with less maintenance. The customer perceives better quality and longer life. The producer experiences fewer rejects, less scrap, and less rework and so perceives lower costs. This illustrates how variability, quality, and costs might impact a manufacturer that implements SPC.

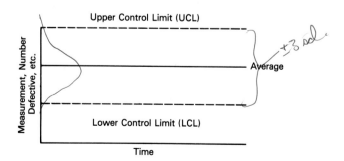

FIGURE 4-4

CONTROL CHARTS 71

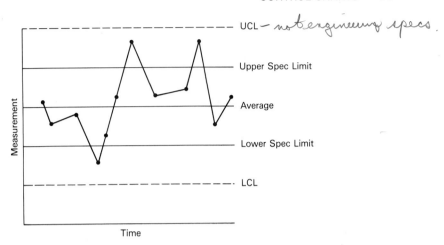

FIGURE 4-5

(UCL annotation: "not engineering specs")

Control charts are a tool for gaining control of process variability. They can

- Identify special causes of variation
- Display the performance of the process
- Monitor improvements.

Again, causes of variation that are not a natural part of the process (special causes) need to be identified and eliminated. Such sporadic unpredictable problems compose about 15 percent of all sources of variation and can normally be controlled by workers. What then remains is the natural variability of the system (common causes). Any one common cause can be insignificant (e.g., slight raw material differences), but their aggregate effect can be considerable. About 85 percent of all sources of variation are from common causes. Usually, only management can eliminate them, since their source is typically beyond the authority of a worker (e.g., poor product design). After special causes have been eliminated, the process is called a "controlled" process. It is predictable, even though it may still produce too many rejects. Once under statistical control, the real work of process improvement can begin.

Control charts are characterized by three features (see Figures 4-4 and 4-5):

- The level at which the process is performing, displayed by the center line representing the overall average of all observations
- The normal distribution of the sample averages, represented by the upper and lower control limits
- The observations, represented by plotted points.

$\overline{X}$ AND R CHARTS

Two different types of data, or observations, are collected, depending on the production process:

- Variable data, generated by actual measurements on a continuous scale, such as width, weight, and temperature
- Attribute data, which is composed of counts of discrete quality-related characteristics, such as defective units produced.

There are control charts for each type of observation. In this section we deal with $\overline{X}$ and R charts, which are used with variable data. Attribute data control charts, P and nP charts, are considered in the next section. To repeat, in this section we are interested in actual measurements, such as length, weight, and thickness, that is, in variable data.

Assume you are destructively testing the life of an electronic component for time to failure. Component samples are picked from the production process randomly at specific points in time. Each of the 20 samples has five components.

Each item is destructively tested, and the time to failure is recorded, as illustrated in Figure 4-6. The average time in sample 1 was $\overline{X}$ = 32.2. The range for

FIGURE 4-6 $\overline{X}$ and R Chart Data. Time to Failure.

Sample Number	1	2	3	4	5	Sample average ($\overline{X}$)	Range R
1	49	27	29	39	17	32.2	32
2	16	29	82	0	2	25.8	82
3	36	3	8	35	64	29.2	61
4	76	62	43	4	97	56.4	93
5	68	17	17	12	77	38.2	65
6	91	92	19	11	85	59.6	81
7	97	30	40	23	39	45.8	74
8	85	38	62	18	47	50.0	67
9	56	12	49	82	9	41.6	70
10	84	38	27	35	44	45.6	57
11	39	7	50	50	33	35.8	43
12	78	56	77	52	1	52.8	77
13	78	17	71	68	10	48.8	68
14	1	91	60	29	93	54.8	92
15	41	83	47	23	68	52.4	60
16	65	81	21	40	86	58.6	65
17	37	55	38	14	53	39.4	41
18	26	60	28	96	37	49.4	70
19	64	5	40	94	90	58.6	89
20	45	21	38	54	22	36.0	33
						$\overline{\overline{X}}$ = 45.55	$\overline{R}$ = 66

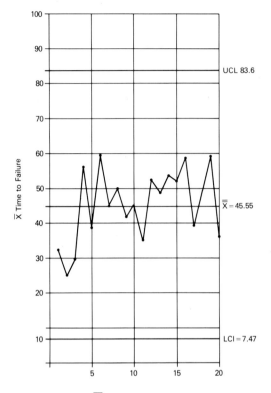

FIGURE 4-7 $\overline{X}$ Chart.   FIGURE 4-8 R Chart.

sample 1 was 32 (the highest less the lowest, or $R = 49 - 17$). The mean of the means is calculated ($\overline{\overline{X}} = 45.55$), as is the mean of the ranges ($\overline{R} = 66$).

The $\overline{X}$ data and the $\overline{\overline{X}}$ calculations are charted in Figure 4-7, and the R and $\overline{R}$ calculations are in Figure 4-8. $\overline{X}$ and R charts almost always appear together, because when you calculate the sample average ($\overline{X}$), the sample spread, or dispersion, is lost. The range (R) chart displays that variability.

The control limits for $\overline{X}$ and R are calculated using the formulas and constants in Figure 4-9, as follows:

$\overline{X}$ chart

$$\begin{aligned}
\text{Upper control limit (UCL)} &= \overline{\overline{X}} + A_2\overline{R} \\
&= 45.55 + 0.577(66) \\
&= 45.55 + 38.08 = 83.6
\end{aligned}$$

$$\begin{aligned}
\text{Lower control limit (LCL)} &= \overline{\overline{X}} - A_2\overline{R} \\
&= 45.55 - .577(66) \\
&= 45.55 - 38.08 = 7.47
\end{aligned}$$

STATISTICAL PROCESS CONTROL

Variables Control Chart: When samples are expressed in quantitative units of measurement e.g. length, weight, etc.
CONTROL CHARTS FOR VARIABLES $\overline{X}$-R Chart = Plotting the Average/Range of Data Collected Calculate the Average $(\overline{X})$ and Range (R) of each subgroup $$\overline{X} = \frac{X_1 + X_2 + \ldots X_n}{n} \qquad R = X_{max} - X_{min}$$ Calculate the Average Range $(\overline{R})$ and the Process Average $(\overline{\overline{X}})$ $$\overline{\overline{X}} = \frac{\overline{X}_1 + \overline{X}_2 + \ldots + \overline{X}_k}{K}$$ $\boxed{K = \text{\# of subgroups}}$ $$\overline{R} = \frac{R_1 + R_2 + \ldots R_k}{K}$$ Calculate the Control Limits $UCL_R = D_4\overline{R} \qquad LCL_R = D_3\overline{R}$ $UCL_{\overline{x}} = \overline{\overline{X}} + A_2\overline{R} \qquad LCL_{\overline{x}} = \overline{\overline{X}} - A_2\overline{R}$

Table of Factors for X & R Charts

Number of Observations in Subgroup (n)	Factors for $\overline{X}$ Chart — From R A_2	Factors for R Chart — Lower D_3	Factors for R Chart — Upper D_4
2	1.880	0	3.268
3	1.023	0	2.574
4	0.729	0	2.282
5	0.577	0	2.114
6	0.483	0	2.004
7	0.419	0.076	1.924
8	0.373	0.136	1.864
9	0.337	0.184	1.816
10	0.308	0.223	1.777

FIGURE 4-9 $\overline{X}$ and R Charts. [From *The Memory Jogger* (Methuen, MA: GOAL/QPC, 1987), p. 52.]

R chart

$$\text{UCL} = D_4\overline{R} = 2.114(66) = 139.5$$

$$\text{LCL} = D_3\overline{R} = 0(66) = 0$$

The control limits indicate that almost all of what you produce should fall between them (assuming your process is under control and only common causes are affecting production). When a point falls beyond the control limits, something more than the chance variation of the process is almost certainly occurring.

This $\overline{X}$ chart shows that the average time to failure is 46 units of time. If this

> Attributes Control Chart:
> When sample reflects qualitative characteristics e.g. is/is not defective. go/no go.
>
> CONTROL CHARTS FOR ATTRIBUTES
>
> the p Chart = Proportion Defective
>
> $$p = \frac{\text{number of rejects in subgroup}}{\text{number inspected in subgroup}}$$
>
> $$\bar{p} = \frac{\text{total number rejects}}{\text{total number, inspected}}$$
>
> $$UCL_p^* = \bar{p} + \frac{3\sqrt{\bar{p}(1-\bar{p})}}{\sqrt{n}} \qquad LCL_p^* = p - \frac{3\sqrt{\bar{p}(1-\bar{p})}}{\sqrt{n}}$$
>
> *This formula creates changing control limits. To avoid this, use Average Sample Sizes $\sqrt{\bar{n}}$ as long as all sample sizes are within 20% of each other.
>
> The np chart = Number Defective
>
> $$UCL_{np} = n\bar{p} + 3\sqrt{n\bar{p}(1-\bar{p})}$$
>
> $$LCL_{np} = n\bar{p} - 3\sqrt{n\bar{p}(1-\bar{p})}$$

FIGURE 4-10 *P* and *MP* Charts. [From *The Memory Jogger* (Methuen, MA: GOAL/QPC, 1987), p. 53.]

is deemed too short a period, management will have to work on the production process to increase it.

The *R* chart shows the range of time to failure. It falls between 32 and 93 units of time for the 20 samples, with an average of 66. (A change in dispersion means an abnormality.) These data suggest that there may be a need for less dispersion; that is, for more consistency in the components so that customers experience a greater, more uniform time to failure. Management would then work on the process to achieve these improvements.

P AND *nP* CHARTS

In this section we are interested in identifying and counting the times that conform (or fail to conform) to some specific requirement, such as defective or not defective, present or absent, or pass or fail. Such data are called *attribute data*. The control charts for attribute data are *P* and *nP* charts:

P charts show the fraction of output that is nonconforming. The center line $\bar{P}$ estimates the fraction nonconforming in the process. *P* charts thus represent proportions (percentages), such as the proportion defective.

nP charts are based on counts of discrete observations, such as the actual number that are defective in the sample (so sample size must remain constant). The center line *nP* estimates the actual number (of defectives per shift, for example). The formulas for calculating *P* and *nP* charts are presented in Figure 4-10.

Some helpful hints for constructing all control charts are as follows.

- The data you collect must reflect how your process runs naturally; so do not change the process during data collection.
- Your data must be kept in the sequence in which you gathered them.
- Use the correct chart for your type of data (i.e., $\overline{X}$ and R charts for variable data and P and nP charts for attribute data).
- Upper and lower control limits are *not* specification limits. Upper and lower control limits reflect natural process variability and must be statistically calculated. Specifications are based on product requirements.
- The variation between the control limits is the natural variability of the process, and only management has broad enough jurisdiction to control it.

CONCLUSION

Many students are required to take one course in statistics, another in principles of management, and a third in systems analysis and design. The connections among these courses are hazy for most of us.

This chapter shows that you are dealing with one integrated whole. W. Edwards Deming lists the requirements for managing complex systems of people and machines so that you can improve quality and productivity while you reduce costs. Statistical process control provides the techniques for quantifying the variability and output of your process. Once defined, everyone can work to constantly improve the entire process, or system. Higher quality and lower costs result, with the dividend of greater productivity.

CASE STUDY

Read the Cutter Laboratories case at the end of this chapter and write out

1. Why can't you obtain quality through technology or through people alone?
2. What SPC charts have to do with the Covina plant's prosperity and the employees' jobs?

SUMMARY

1. American managers who don't learn how to cut costs while raising quality won't survive.
2. W. Edwards Deming's 14 points and his 7 deadly diseases tell how to compete globally.
3. Variability is a critical concept in Deming's approach.
4. Plant and office processes are subject to two kinds of variability: special causes (about 15 percent of all sources of variability, usually correctable by workers) and common causes (about 85 percent of all variability, correctable only by management).

5. A process is in statistical control when the special causes of variation have been removed. Then, the real work of process improvement can begin.
6. A process in statistical control is stable and predictable. It has a definite capability, and you know what specifications it can meet.
7. Control charts help to get a process in control and keep it there. They have three features: observations (plotted points), a center line representing the overall average of all observations (showing the level at which the process is performing), and upper and lower control limits (calculated from the data).
8. When data are from measurements, such as height or weight, the appropriate controls chart is an $\overline{X}$ or R chart.
9. When data come from counts (e.g., acceptable or defective, or present or absent) the proper control chart is a P or an nP chart.
10. Management, statistics, and system analysis are all part of the same entity and are not different topics.

REVIEW QUESTIONS

1. Comment briefly on Deming's 14 points and 7 deadly diseases.
2. If a manager tries to use numerical quotas to improve a system, what will probably happen?
3. Why is variability important here?
4. Explain special and common causes of variation. Who can correct which? Illustrate each.
5. Define statistical control and explain its significance.
6. What are some advantages when a process is in statistical control?
7. Illustrate a run chart.
8. What is a control chart? What are its features? How is it used?
9. Which charts are used for variable data and for attribute data?
10. Why do $\overline{X}$ and R charts usually appear together?
11. Explain how to calculate the control limits for an $\overline{X}$ chart. Why are the constant A_2 and $\overline{R}$ used?
12. Describe the calculation of P and nP charts. Comment on sample size.
13. What are some helpful hints for constructing control charts?

REFERENCES

1. See M. Tribus and Y. Tsuda, *The Quality Imperative in the New Economic Era* (Cambridge, Mass.: MIT, 1985).
2. See M. Tribus and Y. Tsuda, *Creating the Quality Company* (Cambridge, Mass.: MIT, 1985).
3. See UNISYS, *The Third Wave: Statistical Process Control,* 1987 Videotape Training Series.

4. See Mary Walton, *The Deming Management Method* (NY: Dodd, Mead, 1986) p. 51.
5. See W. Edwards Deming, *Out of the Crisis* (Cambridge, Mass.: MIT, 1982) p. 336.
6. *Ibid.,* p. 340.
7. This section draws heavily on the seven modules of UNISYS' training series, *The Third Wave: Statistical Process Control.*
8. This section is from *The Memory Jogger* (Methuen, MA: GOAL/QPC, 1987) pp. 48, 49.

Case Study
CUTTER LABORATORIES*:
DRIVE FOR QUALITY FUELS PARTICIPATIVE STYLE

Cutter Laboratories' Covina, CA, plant management knew top quality was key to recognition of their new product in a marketplace dominated by only one other company.

So when production got rolling back in 1979, they turned responsibility for quality over to employees.

Since then, output's more than doubled despite workforce shrinkage of 15 percent. Direct costs of production have dropped 36 percent.

And the new product, a blood storage bag, has tripled its contribution to Cutter Labs' profitability.

"We're at output and quality levels now we never dreamed we could really reach," said Ben Salumbides, production manager. Perhaps more importantly, however, Covina employees are gaining skills and growing in ways they never before imagined, added Raymond Vierra, senior production manager for the 450-worker facility.

"All of us have enhanced our jobs," said Vierra, a 42-year veteran of Cutter Labs.

CORPORATE BACKGROUND

Cutter Laboratories was founded in 1897 by E. A. Cutter, a self-trained central California pharmacist, to make a variety of human and animal immunological products used, primarily, by local cattle ranchers. The firm's Berkeley headquarters was established in 1903. By 1937, a new method for administering intravenous solutions had helped to push the Cutter Labs' sales to $1 million yearly.

During World War II, Cutter started doing blood plasma processing for the armed forces. In 1974, then-president David Cutter, grandson of the founder, accepted a friendly offer to merge the firm with Bayer Leverkusen, the German pharmaceutical company. In 1983, Bayer merged Cutter into Miles Laboratories, Inc., which Bayer had purchased in 1977. Cutter's five divisions retain their corporate identity as the "Cutter Group" of Miles Labs.

The Covina facility is part of Cutter's biological division, which handles blood collection and storage containers as well as products derived from blood plasma. The 10-year-old plant is one of the largest manufacturers of blood bags in the world.

*Originally published as "Cutter Laboratories: Drive for Quality Fuels Participative Style," Case Study 47, American Productivity & Quality Center, September 1985.

For five years it produced only one type of product, called plasma pheresis bags, used to harvest plasma from whole blood.

In 1979, Cutter decided to take a stab at the so-called "trade bag" market, then dominated by the Fenwall Laboratories division of Baxter Travenol Laboratories Inc. The Covina plant was slated to produce the new product, which is used for collection and storage of whole blood by the Red Cross and other blood banks.

At the same time, organizational changes put three newcomers—Ray Vierra, Ben Salumbides, and Glen Pierce—in charge of the plant.

MANAGEMENT BY NECESSITY

Vierra and Salumbides had worked together at another Cutter plant which had undergone traumatic changes. Pierce had joined Cutter in 1977 to open a Canadian plant that produced a small number of trade bags. The three shared a belief that traditional boss-worker factory relationships could be bettered through employee involvement. But their participative style at the Covina plant evolved as much from necessity as from idealism.

"We recognized that to go into a new product line and to grow with it, our supervisors and managers had to understand what we were up against," Vierra explained. "It was a make it work or we close the plant situation."

Workers' jobs would depend on a quick recouping of high start-up expenses for the new product line, so raising awareness of operating costs became a top priority.

"We also knew that to enter this business we had to have a quality, quality product. That's the only thing that would make a difference to buyers," Salumbides added. Trade bag buyers are the blood banks that supply hospitals and emergency medics. It's not exaggerating to suggest that lives depend on the bags in which blood is stored and collected. A faulty product would be vehemently rejected in the marketplace.

Employee involvement was seen as the catalyst for quality and productivity, survival and, eventually, expansion. "But we'd never heard of the buzzwords back then. We just did it," Vierra recalled, grinning.

"CONTINUALLY TINKER"

The trio set off on several paths in rapid succession, eventually weaving a web of employee involvement activities too numerous to detail. "It's not one thing. It's a whole mess of things you have to continually tinker with," that have made quality "contagious" at the Covina plant, Vierra commented. Among them:

- A task force made up of plant and Group managers began meeting monthly to study and select capital investments to cut critical start-up costs of the new product line.
- An in-plant task force made up of 25 supervisors, line workers and representatives from non-production departments began examining additional cost reductions. Costs of poor quality were prime targets.

- Glen Pierce, director of plant operations, Vierra and Salumbides became frequent midnight visitors to the plant. "We believe we have to know how people do their jobs to help them keep their quality up," Salumbides explained. "So we started coming at 1:30, 2 a.m. to watch processes that only took place then. Ray and I still go religiously to the production floor for a few hours every morning after we open our mail."

  "We want to see what's going on and we want to give those line workers an opportunity to talk to us. I call it my 'good morning situation,'" Vierra added.
- Another in-plant task force, or Quality Review Committee, began meeting monthly to track field performance of Covina-made products and any defects customers find. This group includes representatives from corporate sales, marketing and product development departments, as well as quality engineers.
- Quality Concern Circles were assembled for each of the plant's three production shifts. They're made up of shift supervisors, lead operators, line operators and quality assurance engineers. Circles meet weekly to review rejects, customer complaints and other information passed from or shared with the Quality Review Committee. Their assignment is to tackle day-to-day, on-the-spot quality hindrances.
- First and foremost, middle-level managers and first line supervisors became target groups for intensive training. They, in turn, passed new skills and knowledge on to the Covina plant's 327 hourly employees.

  Covina's supervisors had been behaving more like traffic cops than managers, Vierra explained. "We wanted them to handle problems, rather than just taking them to the next level," he said. "As a first step, Ben and I spent a lot of time trying to define every job in the plant for the new environment we envisioned."

THREE-TIER TRAINING

"We wanted to push responsibility down to the people on the line, the people who build the quality into the product," he continued. "So we started working with the first level of managers, the shift supervisors, who are responsible for daily output of their departments. We set up training to clarify their jobs, to get them to think like managers, and to give them some of the tools they'd need to do that," Vierra said.

A three-tier training program evolved. Vierra, Pierce and Salumbides taught the first classes themselves. First-level managers then helped train line supervisors, and supervisors led classes for top-level hourly workers, the lead operators.

In retrospect, the plant managers acknowledge their strategy was brilliant. By focusing first on middle level workers, they forestalled any of the resentment typical among that group when lower-level employees get a greater say. By stressing the job growth available—indeed, expected—for the shift managers, supervisors and lead operators, they allayed typical fears that mid-level authorities were slipping away.

In short, by "getting them to think more like managers," Pierce, Vierra and Salumbides made strong allies of the mid-level group that's often foiled productivity improvement in other organizations. But they didn't plan it that way. "We just knew we needed those supervisors up to speed to make this new product happen," Vierra said.

As it turned out, the onus now is on the plant's top management to keep hands off supervisory matters. "We have to be careful not to undermine our whole training effort," Vierra said. An open-door policy often brings lower level employees to his office with grievances or ideas, he explained. It's difficult, sometimes, to send the worker back to the supervisor who manages him. The middle ranks keep the chiefs honest, however. "I slipped once and that supervisor was in my office right away, chewing me out for stepping into his area of responsibility," Vierra said.

SKILLS STRENGTHENED

The purpose of the supervisory training was the same for every level: to strengthen skills, broaden knowledge of the plant's operations and prepare the employee for future growth with Cutter Labs.

Every course covered plant production costs, quality requirements, utilization of human resources for methods improvement, manufacturing documentation and problem solving techniques. First line supervisors and shift supervisors reviewed personnel policies. Shift supervisors also were trained in project management.

"We stressed costs of production with the underlying theory that if employees understand the costs involved in what they're doing, they'll better understand the costs of changing the way they're doing things," Salumbides said.

To illustrate the point, examples of the plant's various blood bag products are tacked to huge bulletin boards throughout the three-building facility. Next to each bag is a breakdown on the cost of its components (bag, anti-coagulant solution, plastic stoppers also molded at the Covina facility, tubes and needles) and of the finished product. The breakdown also shows how component costs have risen or—in most cases—fallen since the product-line start-up.

TASK FORCES

The task force created to study cost reductions through capital investments cut across organizational lines. "I chaired that group and sometimes Ray (Vierra) and Glen (Pierce), my bosses, were reporting to me," Salumbides said. The task force also had authority from top Cutter Group management to implement its recommendations, developed over two years, for automating some manufacturing processes.

That group worked so well the plant-level task force was formed about a year later, in early 1980. "Our lower-level workers already were generating lots of productivity improvement ideas. We saw no reason to hold them for action until the higher-level group's meetings," Salumbides said.

The 25 members of the plant-level task force were appointed by Pierce, Salumbides and Vierra to ensure participation by all plant areas. They include representatives from purchasing, engineering maintenance, industrial engineering, accounting, all 16 supervisors and all shift managers. All meet monthly for what Pierce believes to be the plant's most important work toward productivity and top quality. "It's the one meeting I won't allow anyone to miss—ever," he said.

"FEARLESS FORUMS"

The meetings are "fearless forums" where every product rejected at the plant or in later field use is scrutinized to discover the cause of the defect, Pierce explained. At first, the task was daunting. "We started counting our discards as a percentage of quantity produced," he said.

"Now, we count our discards in parts *per million*. Quality improved so much that a percentage number was meaningless." Among the reasons:

- A "No Time for Rework" program that's moved inspection points for quality assurance from finished product all the way back to materials suppliers.
- Recent work with those suppliers to boost the quality of *their* products—solutions, resins and other raw materials.

  "We realized we were treating our suppliers as we used to treat our own people: Assuming the reason we got bad goods was they didn't care," Pierce commented. Instead, Covina management decided to try to spread some of its in-house successes.

  Since late 1984, plant managers have taught three-day seminars on quality control for vendors from throughout the country. Starting in 1985, the plant began to require that vendors supply quality control charts along with the materials they deliver. Compliance is spotty but growing, Pierce said. And response among vendors has been enthusiastic.

  "They appreciate the fact that we're giving them tools to improve *their* business. And the trust level is growing," he added.
- Informal employee testing. Its yearly blood drive brings the local Red Cross to the Covina plant for collections in factory-made bags. "There's no more effective way for employees to judge whether the needles they make are sharp enough," Vierra noted, chuckling.

"CRITICAL BLEND"

In addition, the plant-level task force is another vehicle for employee involvement and job enhancement. "It's the supervisors' first exposure to other departments. It gives them a place to develop the confidence they need to talk about the thing they already know best—how to do their jobs—and it gives them a crack at project management," Salumbides said.

"The program has opened channels for people to work with other departments and get informal cross training," he added.

To ensure *effective* participation, Covina management also provided managers and supervisors with training in statistical process control and on technical aspects of various plant production processes.

"As we went through task force evaluations, we realized we can't get quality through technology or people alone. It has to be a very critical blend of the two. That's the essence of our program," Salumbides explained.

Training in the tenets of statistical process control (SPC, see page 87) started in 1983 for upper level managers. By the end of 1985, all plant managers and supervisors will have completed the courses. All also are required to take on-site training in the use of personal computers to aid their analyses and the technical classes offered on-site since January of this year.

Like the earlier management skills building sessions, all SPC, technical and PC classes now are led by Covina employees.

The technology training is a seven-week course phased through the plant according to which areas needed it soonest. "We track all categories of discards so we can focus on the areas that produce the most," Salumbides said. Both those manning various assembly machines and those responsible for maintaining the equipment attend classes together. Hourly workers are paid overtime for attendance.

The two- to three-hour sessions focus on technical aspects of statistical process control methods. They cover (a) the principles of the assembly process; (b) a breakdown of the process into identifiable steps and customers for those steps, and (c) exploration of practical, technological adjustments that could improve the process and, thereby, quality of the product of each step of assembly.

In practice, the training and involvement programs have "made mini industrial engineers out of all our supervisors," Vierra noted. Supervisors themselves carry out the studies necessary to make a change in the assembly process. A staff engineer merely verifies their work, "so the supervisors own the new work standard," he explained.

EMPLOYMENT SECURITY

In one recent case, a supervisor's work led him to the conclusion his job could be eliminated. Fortunately, Covina's participative management style has created an atmosphere that allowed him to admit so.

Early on, management made it clear that jobs might change, but no jobs would be lost due to productivity or quality improvements. The task force and training programs foster the interaction and cross training necessary to uphold the employment security promise. When attrition opens jobs, they are posted and usually filled from within, Salumbides said. "There have been layoffs due to market forces, but none due to efficiency improvements," Vierra added. "You never want to have a cost reduction plan whereby people can cut themselves out of their jobs."

Perhaps employees' biggest concern, rather, has been the extent to which their responsibilities have expanded.

"What we're hearing from supervisors now is 'our jobs are so much bigger,'" Vierra said. The plant managers say that's because the workers have chosen to make them so.

"Our training is not voluntary, but use of the tools taught is," Vierra maintains. Acceptance and practice of SPC and computer skills varies from supervisor to supervisor and department to department, he added.

POLICY COORDINATORS

In addition to the opportunity to learn and use new skills, however, Covina supervisors have taken greater roles in overall plant management and administration. Since 1980, a number of supervisors have taken on additional responsibilities as plant coordinators for quality, safety, attendance, a formal suggestion system and good manufacturing practices.

"We created these coordinators to head employee teams in the various areas because we wanted these people to get used to working with their peers and to foster cooperation. But we also did it because we (top managers) were overloaded," Vierra said. "We needed the help."

Working with an employee team, the plant's safety coordinator investigates any production accidents and publishes a monthly summary of safety advances or problems. Likewise, the attendance coordinator tracks and reports absenteeism. The coordinators run special promotions and recognition programs to boost employee awareness of their various areas of responsibility. They take part in annual budgeting for funds to support their efforts, and control all funds expended. "It's their baby," Salumbides said.

The strategy to push responsibilities to lower levels of the Covina plant organization has paid off over the years. Absenteeism dropped to 3 percent in 1984 from 10 percent in 1979, before coordinators were assigned. The 1985 target is 2.5 percent. And time lost to on-the-job accidents dropped to one day in 1984 from more than a month two years earlier.

Yet another group of Covina employees meets solely to see that non-production, non-administrative snags are smoothed. The "Communications Committee" is made up of hourly representatives from each section of the plant; it meets monthly with plant production and personnel managers. On the agenda are general problems—those which cross or fall between plant functional lines. Minutes of discussion on the problems are distributed back to the supervisory level of each department for ideas or action.

"It's a delicate situation," Vierra again pointed out. "If we're going to practice what we preach, we have to be careful not to act as a policy-making committee. Everything that can goes back to the supervisors. We really try to *use* that level of management."

"STATE OF THE UNION"

"I see mine as an umbrella type management. I catch all the rain"—the corporate interference or vendor problems that might dampen the energies of those actually running the Covina plant, Pierce added. "We encourage our managers to be entrepreneurs and control their own destinies," he added.

More than once, for example, employee problem solving teams have tested solutions already proven useless, Vierra said. "We knew the suggestion wouldn't work. We'd tried it ourselves. But we let them find out for themselves."

"There's a real educational value in that," he continued. "We tolerate failure. It's part of the process."

When top management does step in, it's on plant-shaking matters.

Pierce spends an 18-hour day each quarter in back-to-back meetings with each department and all work shifts to deliver a "state of the union" type address on sales, business prospects, employee benefits and other company issues. When new designs or work processes are introduced, production stops and all those affected are gathered to learn why, discuss the changes and brainstorm on problems that might come up.

"'Help us make it work,' we tell them. 'Talk to one another and tell us where you see problems, where there are ways to improve,'" Salumbides said.

"Years ago, our first thought would be on the costs of stopping the line," he added. "Now, we don't even consider that." Indeed, supervisors are authorized to stop the line when adjustments are needed to keep process quality high.

MEASURED IMPROVEMENT

Pierce, Salumbides and Vierra measure the success of their wide-ranging employee involvement and quality improvement efforts on a variety of scales:

- *Net savings* from cost-cutting and quality-improvement efforts have let the company hold the line on product prices despite inflationary increases in manufacturing costs. The savings include $50,000 shaved from production costs from a product size change suggested by a plant sanitation supervisor, for example.
- *Defects in manufacturing* of Covina products have dropped by tenfold, "since we're now building quality into the product," Pierce commented.

All is not bliss. Quality Concern Circles and task forces still are examining discards for defects. "And we have our disagreements," Vierra said.

"But they're handled openly. There is no fear of coming to Glen or Ben or me with a criticism. Supervisors are not afraid to protect their turf from interferences. And we have a real spirit of entrepreneurship operating."

Furthermore, top management remains doggedly committed to keeping that spirit strongest close to the ranks. "One of our greatest successes," Pierce commented, "has been in moving our supervisors from roles—and views of themselves—as high paid hourlies to those of management."

STATISTICAL PROCESS CONTROL

"Statistical process control methods help to identify and to correct out-of-control processes. When processes are brought into control, the benefits can be a reduction in downtime, a decrease in rework and scrap costs, a lowering of inspection and testing expenses, a decrease in defect levels, and continuing customer confidence," writes Barbara Kershner Kimball in a 1984 article for Medical Device and Diagnostic Industry magazine. Kimball was manager of Quality Engineering Services at Cutter Labs' Covina plant until she was promoted to headquarters in the spring of 1985.

SPC actually refers to a number of mathematical tools manufacturers can use to assess and correct product quality at each or any step of production, from delivery of raw materials from vendors to shipment of finished widgets to buyers.

Put simply, the idea is to break manufacturing into a series of processes, much as a recipe breaks down the process of cooking. At each step, certain specifications must be met in order to meet final product quality expectations. SPC applies graphic measures to each step so that deviations can be readily seen and corrected. Chief among these are control charts, which display data relative to time so that variations in process behavior can be analyzed using statistical theory.

In making plastic tubing for blood bags, for example, control charts might show lengths and numbers of defects for a given sample over a given period of time. Process behavior would be analyzed relative to a center line, representing the average, and in relation to control limits usually placed at standard deviations from the central line. (See figures)

Such measures can be taken on representative samples of both the *results* of the steps of the manufacturing process (tube length) and of the *step itself* (tube cutting). Analysis of the graphic representations taken over time indicates where and when processes are "out of control," as Kimball says, and allows for projections as to where and when they'll show up as final product defects—and rejections.

With additional analysis, workers can pinpoint causes of deviations and adjust the process to prevent them.

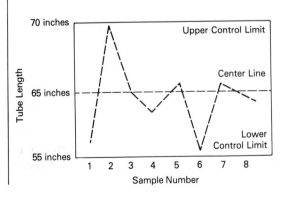
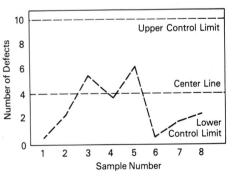

"The existence of control charts often improves communication in a manufacturing plant because everyone speaks the same statistical language and because problems are viewed impartially," Kimball adds.

At Cutter Labs, communication between shifts has improved because the charts provide a complete record of activities, for example, and everyone agrees about when to make a process adjustment. The common language of SPC also has improved communication among research and development, quality and engineering personnel, she adds. Better communication boosts problem-solving and productivity.

Chapter Five

MANUFACTURING AUTOMATION PROTOCOL

After you have read this chapter, it will be clear to you that

- ❏ The manufacturing automation protocol is a set of rules governing how machines of any make should communicate.
- ❏ MAP is based on standards of the International Standards Organization called the open systems interconnection (OSI) model. It has seven layers that take into account the hardware, software, protocols, and network architecture that comprise a telecommunications system.
- ❏ MAP includes all seven layers, but we will discuss only the bottom two in detail (called the local area network, or LAN).
- ❏ LAN standards are set by the Institute of Electrical and Electronics Engineers' (IEEE) Standards Project 802. We discuss 802.4 (broadband bus with token passing) and 802.3 (carrier sense multiple access/collision detection, CSMA/CD).
- ❏ MAP is for multivendor factory automation systems. The technical and office protocol (TOP) is MAP's office equivalent. MAP and TOP are complementary.

Factory machines, such as numerical control (NC) tools, robots, and computer controllers, each have their own software and need expensive translation systems to exchange data. If factories could be wired the way telephone companies wire offices, all the machines could be hooked together regardless of vendor.

That is why General Motors Corporation imposed its own *manufacturing automation protocol* on the industry. MAP is a set of rules governing how machines of any make should communicate. By providing a common communications channel and eliminating special interface equipment and special cabling, MAP can save automation costs.

GM's Pontiac, Michigan, and Fort Wayne, Indiana, plants use MAP-based networks. To illustrate, these systems include:[1]

- The statistical process control system, which keeps track of process trends factorywide
- The flexible scheduling system, which sets up body shop jobs, adjusts vehicle sequences after paint jobs, and sends vehicle option data to terminals and a laser printer on the factory floor
- The shipping control system
- A vehicle-processing system, which tracks the assembly process
- The maintenance management system.

OPEN SYSTEMS INTERCONNECTION MODEL

To plug in the same hair dryer in Quebec City, Canada, and in Paris, France, much standardization of the electrical systems would be required to avoid the need for special adapters. Similarly, much standardization is needed for computer equipment from different suppliers to communicate without special software and hardware.

The national standards organizations of many countries, such as the American National Standards Institute, belong to the International Standards Organization. In 1977, the ISO began work on an open system interconnection model to deal with these incompatibilities. The seven-layer OSI standard was announced in 1979, and it has been generally accepted by the telecommunications industry.

This *OSI model* (Figure 5-1) has seven layers that take into account the hardware, software, protocols, and network architecture that comprise a telecommunications system. These seven layers define the functions needed for any two machines to communicate. The actual connections among computers, robots, terminals, and other nodes are physical. The connections between layers in the model (e.g., the transport layer in system A and the transport layer in system B in Figure 5-1) are logical, not physical.

For hardware and software from various sources to communicate, they have to use these same seven layers, and the data formats and control fields passing between the layers must be compatible. Figure 5-2 illustrates the seven basic tasks (i.e., layers) that are needed for network communication. Messages pass from the

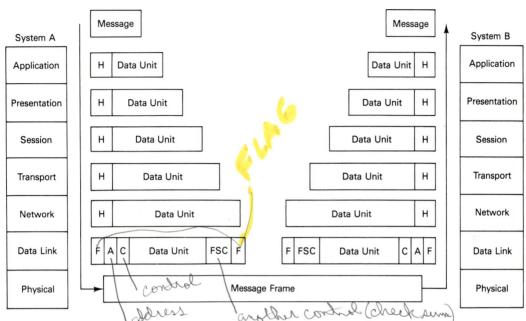

FIGURE 5-1 Open system interconnection standard. In this illustration, a data message is transmitted from an application program in system A to an application program in system B. As it is sent, each communication layer manages or alters the message in some way and adds information for its counterpart in the form of a message header (H). Each layer's header, when added to the original message, forms part of the data unit. In the data link layer, flag (F), address (A), control (C), and checksum (FSC) bits are added. These bits complete the message frame that is transmitted over the physical layer of the network to system B. As the data unit passes through system B, each layer removes and reads the header intended for it, performs the appropriate data conversion, and passes the data unit on to the layer above it. [From *A Primer on Computer Networks,* No. 777-4004, 61 (Lowell, MA: Wang Laboratories, 1982), p. 61. Courtesy Wang Laboratories.]

sender through each of the seven layers and onto the network. At the recipient's end, they then travel back up through the layers, each layer removing and acting on the information intended for it.

The seven layers of the OSI model for network architecture may be characterized as follows.

1. *Physical.* Connects, maintains, and disconnects the physical link between communicating devices. It passes the bits (the zeros and ones which compose the message frame or packet). This layer is concerned with voltages, transmission speeds, connector cable standards, and all the other aspects of the actual physical connection.

92 MANUFACTURING AUTOMATION PROTOCOL

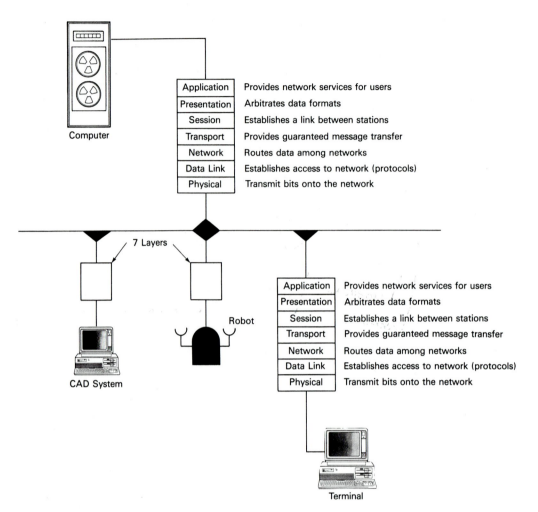

FIGURE 5-2 The OSI communication model spells out the seven basic tasks that must be accomplished before communications can take place on a network. Messages pass from the sender through each of the seven layers and onto the network. They then travel back up through the layers to the recipient.

2. *Data link*. Breaks the raw bit stream into data frames, which are transmitted, received, and acknowledged. It controls the numbering and counting of the frames, detects errors, and retransmits the blocks (when necessary). Essentially, it establishes, maintains, and releases data links.
3. *Network*. Performs traffic control and routing of the packets (i.e., frames), dealing with switching and other aspects of moving data through the network. This leaves the upper layers independent of the transmission

and switching techniques for connecting devices. Layers 1, 2, and 3 operate in chain-link fashion, transferring packets from node to node and never skipping a link.

4. *Transport.* Transmits data from source to destination, ensuring error-free delivery. It allows a program on one device to converse directly with the software of another device, even though they are separated by modems, controllers, front-end processors, and other hardware. Layer 4 is concerned with end-to-end flow control (in contrast with the link orientation of layer 3).

5. *Session.* Interfaces the user with the network (e.g., allows the user to log in by typing a password). It operates from source to destination, as does layer 4.

6. *Presentation.* Converts bit stream characters for tabbing, line feed, data editing, and the like, so incompatible devices (e.g., using different character sets and file formats) can communicate.

7. *Application.* Determines how the programs plug into the OSI environment. The user's software department decides what network statistics will automatically be collected, how file transfers will occur, whether the data base will be distributed, and similar matters. These decisions are then implemented via layer 7.

In summary, the seven OSI layers are roughly as follows.

- The top three are application-oriented:
    7—Application
    6—Presentation
    5—Session
- The next two are interface layers between the application and transmission functions:
    4—Transport
    3—Network
- The bottom two layers provide the data link control for reconciling differences (producing a clean interface between nodes), the physical medium (e.g., twisted wire pairs, coaxial cable), and the standards for physically attaching to the medium plus the techniques for encoding data onto the medium:
    2—Data link
    1—Physical

The manufacturing automation protocol is based on this OSI network model. Diverse equipment from various vendors has to be integrated on the factory floor. MAP is a partial subset of the OSI standards, specifically for a tightly coupled factory environment. Note that as MAP develops, newer versions are announced (e.g., MAP 2.0, 2.1, 2.2, and 3.0). While MAP includes all seven layers, we will discuss only the bottom two in detail. These two are termed the *local area network layers.*

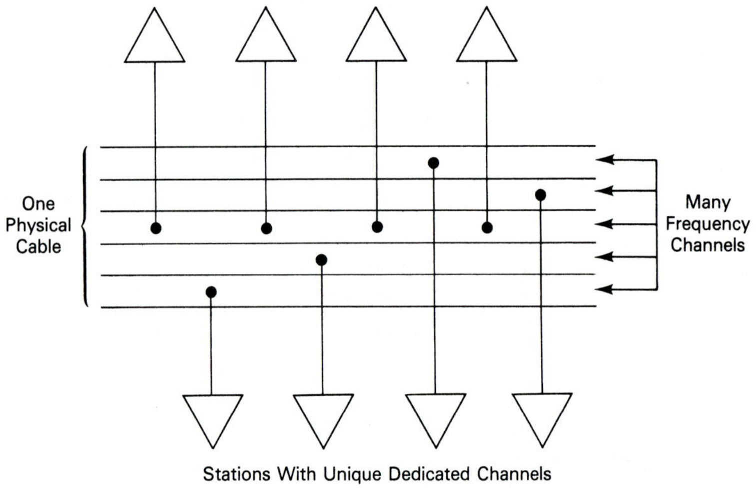

94 MANUFACTURING AUTOMATION PROTOCOL

FIGURE 5-3 **Broadband systems**—frequency division multiplexing (when more than one device can transmit over the same cable). [From *An Introduction to Local Area Networks,* Publication No. GC20-8203-1 (IBM, 1984), p. 3-8. Courtesy of International Business Machines Corporation, White Plains, NY.]

LOCAL AREA NETWORKS

The Institute of Electrical and Electronics Engineers endorses the OSI network model. IEEE Standards Project 802 further defines standards for the bottom two ISO layers, the physical and data link layers. Since these 802 standards are part of MAP, they are discussed next. Critical characteristics of MAP's bottom two layers are their ability to move data (bandwidth), the geometric shape of the network (topology), and who obtains access and when (access protocols). The discussion of MAP's first and second layers is in terms of the following three topics.[2]

BANDWIDTH

Bandwidth concerns the network's ability to move data and how this capacity is used. There are two techniques:

- *Broadband,* which provides multiple communication paths with a broad range of frequencies (Figure 5-3). One cable carriers several frequencies, which are assigned to specific devices connected to the cable.
- *Baseband,* which allows several devices to share one cable using time sharing (Figure 5-4). Each device is assigned a specific time slot (e.g., a few millionths of a second) in which to transmit, and only this device can use that slot.

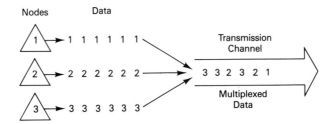

FIGURE 5-4 Time division multiplexing (TDM). [From *An Introduction to Local Area Networks,* Publication No. GC20-8203-1 (IBM, 1984), p. 3-10. Courtesy of International Business Machines Corporation, White Plains, NY.]

TOPOLOGY

Topology is the physical layout of the transmission medium (e.g., wires; see Figure 5-5). Topology matters because it affects the network's reliability and expandability. *Nodes* are points where devices connect to the medium. Most LANs broadcast data, so every message goes to every node and individual nodes ignore all messages not addressed to them. Bus and ring topologies are common broadcast layouts. A non-broadcast topology is the star.

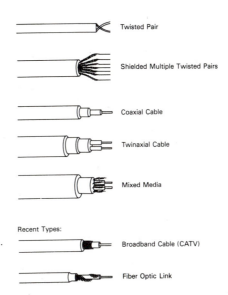

FIGURE 5-5 Transmission media. [From *Local Area Networks,* Publication No. G320-0108-0 (IBM, 1983), p. 10. Courtesy of International Business Machines Corporation, White Plains, NY.]

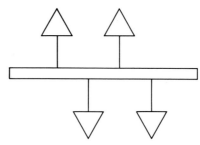

ADVANTAGES
- Uses the least amount of cable because it provides the most direct cabling routes.

DISADVANTAGES
- Requires a means of bidirectional traffic control along the bus to prevent simultaneous transmissions.
- A break in the cable cannot be easily detected.

FIGURE 5-6 Bus topology. [From *An Introduction to Local Area Networks*, Publication No. GC20-8203-1 (White Plains, NY: IBM, 1984), p. 3-26. Courtesy of International Business Machines Corporation.]

- *Bus* refers to a cable not connected in a ring or a star. Devices connect to it, and when one device broadcasts, its signal goes in both directions and to all other devices (see Figure 5-6).
- *Ring* refers to transmitting in a circular, unidirectional flow (see Figure 5-7).
- *Star* refers to the transmission of all signals through the central controller to the receiving device. The central controller manages the communications (see Figure 5-8).

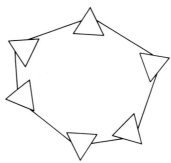

ADVANTAGES
- A break in the cabling can be readily detected.
- Communication control is simplified because the ring is unidirectional and a closed circuit.
- More distance can be covered by the network because each node regenerates the signal to full strength.
- Lends itself to the use of fiber optics because of its unidirectional nature.

DISADVANTAGES
- Modifying the ring to accommodate changes may be difficult.
- Uses more cable than bus topology, but less than star.

FIGURE 5-7 Ring topology. [From *An Introduction to Local Area Networks*, Publication No. GC20-8203-1 (White Plains, NY: IBM, 1984), p. 3-26. Courtesy of International Business Machines Corporation.]

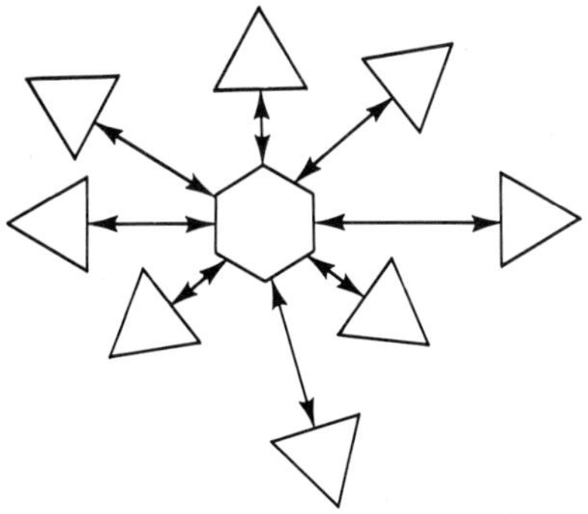

ACCESS PROTOCOLS   97

ADVANTAGES
- Cable is easily modified to accommodate changes and moves.
- Defective nodes are easily detected and isolated.

DISADVANTAGES
- Uses the most cable.
- Failure of the central controller disables the entire network.

FIGURE 5-8   Star topology. [From *An Introduction to Local Area Networks,* Publication No. GC20-8203-1 (White Plains, NY: IBM, 1984), p. 3-26. Courtesy of International Business Machines Corporation.]

ACCESS PROTOCOLS

There are two basic types of access methods employed in LANs: contention methods and noncontention methods. Contention network users attempt to gain access to all of the bandwidth for short periods of time. Because each user contends for the available bandwidth, the sytem is therefore probabilistic. In other words, there is some probability that when a user needs the LAN, it will not be immediately available.

Noncontention systems are different in that they allocate some part of the total bandwidth to each user of the network on a guaranteed basis. This results in a more deterministic, or predictable, performance of the LAN.

A common contention type of access method is the CSMA access method. *Carrier sense* simply means listening before sending, and *multiple access* means having once listened anyone can send as long as the cable is not being used. (See Figure 5-9.)

CSMA

Carrier Sense:	Listen Before Sending
Multiple Access:	Send When Channel Is Free

CSMA/CD

Collision Detection:	Delay Allows Collisions Detect and Retry Uses a Statistical Back-off Algorithm
Advantages:	Efficient Under Normal Conditions Up To 90%
Disadvantages:	Not Deterministic and Quickly Slows Under Heavy Load

FIGURE 5-9   [From *LAN Protocol Analysis* (Colorado Springs, CO: Hewlett-Packard, 1987), p. 2-16.]

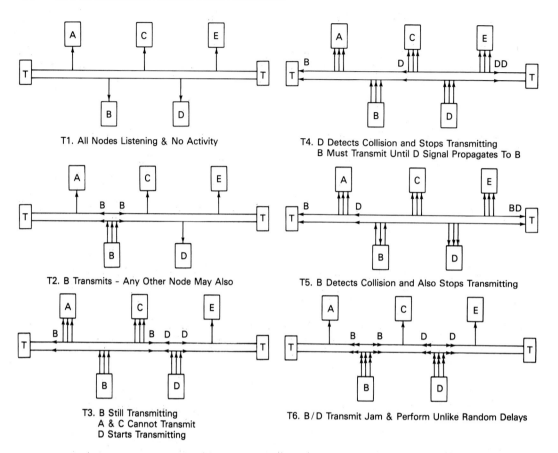

FIGURE 5-10 CSMA/CD bus operation. [From *Local Area Network Concepts*, Publication No. G320-0161-0 (White Plains, NY: IBM, August 1984), p. 34-36. Courtesy of International Business Machines Corporation.]

A good analogy to CSMA is the old telephone party line system where you would pick up the telephone before making a call and listen to make sure your neighbor was not using the line. If someone else was on the line, you would hang up and try later.

A frequently encountered version of this system is the carrier sense multiple access with collision detection system. There is a delay associated with the transmission signal. One node can listen to the cable and determine that no one is using it, when in fact someone far away has begun to use it but the signal hasn't reached the node yet. In the meantime, the node begins transmitting and the signals of the two users collide.

The collision is detected electronically. Each node then stops transmitting immediately and waits a specified amount of time. The delay at each node is statisti-

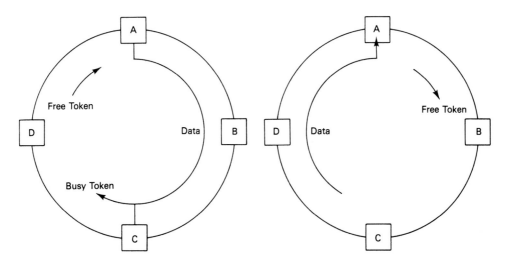

FIGURE 5-11   Token passing ring. In this example, node A is ready to send data and looks for a free token. Node A changes the free token to a busy token and appends the data to the token, addressing it to node C. Node C receives the busy token and copies the data addressed to it. Node A then removes the busy token and data from the ring and generates a free token to replace the busy token. [From *Local Area Network Concepts,* Publication No. G320-0161-0 (White Plains, NY: IBM, 1984), p. 39. Courtesy of International Business Machines Corporation.]

cally calculated so that both do not try to transmit again at the same time. This decreases the possibility of additional collisions. (See Figure 5-10.)

The most important noncontention access method for LAN is token passing. In token passing, a token message gives permission for a node to talk. This token (a number of bits controlling transmission) is passed around the network. If a node has a message to send, it acquires the token, sends the message, and releases the token to the next node. If a node has no message to send, the token is immediately sent on to the next node. Token passing is similar to the situation in a meeting room where people have made an agreement to talk only when a person has the timer. The timer is set for 1 minute. When you have the timer, you have permission to talk for a minute, and when the timer goes off, you must reset it and pass it to the next person. (See Figures 5-11 and 5-12.)

Figure 5-13 summarizes the relationship between the OSI model and the IEEE 802 Standards. The OSI and IEEE models are both layered approaches to network architecture. If we simplify the OSI model, we will see three major levels: the physical, data link, and network layers. The IEEE 802 specification (which covers only the bottom two OSI layers) is also layered. However, in this case, while the physical layers match exactly, the data link layer has been divided into two sublayers. These are called the logical link control and media access control layers. The IEEE is the

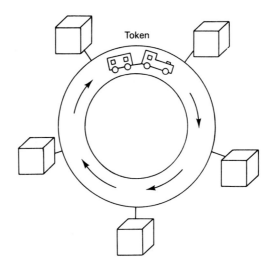

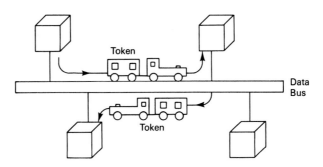

FIGURE 5-12 Token passing. [Fron *An Introduction to Local Area Networks,* Publication No. GC20-8203-1 (White Plains, NY: IBM, 1984), pp. 3-32, 3-33. Courtesy of International Business Machines Corporation.]

major standardizing body defining LAN standards, specifying the protocols that will perform the functions of the data link and physical layers.

MAP specifies selected protocols from all seven ISO layers. For the bottom two layers, it specifies IEEE 802.4: use of a broadband coaxial cable bus with token-passing access. Real-time devices need to be controlled with guaranteed access, which the token-passing option provides. A relatively low cost, mature technology (closely related to cable TV), the bus is easy to tap into, which is especially signifi-

OSI and IEEE 802

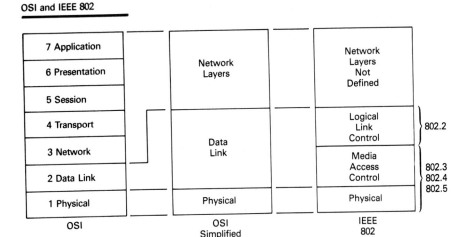

FIGURE 5-13 [From *Lan Protocol Analysis* (Colorado Springs, CO: Hewlett-Packard, 1987), p. 2-9.]

cant when factory equipment is frequently moved. The cable is shielded from factory "noise." It offers multiple channels so robots, programmable controllers, NC machines and other equipment can communicate. It also supports file transfer from one station to another.

TECHNICAL AND OFFICE PROTOCOL

Boeing's horrendous problem involves tracking the 3.5 million individual parts used in an airliner (a car has about 30,000). Boeing designed its technical and office protocol to help with this problem and to support engineering, accounting, marketing, and other office functions. Based on the seven OSI layers, TOP specifies IEEE 802.3 for the lower two layers (i.e., CSMA/CD access), baseband cable with bus topology.

TOP is MAP's equivalent for the office and for engineering functions. It can, for example, connect word processors from various vendors, merge text and graphics (desktop publishing) and move files among stations. MAP and TOP networks can be connected through routers, which can also connect them to (outside) wide area networks.

MAP and TOP are complementary. MAP is for multivendor factory automation systems, and TOP is for office automation such as electronic mail, graphics, and document interchange. The combination of MAP and TOP technologies can help save time, cut costs, raise productivity, and improve quality. There are now enough joint MAP/TOP installations to justify the above remarks and to alert readers to this development.

Developed to reduce the islands of automation mentioned previously, MAP/TOP is linking factory and office communication lines to make computer-integrated manufacturing a reality. Within a company, MAP/TOP might integrate the following:

Product design

Engineering

Order entry

Job scheduling (e.g., raw material planning)

Manufacturing (e.g., robots, drilling)

Inspection

Maintenance/warranty (e.g., spares)

Marketing and sales

MAP/TOP can connect the firm to its vendors and to its customers, both large and small.

In conclusion, proprietary designs (protocols) cannot easily pass information to competing products. Such communications incompatibility is no longer acceptable. Common communication standards are required which allow equipment and networks to function together, thereby eliminating the islands of automation. MAP and TOP do this, integrating office and engineering functions with the plant. Such efficient communication provides better information for earlier decisions, raising productivity and quality, while lowering costs.

CASE STUDY

Use "The Town That Saved Itself" at the end of this chapter as the basis for a brief discussion on motivating people.

SUMMARY

1. Manufacturing automation protocol is a set of rules governing how machines of any make should communicate.
2. MAP is based on standards from the International Standards Organization. The standards are called the open systems interconnection model.
3. The OSI model has seven layers that take into account the hardware, software, protocols, and network architecture that comprise a telecommunications system.
4. These seven layers can be characterized as follows:
   — The top three are application-oriented.
   — The next two are interface layers between the application and the transmission function.
   — The bottom two layers provide the data link control and the physical link.

5. MAP includes all seven layers, but we have concentrated on the bottom two, called the local area network.
6. LANs can be described in terms of
   — Their ability to move data and how they do it (bandwidth)
   — The physical layout of the transmission medium (topology)
   — How devices access the LAN (access protocol).
7. LAN standards are set by Standards Project 802 of the Institute of Electrical and Electronics Engineers.
8. The relevant standards for this chapter are 802.4 (broadband bus with token passing) and 802.3 (carrier sense multiple access/collision detection).
9. Technical and office protocol is MAP's office equivalent. MAP and TOP are complementary.

REVIEW QUESTIONS

1. Define MAP and explain why GM embraced it. Give a couple of illustrations of what MAP does.
2. Explain the OSI model in terms of Figures 5-1 and 5-2. What is the packet or message frame? Look up SDLC and note any packet similarities. What does this imply?
3. Characterize OSI's seven layers. Specifically, what do the bottom two layers do? What are they called (together)?
4. Name and discuss three characteristics of MAP's bottom two layers.
5. Define and explain:
   a. Bandwidth (broadband and baseband)
   b. Topology (bus, ring, and star)
   c. Access protocols (contention and noncontention).
6. Explain Figures 5-3, 5-4, and 5-6 to 5-9.
7. Follow through on the logic of Figure 5-10 from time T1 to time T6.
8. Explain token passing. For ring topology. For bus.
9. Define and explain 802.3 and 802.4.
10. Why does MAP use 802.4?
11. Look up Ethernet. What is its relationship to 802.3?
12. Compare and contrast TOP and MAP.
13. Comment on the relationship among CIM, MAP, and TOP.

REFERENCES

1. See *MIS Week,* August 3, 1987, p. 47.
2. See F. Greenwood et al., *Business Telecommunications* (Dubuque, IA: Brown, 1988), Ch. 8.

Case Study
THE TOWN THAT SAVED ITSELF*

by Dotson Rader

Five and a half years ago, when I first traveled to Weirton, W. Va. (population: 25,370), it was a dying mill town in the Ohio Valley—dying because its economic heart, Weirton Steel, was on the verge of being shut down by its owner, the Pittsburgh-based National Steel Corp. Weirton was in many ways similar to other distressed communities in the Rust Belt, its jobs being lost to foreign competition, its sons and daughters laid off by the mills and leaving to seek a future elsewhere.

Everywhere in Weirton were houses that had been foreclosed on by the banks and put up for sale—with no buyers. Empty shops stood near parking lots filled with repossessed cars, while the unemployed went from door to door seeking odd jobs so they could feed their families. Anguished parents watched helplessly as their families broke apart.

But this was no ordinary steel plant. It produced some of the best tinplate in the world. And this was no ordinary town.

About 27 percent of Weirton's residents worked for Weirton Steel, and they had only one remote chance to save the plant: to buy it under an ESOP (Employee Stock Ownership Plan). A majority of the unionized workers had to vote for givebacks. These included a 20 percent cut in hourly wages, a no-strike clause and no cost-of-living increases. National Steel would cover employees' pensions through Nov. 1, 1988, should the plant fail under ESOP prior to that date. There was every possibility of failure: The antiquated plant needed hundreds of millions of dollars in new capital investment, and an ESOP never before had been attempted in a company so large. In effect, the people of Weirton were being called upon to walk alone in the dark toward a future no one could predict.

When I left Weirton that autumn in 1982, the town was bitterly divided: Some older workers wanted to take their pensions and let the place close. Others wanted to risk what they had in the hope of buying a secure future for their kids. I was sure that the town would go under. Too much was being asked of it; the people were too fearful.

However, on Sept. 23, 1983, by a vote of 5273 to 731, the workers decided to accept ESOP and to buy the company. They had stepped into the unknown.

Last fall, I returned to Weirton—but it was a different place.

Guido and Eudora "Doedee" Magnone still live in the same house where, five

*Reprinted with permission from *Parade,* copyright© 1988.

years before, Guido had angrily told me, "The fat cats don't want us around! They don't want us to survive!" This time, I sat with the Magnones in their kitchen and asked them to look back.

"Everybody was fighting for their lives," recalled Guido, now 52. "We were scared to death. In 1982, people were leaving . . . the family was breaking up. There's nothing more important to us than the family." But things got better, and now 31 percent of Weirton's residents are employed by the company, which is thriving. "I could see a big difference when Mr. Loughhead came in," Guido said. Robert L. Loughhead was brought in as chairman, president and chief executive officer of Weirton Steel in July 1983. He succeeded Jack Redline, now retired. "Redline," said Guido, "was more responsible than anyone for the passage of ESOP. Now we have the EPG [Employee Participation Groups, begun by Loughhead]. They meet in different departments once a week. And then they come into the mills, and mill workers and management sit together solving problems.

"Then there's SPC—Statistical Process Control—an idea that comes from Japan. Weirton is trying to give its customers 100 percent quality steel, so that when it gets to your plant, you don't have to inspect it, like you had to before. It means continuous quality control. And then there's constant communication between the employees and management."

Throughout the plant there are TV sets and VCRs for which a new tape, like a newsletter, is produced each week. It informs everyone about problems at the plant, management planning, the financial state of the business.

"These are good things," said Guido. "There are a lot of good things happening. We're gradually breaking the line dividing employees and management. Middle management is starting to listen to us, because top management is telling them, 'You better listen.'"

In 1989, the employees will begin to elect members of the board of directors.

The new president, chairman and CEO is Herbert Elish, 54, who succeeded Loughhead last June. He visits a different division of the mill weekly and often has breakfast with the workers. If management and employees cannot agree on a problem, management's decision is accepted. And at Weirton Steel, management is acutely conscious that the employees ultimately will elect the directors who make the major decisions and who hire and fire top management.

I asked the Magnones about their children, whose layoffs and leaving had so wounded them. They were happy to report that all had returned to the mill.

"So *many* people were laid off when you were here," recalled Doedee, 50. She added that some had gone to California, Florida and Texas to find work. "And now they're back. Oh, it's happier times now," she said, shaking her head and smiling.

Herbert Elish has been on the board of directors since ESOP began. He called "extraordinary" the workers' achievements for, in his words, "creating a company for themselves and saving this community where, in most cases, it would have been lost." He added, "There's a community involved and people involved who are worth working with to make sure this success is permanent."

And success reigns at Weirton. There have been 16 straight profitable quarters since it began operating under employee ownership on Jan. 11, 1984. Last year, for example, Weirton Steel earned $120.8 million—before $40.2 million in profits were shared by employees—on sales of $1.3 billion and shipments of 2.8 million tons of steel.

The workers' decision to adopt ESOP was particularly blessed, in light of the subsequent rise in value of the Japanese yen and U.S. restraints on steel imports (primarily from Japan and Europe). In 1984, according to the American Iron and Steel Institute, imports supplied 29.8 percent of the United States' demand for steel. In 1987, the figure had dropped to 21.3 percent. The company today is earning record profits—more than double those of 1986. Weirton Steel now employs 8100 individuals and has an annual payroll of $280 million. The average steelworker's hourly pay at the mill is about $15, plus benefits.

In 1987, the company paid $14.8 million in state and local taxes, and its shipped tonnage made Weirton the nation's seventh-largest steel company in terms of sales production and shipment. It is *the* largest 100 percent employee-owned industrial company in the nation and fully finances its own pension plan. In the United States today, there are more than 8000 ESOP companies, employing 8 million people.

Said Elish, "To me, the way this company works is really an example of industrial democracy. . . . In other companies, decisions are made at high levels and communicated down. Here, the employees vote and participate in decision-making. . . . The purpose of business is a lot of things. It's to make people money and all that, but there's a greater purpose: It's to allow the people who work in the company good lives."

As to the future, Elish said, "If we do the right thing—all of us together—I think our future and Weirton's is great."

The night before I left Weirton, I went to the Hideaway Club, where a fundraiser was being held for the United Way. It was crowded with Weirton Steel employees and other townsfolk. And, working side by side as volunteer bartenders, were Charles Cronin, Weirton Steel's director of corporate public relations, and Walter Bish, president of the Independent Steelworkers Union.

I sat for a while with Cronin, 55, who has been at Weirton Steel for 24 years. "My faith in the company has never wavered," he said. "Even through the dark days of '82 and '83, when there was doubt that we would ever survive, I kept the faith. And I was one of many." He credited ESOP with the new friendliness between management and labor and said he once had seldom talked with union leadership. "I can now pick up a phone and call union people," he said. "We go on trips together. We go to meetings together."

"We're together now," added Cronin, "because in the beginning we *had* to be. And we finally learned: If we didn't stand together, we'd all sink alone. Those were frightening times, but they scared some sense into us. We learned a bitter lesson, but we learned it well."

Chapter Six

COMPUTER-AIDED DESIGN

After you have read this chapter, it will be clear to you that

- ❏ Design is a strategic weapon.
- ❏ Computer-aided design helps to create, analyze, and modify designs.
- ❏ CAD workstations have five components: the computer, video controller, input device, output device, and video display.
- ❏ CAD software implements the typical CAD functions: design, analysis, and drafting.
- ❏ CAD-created designs are stored in data bases where they are kept up to date and can easily be accessed.

Manufacturing includes the following stages:

- Product planning—estimating the demand for certain functions at a given price
- Product design—designing the product to have the functions defined during planning
- Production—planning and executing the production process
- Marketing and sales—informing the market of the new product and all such related tasks.

None of these stages is more crucial than design. Design blends function, style, quality, engineering, and art, and is at the heart of competitiveness. A well-designed product is appealing; it is also easy and economical to operate and service and simple to manufacture. Design and quality are congruent, and so design impacts directly on profits.

Design is one key to cutting costs and raising quality simultaneously. For example, assembly typically accounts for two-thirds of manufacturing costs. Accordingly, design that reduces the number of fasteners (e.g., screws, bolts) can cut assembly costs in half. Design that eliminates parts not only lowers production costs, but also tends to reduce failure rates. Design can thus win market share from competitors, but only when it honors the needs of manufacturing and other departments while presenting an appealing style to the market. In sum, design is a strategic weapon.

Computer-aided design is the use of computers to create, analyze, and modify designs. The *CAD package* is the software (computer programs) used to create a design. The *CAD system* is the hardware and software used by the designer.

What a word processor (WP) is to text, a CAD package is to drawings. Just as a WP uses a text editor, CAD has a *drawing editor,* which allows you to modify a drawing. A CAD system handles the routine, repetitive aspects of design, thereby increasing productivity and freeing designers to use their technical ingenuity and creativity.

CAD helps to draw subassemblies which can then be magnified so clearances can be checked (without building a prototype). Further, drawings can be layered, so building plans, for example, can show wiring and plumbing separately or together. This allows a general contractor, for instance, to provide appropriate drawings to electrical and plumbing subcontractors with minimal effort.

CAD allows you to build blocks from basic elements, such as lines, arcs, and circles, and these blocks can be moved around the drawing. You can also build a data base of existing parts, modifying them to create new parts. Drawings (i.e., models) can be manipulated by the CAD system to check clearances or to predict bending and twisting, for example. The model can then be modified repeatedly until it performs acceptably.

Digital computers appeared in the 1950s. Huge, electromechanical machines using relays and other moving parts, they were soon replaced with vacuum tube computers. In the 1950s, transistors took the place of vacuum tubes, and in the

1970s, integrated circuitry further reduced costs and size. Today, computers are more compact, cheaper, and much more powerful than the earlier models. CAD developed along with computers.

CAD started as interactive graphics at Massachusetts Institute of Technology (MIT) in the early 1960s with the Sketchpad Project. Data were entered with a hand-held lightpen, and by lighting points on the scope, figures could be generated. The image could be manipulated and produced as *hard copy* (printed), and communication with the computer was in *real time* (i.e., immediate interaction). The drawing was stored as a *bit map,* where each element of the screen drawing (pixel) occupies a corresponding memory location. It takes a low level of computer power to manipulate a bit map, but such drawings are machine-dependent and cannot be transferred between computer types. Interactive graphics in this context was simply automated drafting which only large firms could then afford.

As computer hardware and software developed, so did these graphics systems. Faster and friendlier extensive menus now offer wide choices of manipulation and analyses (see "CAD Software"). Today's CAD packages use data bases in contrast to bit maps. These data bases are normally machine-independent and are transferable between computers. Also, drawing accuracy is not dependent on the screen resolution (as it is in bit maps). By the 1970s, graphics could be done with minicomputers, which cost considerably less than the earlier mainframes. Now, computer-assisted design can be done with personal computers (PCs).

Productivity usually drops for the first few months as people are trained to use a CAD system. Then a 3-to-1 or a 4-to-1 increase in productivity is common, which pays for the system in a couple of years.

We have thus moved from the automated production of engineering drawings in the 1960s to today's CAD systems which design a part, analyze its movements, and produce engineering drawings automatically. From the description stored in the data base, processing plans, machine programming, and production planning can be carried out. That is, a design can be created, and the manufacturing process can be executed with the same computer system (see Figure 6-1). We thereby move closer to automated factories with computer-assisted design.

CAD HARDWARE

CAD workstations have the five basic components shown in Figure 6-2. The CAD system's performance depends on their interaction, so the whole can be no stronger than its weakest hardware element. We'll discuss these elements next.

The *video display* is the TV-like screen that the user "draws" on with a lightpen, an electronic stylus, or a similar device. The design can be quickly erased and redrawn, so changes are seen immediately. The image disappears when the power is turned off and is termed a *soft copy* of the design (in contrast to a paper version, which is called a *hard copy*). The screen image is built from electrical signals from the video controller, so the results depend on both the quality of the display device and the controller, plus the quality of their interaction.

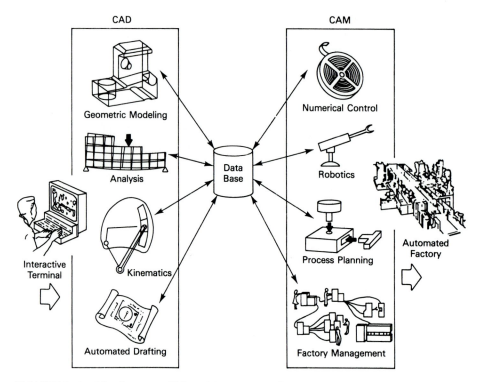

FIGURE 6-1 Ideally, we will be able to move from an initial concept to a finished part in one integrated system. (Courtesy of *Machine Design Magazine,* Cleveland, Ohio.)

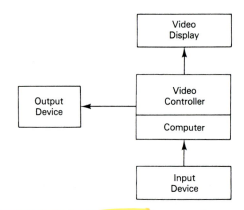

FIGURE 6-2 CAD workstation components.

CAD HARDWARE 111

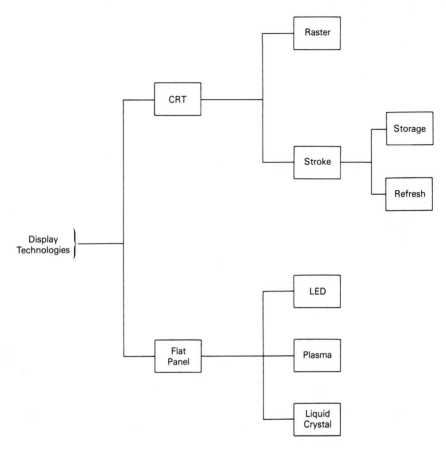

FIGURE 6-3 Display technologies. LED, Light-emitting diode.

Most CAD video displays use *cathode ray tube* (CRT) technology (see Figure 6-3). The CRT is a large vacuum bottle (see Figure 6-4) containing an element that generates the electron beam (the gun), a beam control unit, and a phosphor-coated screen. The high-speed electron beam writes on the screen as it is guided by the controller. The gun would burn out rapidly without the vacuum.

The CRT screen glows (i.e., fluoresces) when electron beams hit its phosphor coating. Color depends on the type of phosphor and the intensity of the beam. Without the beam, the phosphor glows briefly (i.e., phosphoresces). Flicking images result when the glow is allowed to fade before it is refreshed.

Some CRTs use *stroke technology;* that is, the electron beam writes short lines on the phosphor screen, approximating arcs, circles, and other curves by connecting short lines. An advantage of building the screen image this way is that it requires relatively little memory in the video controller.

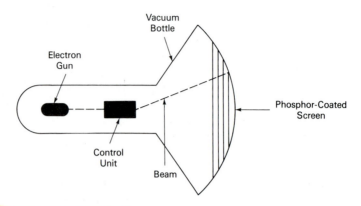

FIGURE 6-4 Cathode ray tube.

Stroke CRTs maintain screen images in one of two ways:

- *Refresh stroke.* The image is constantly redrawn. When the image is complex, it takes longer to refresh, so that too much complexity can create flicker.
- *Stroke storage.* The image is maintained by flooding the screen with extra electrons from flood guns at the wide end of the CRT. These electrons have just enough energy to maintain the phosphorescence. The image cannot be selectively erased, however, so it must be completely erased and redrawn when editing.

Other CRTs use *raster technology,* which traces a field pattern on the screen (rather than drawing the image at random locations). See Figure 6-5. The electron beam is turned off and on as it traces its pattern, thereby turning the picture elements, or *pixels,* off and on. Each pixel corresponds to a specific part of the video display memory. The video display and video controller must, therefore, exchange large amounts of information at the proper rate. Pixels create jagged displays, but this CRT weakness is not part of the data base, so when a hard copy of the design is plotted, there are no such inaccuracies.

Flat panel technologies (Figure 6-3) are not yet common in CAD workstations and are mentioned just to note that alternative technologies exist.

VIDEO CONTROLLER

The *video controller* is between the computer and the CRT (see Figure 6-6), receiving information from the computer, processing it for display, and sending it, along with control signals, to the CRT. For example, a PC-based workstation might have 144,000 individual pixels (see Figure 6-5), and the video controller must monitor the status of each pixel 60 times a second, which is a lot of information to handle precisely.

VIDEO CONTROLLER   113

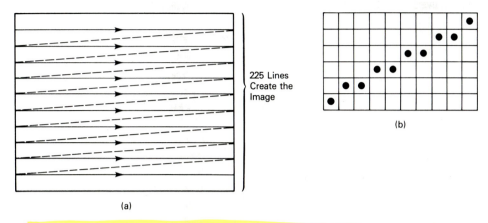

FIGURE 6-5   (a) Raster scan screen. (b) Images are built from pixels. A PC might have 144,000 pixels (640 × 225).

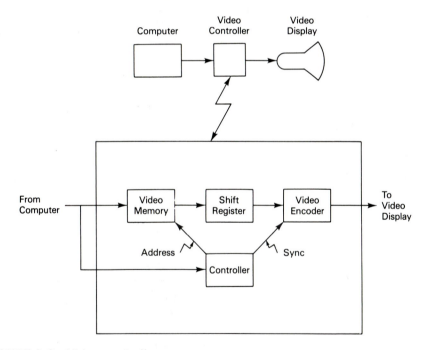

FIGURE 6-6   Video controller.

The resolution of the video monitor refers to the detail of the display. Resolution relates to the number of addressable points on the screen to which light can be directed under program control (i.e., the pixels). An alphanumeric monitor might have 65,000 points, while a graphics monitor might have 250,000. Color grapics monitors can help display layers; for example: a building plan might show the wiring

114 COMPUTER-AIDED DESIGN

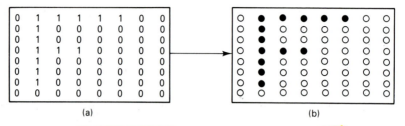

FIGURE 6-7 (a) Video memory (bit map). (b) CRT screen (pixels).

drawings in one color and the plumbing details in another color, separately or superimposed.

Digital data from the computer (i.e., binary 0s and 1s) is stored in the video memory. Then, it moves through the shift register to the encoder, which processes information from the register and control data (SYNC signals from the controller), sending both to the video display. Each video memory location (the *bit map*) corresponds to a CRT pixel, as illustrated in Figure 6-7. The *shift register* receives binary data in parallel and sends it to the encoder in serial form. The *encoder* combines the data from the register with control signals from the controller and sends them together, in the correct sequence, to the CRT.

COMPUTER

In the 1950s computers were made with vacuum tubes, perhaps 3000 of them in a large $5 million machine. They filled entire rooms, requiring special air-conditioning systems and large supplies of power. By the early 1960s, computers were transistorized, with discrete components soldered onto printed circuit boards. By then a large machine cost $2.5 million. In the late 1960s these transistor circuits became part of small integrated semiconductor circuit packages called chips. In the 1970s microminiaturization created complete microprocessors that were less than a quarter-inch square (computers on a chip), selling for a few dollars and using less energy than a 100-watt lightbulb.

A quarter-century of technological developments has brought among others, these changes:

- Computer logic costs are declining 25 percent a year, costs of communication are falling 11 percent a year, and memory costs are plummeting 40 percent a year.
- The number of components on a silicon integrated chip is doubling every other year.
- Hardware worth a million dollars in the 1950s costs less than $20 today.
- Some of today's systems are a 100,000 times faster than those of the 1950s.
- Today's solid-state circuits are 10,000 times more reliable than the vacuum tube technology of the 1950s.
- The ratio between cost and performance has improved roughly 100 times each decade since the 1950s.

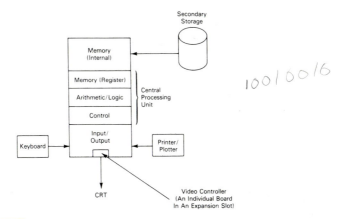

FIGURE 6-8 Computer.

Because of such technological developments, you pay far less for equipment now, and it can do much more. A computer can do simple repetitive tasks more accurately, remember things better, and calculate numbers much faster than people can.

A microcomputer, for example, is a small but powerful, versatile, low-cost, general-purpose machine. It can be programmed (usually in BASIC) to perform specific tasks with great accuracy and speed. Preprogrammed software packages are available to help business people keep track of inventory, invoices and bills, provide cost analyses, and so on.

The computer usually works with data in *binary* form. People still use the digits 0 through 9 to calculate, ultimately because we were born with 10 fingers. Computers run on electricity and have only two "fingers": on and off. Computers therefore do arithmetic in the binary system, using only the digits 0 and 1. Accordingly, the presence of an electrical current represents a 1 to a computer, and its absence a 0. Any number, letter, or punctuation mark can be coded into a series of 1s and 0s.

If you had a row of eight light switches next to one another in front of you, you might turn on every other one, leaving the rest off. This pattern, 10101010, means something to the computer, because this is how you "talk" to it. Each switch, 0 or 1, is a *bit* (combining the *b* from binary and the *it* from digit).

A series of 8 bits is called a *byte*. A byte forms a "word" that an 8-bit computer understands. That is, each byte consists of 8 bits and is equivalent to a single letter or number. In a 16-bit computer, 2 bytes of information form a word. The computer's *word length* is thus the number of bits of information it handles in a single operation. Generally, the longer the word length, the more powerful the computer. Many CAD workstations have a 4-byte word (32 bits).

The microcomputer (or microprocessor) system has both internal components and external *peripheral** equipment (see Figure 6-8).

---

*Microcomputers are usually smaller and cheaper than minicomputers. Peripherals work with the computer, but are not part of the central processing unit, such as a printer.

The external peripheral equipment enables the microprocessor to communicate with the outside world, that is, the printer or the cathode ray tube. Information might be provided to the computer via the keyboard, and it could then "answer" by means of the CRT.

The microprocessor chip (also called the *central processing unit,* CPU) contains the *arithmetic logic unit* (ALU), which does the calculations, and the control unit, which moves the binary data around. The CPU also has small, fast-access storage areas (for temporary results or for transient data) called *registers*.

These registers, the ALU, and the memory together process information in cycles. Each time the CPU returns to the memory for a new instruction, it completes a *fetch cycle* (i.e., it gets new instructions). The memory holds a sequence of instructions (the program for the registers to process). Timing is provided by the electronic clock's pulses (about 1 million each second). Movements of instructions between memory and the CPU and of data and results from the CPU to memory are timed by these pulses.

The computer's memory stores data and programs. Memory is measured in *kilobytes. One kilobyte* (1K) *is equal to 1024 bytes.* A computer with 64K of main memory can store more than 64,000 bytes of information.

Essentially, the computer is composed of the microprocessor chip, the electronic clock, and the main memory. But you have to be able to communicate with it. This is achieved by way of input/output (I/O) devices such as the CRT, the keyboard, and the printer. The I/O interfaces are the communication channels between the computer and the keyed input or the printed output devices.

These I/O interfaces are interconnections (called *buses*) for transmission of data or control signals. Three types of buses transmit data into and out of the computer:

- Data bus, transmitting data between the CPU and memory
- Address bus, selecting locations to which data are transferred
- Control bus, stopping or resetting the CPU, and so on.

In other words, a bus is a set of lines grouped by function.

Transmission along these I/O interfaces may be parallel or serial. In *parallel transmission,* all the bits of a word are sent at once over several parallel wires. This method is fast but can be used only where the distance between the CPU and the I/O device is short (i.e., 20 feet). In *serial transmissions,* bits are sent one after another in sequence. Usually slower than parallel transmission, it lowers costs and reduces susceptibility to interference where distances exceed, say, 20 feet. Serial transmission speed is the number of bits per second transmitted or received.

CAD workstations built with personal computers usually include the video controller as a card in one of the expansion slots, as suggested by Figure 6-8. As noted, the controller accepts data from the computer, generates the signals needed by the CRT, and sends them in the form the display requires.

INPUT DEVICES

Keyboards are a part of almost all CAD workstations. They are good for alphanumeric input but not ideal for graphical input. Therefore, some kind of pointing device is also used to trace designs electronically. Together, input devices have three functions: selecting commands from a menu, tracking the cursor for the user, and tracing designs (also called digitizing). An image is scanned with the digitizer's stylus to convert it into digital data that the computer can handle.

The digitizer allows the designer to move a hand-held device along the flat surface, just as is done by an artist sketching. A grid of wires is embedded in the table. The device generates a magnetic field over the wires. The field's location can be tracked and a corresponding light dot on the screen shows the stylus' location. The designer then pushes a button on the stylus to record its position. Besides the stylus, common input devices are the mouse and a puck. Obviously, before a design can be produced on an output device, it must first be placed in the CAD system.

OUTPUT DEVICES

Ultimately, all designs are normally made into hard copies by some kind of output device, such as a pen plotter.

Plotters have buffers to receive workstation signals. There is a drawing mechanism (normally a pen) which is electromechanical and slower than the computer (hence the buffer). There is also a controller which runs the drawing mechanism and also runs diagnostics to check the plotter's electronics.

Pen plotters display computer-generated line drawings, charts and graphs as high-precision hard-copy output (i.e., permanent, in contrast to the temporary, softcopy displays on the monitor's screen). Plotters used with micros typically employ one, or several, pens that move as the paper moves to make the drawing. The pens move under computer control. Several pens may be required to vary color and width of the lines.

Printers are part of most workstations. Dot matrix printers are fast and relatively inexpensive. Laser printers are fast and produce a better quality of output (but not as good as that of a plotter).

All these separate devices must work together for the CAD system to function effectively. This includes

- Mechanically, such as compatible cables, plugs, and sockets
- Electrically, so the correct wires carry the proper signals at the right times
- Hardware, so each device can put information on the communication channel at one end and take it off at the other
- Software, so that devices agree on what information to exchange and how to talk.

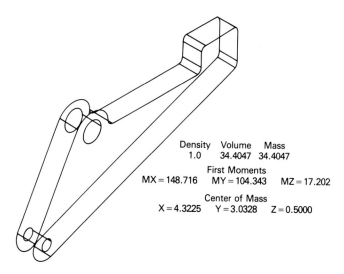

FIGURE 6-11 Simple instructions to the CAD package can trigger analyses of the drawing, as this suggests. (Courtesy of Prime Computer, Inc., Natick, Mass.)

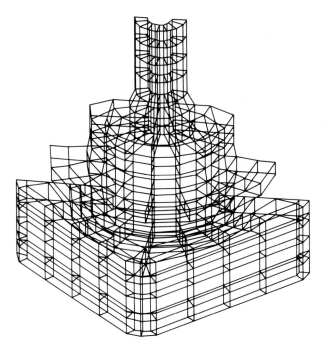

FIGURE 6-12 A network of simple elements, such as the rectangles and triangles above, represents the structure in the data base. (Courtesy of Control Data Corporation, Minneapolis, Minn.)

INPUT DEVICES

Keyboards are a part of almost all CAD workstations. They are good for alphanumeric input but not ideal for graphical input. Therefore, some kind of pointing device is also used to trace designs electronically. Together, input devices have three functions: selecting commands from a menu, tracking the cursor for the user, and tracing designs (also called digitizing). An image is scanned with the digitizer's stylus to convert it into digital data that the computer can handle.

The digitizer allows the designer to move a hand-held device along the flat surface, just as is done by an artist sketching. A grid of wires is embedded in the table. The device generates a magnetic field over the wires. The field's location can be tracked and a corresponding light dot on the screen shows the stylus' location. The designer then pushes a button on the stylus to record its position. Besides the stylus, common input devices are the mouse and a puck. Obviously, before a design can be produced on an output device, it must first be placed in the CAD system.

OUTPUT DEVICES

Ultimately, all designs are normally made into hard copies by some kind of output device, such as a pen plotter.

Plotters have buffers to receive workstation signals. There is a drawing mechanism (normally a pen) which is electromechanical and slower than the computer (hence the buffer). There is also a controller which runs the drawing mechanism and also runs diagnostics to check the plotter's electronics.

Pen plotters display computer-generated line drawings, charts and graphs as high-precision hard-copy output (i.e., permanent, in contrast to the temporary, softcopy displays on the monitor's screen). Plotters used with micros typically employ one, or several, pens that move as the paper moves to make the drawing. The pens move under computer control. Several pens may be required to vary color and width of the lines.

Printers are part of most workstations. Dot matrix printers are fast and relatively inexpensive. Laser printers are fast and produce a better quality of output (but not as good as that of a plotter).

All these separate devices must work together for the CAD system to function effectively. This includes

- Mechanically, such as compatible cables, plugs, and sockets
- Electrically, so the correct wires carry the proper signals at the right times
- Hardware, so each device can put information on the communication channel at one end and take it off at the other
- Software, so that devices agree on what information to exchange and how to talk.

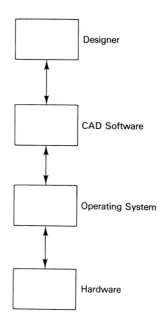

FIGURE 6-9

CAD SOFTWARE

With a CAD system, you can design a part (geometric modeling), analyze stresses (analysis), study mechanical action (kinematics), and create engineering drawings (automated drafting). These functions all depend upon CAD software (see Figure 6-9). The operating system, the collection of programs through which the computer manages its own resources, interfaces with the hardware, while the user works directly with the CAD package. The CAD software interacts with the operating system; that is, the designer controls the CAD system, which does its job through the operating system, which ultimately controls the hardware.

We will now discuss typical CAD functions.

DESIGN

A CAD system can help create and modify designs, and both two- and three-dimensional CAD packages are available. Most packages tend to have similar commands and functions. For example, the CAD drawing editor, which is analogous to the text editor of a word processor, defines the drawing environment. Figure 6-10 is the main menu for "AutoCAD," a widely used CAD package. The user constructs a design (a geometric model) on the CRT, which describes a shape to the computer. The computer converts this design into a mathematical model, which it stores digitally in the data base. The shape can be recalled by reconstructing it on the screen from the data base information. The design can then be modified, serve as the input

```
                    Main Menu

              0. Exit AutoCAD
              1. Begin a NEW Drawing
              2. Edit an EXISTING Drawing
              3. Plot a Drawing
              4. Configure AutoCAD
              5. Make Drawing Interchange File
              6. Load Drawing Interchange File
              7. File Utilities
              Enter Selection:
```

FIGURE 6-10 Main menu of autoCAD's drawing editor.

for stress analysis, become the basis of automated drafting, or be used to produce NC tapes for machining the part. The data base is crucial. Each CAD drawing has its individual elements stored digitally (e.g., lines, directions, prices, ID numbers). This amounts to a single product definition stored in one central location—the data base. Everyone who needs the information accesses the same data, and this implies (among other things) that

- All design changes are immediately and automatically reflected wherever appropriate (which reduces the volume of engineering change notices).
- A technical writer preparing maintenance manuals always has up-to-date information (in contrast to instructing the reader on the maintenance of an earlier, different version of a product).
- Parts lists and bills of materials are always accurate, which matters to the manufacturing department especially.

The Appendix to this chapter is a primer for those readers wanting more information on data bases.

ANALYSIS

Manufacturers sometimes used to build prototypes of intended products to test them (perhaps destructively). Much of this can now be achieved with a CAD system. Deflections, stresses, and other analyses can be performed, often simply by pressing a couple of keys (see Figure 6-11). As the figure suggests, CAD packages are often able to analyze volume, center of gravity, and moments of inertia.

Finite-element analysis (FEA) is also common. FEA represents the geometric model as a structure of simple elements (usually by creating a mesh of rectangular or triangular areas; see Figure 6-12). The FEA program analyzes forces within the smaller areas and then computes the aggregates for the entire model. This typically results in a drawing showing stresses in different colors.

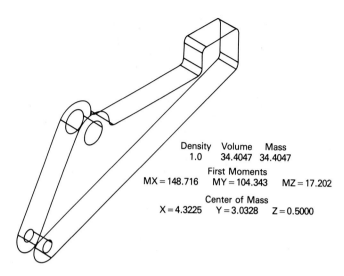

FIGURE 6-11 Simple instructions to the CAD package can trigger analyses of the drawing, as this suggests. (Courtesy of Prime Computer, Inc., Natick, Mass.)

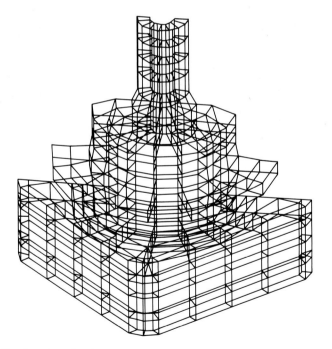

FIGURE 6-12 A network of simple elements, such as the rectangles and triangles above, represents the structure in the data base. (Courtesy of Control Data Corporation, Minneapolis, Minn.)

SIMULATED MOTION

CAD programs can usually animate the motion of parts (these are called *kinematics programs*). This helps the designer because such computer simulation speeds the work. For example, a new subassembly may be designed, and dynamic simulation can check the clearances in motion (without building a prototype). The design can then quickly be modified.

Wire-frame representations (see Figure 6-12), and two- and three- dimensional drawings, or solid figures with shading, can help engineers (computer-aided engineering, or CAE). For example, intersections of the lines in wire-frame drawings might represent stress. Computer simulation could deform the part, revealing areas subject to failure. Stress and other characteristics (e.g., temperature) might be displayed using different colors, assuming appropriate hardware and software.

DRAFTING

Just as you generate text with word processors, so you generate drawings with CAD packages (see Figure 6-13). With such automated drafting, changes are fast and productivity is high. Drawings can originate from the data base, or they can be entered via the terminal.

DATA BASES

Our plants are imperfectly lurching toward manufacturing information systems. These systems begin with product designs which are stored in computerized data bases. These designs can be accessed to help plan the manufacturing processes. This data eventually ties into the management information system. Numerical control (NC) tools, robots, and computer-assisted design (CAD) are steps along the way.

We are thus dealing with a flow of information from the CAD workstations to the data base and from the data base to the factory machinery and so on to the administrative information systems. Figure 6-14 illustrates how the data base connects design and manufacturing.

CAD packages can (ideally) design the product, analyze the stresses, simulate its operation, and automatically produce engineering drawings. This can all be stored in the data base. In a perfect world, this information then serves to produce NC tapes, robot programs, processing plans, and factory management reports.

You may be thinking that this will happen when dogs begin to whistle. Maybe, but you don't have to look very far for manufacturers which use CAD, NC, or robots.

There are manufacturing operations today relying on a (semi?) smooth flow of information from their customers to marketing to designers to suppliers to production and assembly to distribution and on to management. This information has to flow over something. The something it flows over is MAP (Manufacturing Automation Protocol) in the plant and TOP (Technical and Office Protocol) in the office, discussed in Chapter Five.

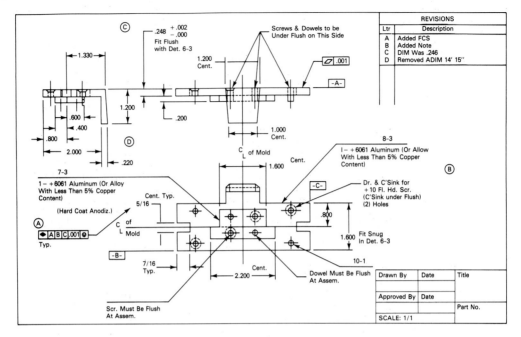

FIGURE 6-13   CAD packages produce drawings fast. (Courtesy of Prime Computer, Inc., Natick, Mass.)

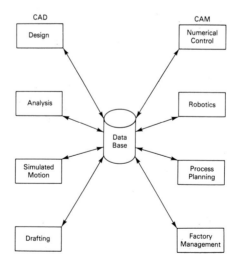

FIGURE 6-14   This suggests the CAD data base in different functional areas. Implicit here is the necessity for accuracy in the initial design phase.

SUMMARY

1. Design is a strategic weapon.
2. Computer-aided design is the use of computers to create, analyze, and modify designs.
3. CAD designs are stored in data bases and can be accessed to help with manufacturing processes.
4. CAD hardware is composed of a computer, input and output devices, a video display, and a controller.
5. Every TV viewer is familiar with the cathode ray tube video display.
6. The video controller receives information from the computer, processes it for display, and sends it to the CRT along with control signals.
7. Plotters are common output devices with a drawing mechanism.
8. The user at a CAD station works directly with the CAD software package. The CAD package interacts with the operating system, which ultimately controls the hardware.
9. Typical CAD functions include design, analysis, and drafting.
10. The CAD drawing editor is analogous to a word processor's text editor.
11. CAD packages can usually analyze deflections, stresses, and the like, by pressing a couple of keys. They can also simulate the motion of parts, quickly modifying any deficiencies.
12. Just as word processors generate text, CAD packages generate drawings.

REVIEW QUESTIONS

1. How does design fit into the four manufacturing stages mentioned early in the chapter?
2. Design is a strategic weapon. Explain.
3. What is a drawing editor?
4. Explain: bit map, pixel, fluoresce, phosphoresce, raster technology, and stroke technology.
5. What does the shift register do in the video controller? What is the function of the encoder?
6. What is the importance of word length to computer users?
7. Essentially, the computer is composed of the microprocessor chip, the electronic clock, and the main memory. Explain.
8. Briefly describe the software between the CAD user and the hardware.
9. Comment on the place of the data base in CAD.
10. CAD can perform analyses. Explain.

Appendix
DATA BASE PRIMER

A data base is an organized collection of related items of information, such as the yellow pages, an accumulation of recipes, or an address book. This information is often maintained on paper files in folders and kept in cabinets. But computerized data bases are also common.

A big advantage of computerized systems is the speed with which inquiries about the data can be handled. A query can be answered in seconds with a computer, which might take 20 minutes to calculate manually. For example, How many students have majored in Business Information Systems each term for the last five academic years?

Early computer processing was achieved by writing specific programs, perhaps in COBOL (a programming language), to manipulate certain data lists, for instance, converting current time cards into payroll data such as gross pay, deductions, and net pay. These file management systems require that all the information for the application be contained in that file.

This creates duplication. To illustrate: Payroll and retirement applications would contain much identical information (e.g., name, social security number, deductions). Each file management system would have to enter and maintain such data separately. So, when a woman marries, the name field would be changed in each different file, individually. Consequently, there would be considerable duplication of effort.

A data base on a computer is implemented using a set of programs called a data base management system (DBMS). The DBMS provides for storing, manipulating, and retrieving information. It confers data independence, so that programs are independent of the data on which they work. That is, different applications can share the same set of data (making it unnecessary to store the information more than once).

With file management programs, you work with one file of information at a time. Using a DBMS, you can work with two or more files at once. This creates a single data base, even though the data may come from marketing, manufacturing, or accounting files. An update by the file "owner" is immediately available to all data base users.

Data base management systems supply tools for manipulating information to meet your needs, putting processing power at your disposal. The trade-off is that they are usually more difficult to use than file management programs. File managers are menu-driven, and DBMSs are command-driven. For example, you have to learn the query language to express the DBMS commands for:

    Creating the data base
    Adding records

Retrieving information
Updating information
Deleting information
Calculating information.

dBASE IV PLUS is a DBMS. It can do simple tasks, such as storing records in a particular file, and complex jobs, such as creating a paycheck file from two other files (e.g., the employee information file and the file of time cards for that period). It is a relational data base management system, which means it stores data in tables that it can link when these tables share a common data field.

A file (table) of employee records might be as follows:

Emp. No.	Name	Hired	Salary	Dept.
10	ARROW, ALAN	4/19/88	24000	WHSE
6	BLACK, BOB	10/12/84	27000	ACCTNG.
5	COOK, CAROL	2/3/84	26000	MFG.
4	DURO, DOUG	6/25/83	30000	MFG.
7	EAGAN, ELLEN	5/23/85	29000	ACCTNG.
3	FROST, FRANK	7/9/82	42000	SALES
1	GREEN, GLORIA	3/13/81	38000	SALES
9	HUNT, HARRY	8/2/86	25000	MFG.
2	ING, INGRID	9/22/81	45000	SALES
8	JOS, JOAN	1/29/87	33000	ACCTNG

Such files can be thought of as tables composed of rows and columns of information. For each item about which dBASE maintains information, a row in the table is created. These rows are referred to as *records*. Each record contains a number of elements (e.g., in an address file, each record might contain a street address, city, state, and zip code) which are referred to as *fields*.

A payroll system might contain two files, one with employee information such as address and social security number, while the other contains records releating to actual pay amounts. The two files are related to each other by a field referring to the employee number, which appears in each file.

In addition to these capabilities of dBASE IV, the facility exists for programming the software. An experienced user can apply dBASE's own programming language to create sophisticated systems to handle such business problems as accounting and inventory control.

As displayed in the file, the name field is arranged alphabetically. dBASE IV PLUS can rapidly sort the file (table) by employee number or by department, for example. Further, assuming there is a pension file and another for payroll deductions, the benefits data for Gloria Green can quickly be extracted (via the common name field or Gloria's employee number) using all three files.

dBASE requires users to learn how to give commands and how to ask questions about the data. In return, users get speedy access to data base information, which can be displayed in a flexible fashion. Because dBASE can work with two or more files (actually, tables) simultaneously, data duplication is unnecessary; you don't need the same data in two or more places. dBASE links two or more files through a common field (e.g., social security number). So, dBASE handles a broad range of applications, from mailing lists and labels to entire accounting systems and sophisticated inventory mangement systems. The package can be used on a stand-alone basis or on a local area network.

Chapter Seven

NUMERICAL CONTROL

After you have read this chapter, it will be clear to you that

- ❏ We are dealing with a flow of information from the CAD workstation to the data base and from the data base to the factory machinery and on to the administrative information systems.
- ❏ Numerical control is a technique for controlling factory machinery.
- ❏ Machine centers are NC tools that can perform several different operations on the work piece.
- ❏ NC programs control machine tools by specifying locations with coordinates.
- ❏ NC is moving toward an overall system for managing production from raw materials to finished products.

128   NUMERICAL CONTROL

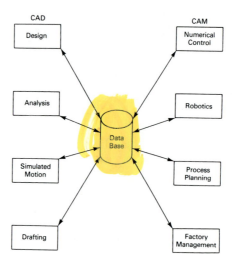

FIGURE 7-1   CAD/CAM functions.

Computer-aided design uses computers to help design products. Computer-aided manufacturing uses them to manage and operate factories. A suggested by Figure 7-1, CAD/CAM can help to design a product, analyze its stresses, simulate its movements, and automatically produce engineering drawings. From the product's description in the data base, an NC program can be generated, robots can be programmed, manufacturing processes can be planned, and plant operations can be managed.

Further, the data base might integrate operations by serving the following functions[1]:

- Engineering
  Design
  Analysis
  Documentation
- Planning
  Parts planning
  Production and inventory planning
- Control
  Process, shop and materials control
  Inspection, testing and quality
- Production
  Parts and tool production

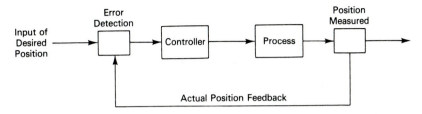

FIGURE 7-2 Servomechanism.

   Assembly
   Handling and storage
- Support
   Facilities engineering and maintenance
   Personnel management
   Data processing
   Order processing
   Accounting

  CAD/CAM impacts almost every area of manufacturing, helping to ease the drudgery of repetitive routines while raising productivity. Its driving forces include a shorter life cycle for many products, growing needs for customization, and increasing global competition.

  CAM includes computer-related tools, such as NC machines and robots, combining them into a manufacturing system that is more productive than using stand-alone tools. The system has a communication component (i.e., MAP, discussed in Chapter 5) that connects all its parts to a data base (which contains digital descriptions of products; see Chapter 6). Conceptually, the whole system can be regarded as a flow of information from the design workstation to the data base and then from the data base to the factory machinery and on to the administrative information systems (e.g., TOP, as described at the end of Chapter 5). We start by taking a look at numerical control.

  Numerical control is a technique for controlling a machine process with prerecorded coded information. NC instructions are often stored as holes punched into *paper tape,* which program controls the machine tool. NC is one of the more mature CAD/CAM technologies.

  NC is not a machine; it is a technique for controlling machines with servomechanisms. A *servomechanism* is an automatic control system which compares output results to input instructions. The difference between the two is the basis for any control adjustments. That is, you have a closed-loop system that automatically provides data on its output position which it compares to the input instructions so the process can be adjusted for greater accuracy. See Figure 7-2.

NC started about 1947. A set of patterns was developed to check helicopter rotor blades for the Department of Defense using punch-card tabulating and computing capabilities. Essentially, a milling machine* was operated with constant feedback about the location of its cutters, which indicated how a tool controlled by numerical data could produce more accurate rotor blade airfoil contours. This illustrated the usefulness of a device that could provide constant feedback on the actual position of the tool for comparison with its programmed position so the process could be adjusted for greater accuracy. A servomechanism uses the difference between these two quantities to achieve control and precision, as noted.

With NC, the programmer works from drawings to program the motions that produce the part. That is, the design, which is defined mathematically in the data base, is programmed into a control mechanism that executes a series of machine tool motions to do the machining. This changes the role of the operator, who used to study the engineering drawing and then manually direct the machine tool. Nevertheless, machine operators must still be good machinists, even though the NC program controls the machining (e.g., they need to know how to handle emergencies). Operators now usually supervise several machines, for example, mounting the workpiece, loading the program, starting the sequence, and suggesting program improvements.

MACHINE CENTERS

Machine tools are power-driven semiautomatic devices that manufacture machine parts. They perform one of two basic functions:

- Forming metal with pressure (e.g., punch presses).
- Shaping metal by removing chips (e.g., mills or drills).

Although differing widely, machine tools share these features: a table to hold the work, a spindle to hold the tool, drive motors to move the table and spindle, and a frame which holds everything. See Figure 7-4. NC machine tools also have servomechanisms.

Machine tools used to be single-purpose, so the work was moved from machine to machine when it required several operations. Programmable automatic tool changes have altered this. Now one machine can perform several different operations on the workpiece. These multipurpose NC tools are called *machine centers*. A typical machine center has a tool magazine of 18 to 60 tools, which a programmable arm changes, so the machine can mill the piece after drilling it, for example. By thus automatically taking tools from the magazine and inserting them into the spindle as needed, the time and effort required to move and set up the workpiece on different machines are eliminated.

---

*The work is secured to a carriage and fed against the milling machine cutters for shaping and dressing.

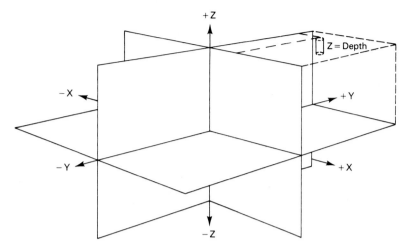

FIGURE 7-3 Three-dimensional coordinates in this illustration depth is measured along the z axis. (Courtesy of *Modern Machine Shop 1988 NC/CIM Guidebook,* Cincinnati, Ohio.)

COORDINATES

Any geometric shape can be defined mathematically and programmed. The program controls the motions of the machine tool axes; that is, it controls the relationship of the workpiece to the cutting tool, thereby machining the workpiece.

The usual way to define machine movements and workpiece geometry is with *Cartesian coordinates* (see Figures 7-3 and 7-4). Three-dimensional coordinates typically measure depth on the Z axis. For many machines, the Z distance starts from the point where the spindle is fully retracted. The X and Y axes are movements on the table, and the Z axis advances and retracts the spindle. There might be other axes of motion, too, such as tilting the swivel or rotating the table.

Positions can be identified with reference to the fixed origin (*absolute*) or with reference to a known position other than the origin (*relative or incremental*). An incremental coordinate location is expressed in terms of the distance and the direction from the preceding point. For example, X2 Y5 in incremental program notation means 2 units along the positive x axis and 5 units along the positive y axis from the preceding program point. NC programmers choose absolute or incremental dimensioning depending on the particular problem.

Polar coordinates are also used. They define positions in terms of distance and angle from another position. Polar coordinates might be employed, for example, in directing a robot with a cylindrical base in its right and left motions about its control axis.

132　NUMERICAL CONTROL

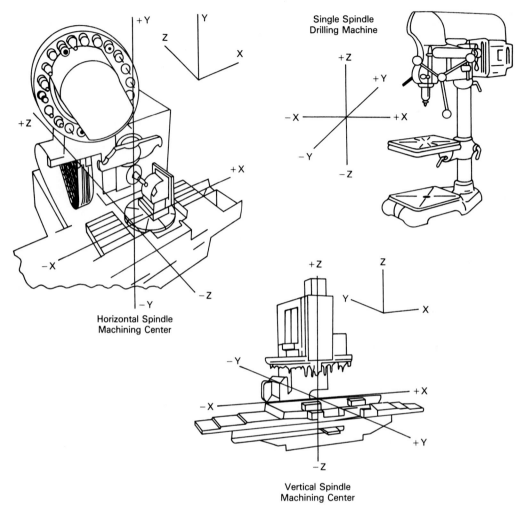

FIGURE 7-4　Some axes of motion the NC program controls. (Courtesy of *Modern Machine Shop 1988 NC/CIM Guidebook,* Cincinnati, Ohio.)

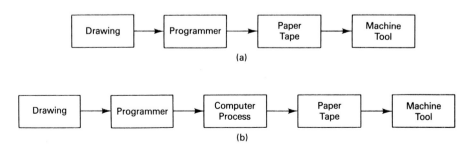

FIGURE 7-5　(a) Manual. (b) Computer-assisted.

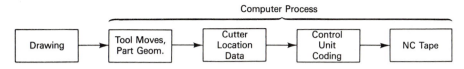

FIGURE 7-6   Computer-assisted programming.

PROGRAMMING

The programming is done by an unassisted programmer (manual) or by a programmer working with help from a computer. Working manually, the programmer has to code every detail of the machining. For jobs other than the simplest, computer assistance is normal. See Figure 7-5. Actually, it is the software (running on the computer) that helps. The software was authored by people who understand machining and machine tools, and they embedded this knowledge in the package. One of the most widely used such processor languages is *automatic programming of tools* (APT).

That is, NC instructions are commonly written in the APT language. There are three types of instructions:

- For the controller (i.e., operational sequence)
- For the path of the tool
- For the table (e.g., rotate).

Lack of standardization means separate NC programs have to be written for each specific tool and that they won't run on different makes of computers.

Computer-assisted programming begins with creation of the engineering drawing, and then (see Figure 7-6)

- The programmer uses, say, APT to create a program that generically defines the geometry of the workpiece and the movements of the tool.
- This program is run against the APT software to generate a file of cutter location data defining generically the cutting tool path.
- The process ends with a machine-specific postprocessor run for that particular tool. This produces the paper tape containing the coding for the controller. Note that magnetic tape and floppy disks are also used to store the NC program.

CONTROLLER

The *controller* is between the program and the machine tool (see Figure 7-7). It reads the tape, storing the program and then executing it. Also, the controller processes information from the feedback unit, performing its servomechanism function.

FIGURE 7-7   NC components.

134 NUMERICAL CONTROL

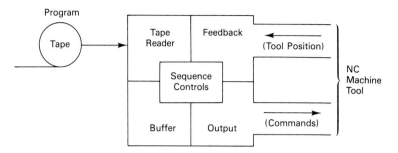

FIGURE 7-8 Controller.

Figure 7-8 suggests how the controller works. The program is read into the controller and stored in the buffer. Instructions are sent to the machine tool drive motor(s) as needed. When the feedback signals that execution is complete, the controller begins another instruction cycle. Sequence controls coordinate these activities. Again, the controller accepts and stores the NC program and processes it to provide output signals that control the servomechanism drives on the machine tool.

NC DEVELOPMENTS

In the 1960s, *direct numerical control* (DNC) developed. DNC is defined as a system where one or more NC machine tools is connected to a remote computer. The NC machine gets its program directly from the computer (rather than from a paper tape reader). See Figure 7-9. Individual machine status can be monitored, so there is current information about factory floor activities.

A more recent development is NC tools that have built-in computers. This is termed *computer numerical control* (CNC); see Figure 7-10. CNC machines have keyboards and CRTs. Once the program is read from the paper tape, it is stored in the built-in computer and is available as needed. This results in a tool with its own "intelligence," so that it is very flexible. Another big advantage of CNC machines is their capacity to communicate in a computer-based environment.

This led to connecting several CNC machines to a remote computer, thereby combining the advantages of CNC equipment with the benefits of direct numerical

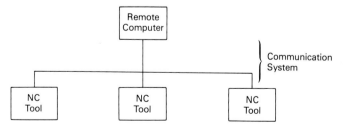

FIGURE 7-9 Direct numerical control.

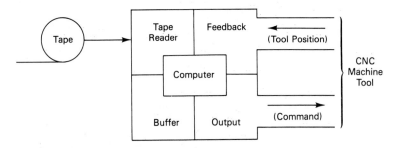

FIGURE 7-10 Computer numerical control.

control. This is called *distributed numerical control;* see Figure 7-11.

Distributed numerical control provides real-time feedback on manufacturing processes and allows for more precise adjustments. Combining distributed numerical control tools with other intelligent machines (e.g., robots) is a big step toward computer-integrated manufacturing. The overall system manages production from raw materials to finished products. Lower-level systems manage the operators and machines of control centers. Requirements are detailed down the hierarchy, and results are summarized upward. Each level plans and allocates its resources with computer support.

Computer-aided testing (CAT) illustrates feedback on manufacturing processes. Inspection and testing were historically manual operations using gages and other instruments. In a CAT environment, computers and various sensors are employed to measure the parts and to control the fabrication process itself. Optical scanners, such as machine vision and lasers, and non-optical devices (including ultrasonics and radiation) can monitor flatness, circularity, and shape, for example, more effectively than manual methods.

JUST-IN-TIME PRODUCTION

Readers who want to review the ideas of Just-in-Time production are referred to the article at the end of this chapter. JIT is concerned with producing only what is required, when it is needed, and in just the correct amount.

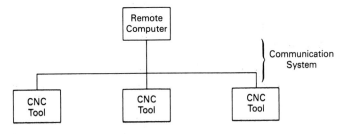

FIGURE 7-11 Distributed numerical control.

SUMMARY

1. CAD provides the product description in the data base from which an NC program can be generated.
2. NC is a technique for controlling machines with prerecorded coded information.
3. The technique relies on servomechanisms, which automatically compare output results to input instructions.
4. NC machine tools can perform several different operations on the workpiece. These multipurpose NC tools are called work centers.
5. The NC program machines the work piece by controlling the relationship of the workpiece to the cutting tool. Machine movements are defined with Cartesian coordinates.
6. NC instructions are commonly written in a programming language such as APT.
7. Such programs include three types of instructions: for the controller (i.e., the operational sequence), for the path of the tool, and for the table (e.g., rotate).
8. The controller works between the program and the machine tool. It reads the program from the tape, stores it, and executes it. It also processes information from the feedback unit, performing the servomechanism function.
9. NC machines have moved from stand-alone units that obtain their programs by reading paper tape to tools connected to a remote computer (from which they get their programs). Next was equipment that has its own built-in computer and, finally, we have NC machines with internal computers that are also connected to a remote computer.
10. We are thus moving to an overall system that manages production from raw materials to finished products.

REVIEW QUESTIONS

1. CAD and CAM are connected by the data base. Explain.
2. The information system runs from the CAD workstation through the data base to the factory machinery and on to the administrative management systems. Comment.
3. Explain how MAP and TOP relate to Question 2.
4. Define NC and explain both the programming and servomechanism aspects.
5. What is the role of machinists in NC shops?
6. Explain machine tools and their basic functions.
7. What are machine centers?
8. Describe the NC coordinate system (both absolute and relative).

9. Name the three types of NC instructions and one example of an NC programming language.
10. Describe the creation of an NC program (e.g., generic and machine-specific parts).
11. Explain what the controller is and how it works.
12. Review the NC developments leading to computer-integrated manufacturing.

REFERENCE

1. Lee Hales, CIMPLAN: The System Approach to Factory Automation (Cutter Information Services, 1986)

Appendix
JUST-IN-TIME INVENTORY/ ZERO INVENTORY*

INTRODUCTION

Productivity inprovement continues to be the guiding principle for business and industry. A long-acknowledged way to increase productivity is to reduce waste. When less scrap—ideally no scrap at all—is created, the productive resources of the organization are used more effectively. Instead of using effort for no return, that effort—materials, labor, handling—is used for creating a product that has value.

One way to achieve this has been used in some Japanese manufacturing facilities for many years. It is known as just-in-time (JIT) production.

> **Definition:** *Just-in-time production* involves getting the correct amount of the correct material at the correct time to the correct production location. ("JIT and MRP II," p. 58)

JIT has evolved into a distinct philosophy. The American Production and Inventory Control Society has given this philosophy the name *zero inventory*. "Zero inventory is for manufacturing excellence. Inventory levels cannot be reduced without it. Just-in-time production and flexible manufacturing systems are the culmination of years of effort to rethink and upgrade every aspect of management in each company that has been successful with it" (Hall 1983, p. 1).

THE PHILOSOPHY

The just-in-time philosophy is a long term commitment to the pursuit of excellence in all phases of manufacturing (Monden 1983). It represents a major shift from the traditional view of management that success is measured by short term return on investment. American workers are among the best in the world. When properly directed and motivated, they are the most productive in the world. It is management's responsibility to provide that direction and motivation to its workers.

> It is important to emphasize that the success of JIT is not the result of cultural, structural, or environmental factors, but rather it stems from planned management actions that any manufacturer can implement. . . . It is the discipline, understanding, dedication, confidence, and continuous striving for improvements which brings a successful JIT system into being. (Sepehri 1985, p. 50)

*From: Lawrence F. Aft, *Production and Inventory Control* (Harcourt Brace Jovanovich, 1987), Chapter 12, pp. 203–219.

The following list, from Hall (1983), enumerates the specific aspects of the JIT or zero inventory philosophy:*

1. Eliminate all waste. Waste is any activity that does not add value to the product.
2. Learn as you work. Develop ideas for improvement from the results of actions taken. Do not develop elaborate plans for improvement without trying ideas as you go.
3. Establish visible methods of control on the shop floor. Allow everyone to see what is to be done by rapid and simple methods. These might or might not incorporate computer methods. Allow everyone to see problems first hand with a minimum of long reports written about problems.
4. Organize the plant floor so that only what is necessary is kept there and everything is kept in its place. Good organization and good housekeeping promote the ability to see problems directly.
5. Stop the process whenever necessary to avoid making defective material, but try to anticipate problems to avoid stopping. Learn from the process stops.
6. Strive for a minimum lot size. Never make anything that is not needed right away. The ultimate goal is a lot size of one piece. That develops economical ways to manufacture at any level of production.
7. Minimize set-up times in all operations.
8. First improve the operation with existing equipment as much as possible. Then get new equipment and facilities when you understand from experience exactly what you need—and why.
9. Reduce the deviation of actual operation times from desired operation times:
   —First, by physically improving operations to eliminate defects, breakdowns, etc.
   —Second, by not allowing deviations to accumulate. Absorb them within the shortest possible time periods.
10. Develop the flow of material through the production network to be as smooth and fast as possible. In that way keep the lead time of production operations as short as possible (pp. 1-9).

The JIT philosophy is a total commitment by the organization. It is a commitment to excellence demonstrated by a complete willingness to achieve total quality through effective problem solving. *The key is commitment.* Simply adopting the techniques that will be described in the following section will not guarantee success. As Sepehri (1985) put it, "The implementation of JIT can affect productivity unfavorably in the short term because the attention is focused on solving manufacturing problems. The productivity will increase rapidly once the roots of the problems have been identified and corrected" (p. 51).

*Third Quarter, 1983, *Production and Inventory Management,* Journal of the American Production and Inventory Control Society, Inc., pp. 1-9. Reprinted with permission.

CHARACTERISTICS OF JUST-IN-TIME PRODUCTION

As stated earlier in this chapter, just-in-time production involves getting the correct amount of the correct material to the proper place at the proper time. This type of manufacturing scheme has several distinct characteristics.

The first of these characteristics is work stations that are relatively close together (Schonberger, 1984a). Placing work stations close to each other works to reduce waste. Specifically, waste, or unnecessary cost, is reduced in this manner by

- Reducing transit time between operations. Material is not productive when it is being handled.
- Reducing the time parts spend waiting for processing. Material gains no value waiting to be processed. Instead, it represents a waste of resources that might be used more productively in other fashions.
- Reducing space required for production. Without transit and queue inventories taking up space, alternative uses can be found for this asset. Producing more with the same resources is an ideal way to increase productivity.
- Reducing the time between the creation of a defect and its discovery. A bad product is discovered more quickly when it is manufactured. Hence it will often require a smaller investment of resources to correct the problem.
- Increasing communication and teamwork among the workers producing the product. People deal directly with the other people producing the product, not with mountains of inventory.

A second characteristic often associated with JIT is the cellular manufacturing concept, also known as *group technology*. (See the November, 1983, issue of *Industrial Engineering* for a complete discussion of cellular manufacturing.) This is most effective for small production runs of large quantities of similar parts. The key words are *similar parts*. The benefits associated with the flexibility of cellular manufacturing include the following.

First is reduced set-up time. Similar products have similar set-ups, and the learning curve concepts apply here as well as in production. Second is increased maintenance for machines in each cell. Failure of one machine within a cell can cause the entire cell to cease production. The people responsible for each cell generally take better care of their "own" equipment. The result is a quicker throughput.

A third major characteristic of JIT is automation. This is not the piecemeal automation that many organizations have undertaken, however. JIT automation is introduced as solutions to problems. While robots can be very effective, they are inflexible and can be reprogrammed only with considerable effort. Automation that is typically associated with JIT includes automatic inspection devices and servo mechanisms for part adjustment. The key to JIT automation is flexibility, which can best be attained by using an appropriate mixture of dedicated machines and people (Schonberger 1984a).

The fourth characteristic of JIT is a smooth production flow within each manufacturing organization. The best illustration of this is the system of shop floor control used at Toyota.

> Each production department will be informed of this necessary quantity per day and the cycle time from the central planning office once in each previous month. In turn, the manager of each process will determine how many workers are necessary for this process to produce one unit of output in a cycle of time. The workers of the entire factory then must be repositioned in order that each process will be operated by a minimum number of workers. (Monden 1983, p. 9)

Within requirements of the organization, the responsibility lies with the individuals who are actually producing the product.

A fifth characteristic often associated with JIT is the use of quality circles. Much of JIT involves solving production problems as they arise. The participative management philosophy that quality circles has embodied stresses that the people who regularly perform the work are best qualified to identify and solve work-related problems. This provides an ideal complement to JIT production.

The sixth and final noticeable feature of just-in-time is the lack of inventories. The elimination of transit and queue inventories has already been mentioned. Also absent in a JIT setting are stocks of raw materials and finished goods.

The characteristics of JIT are distinct and quite obvious when they are present in an organization. While they are the end product of the management philosophy that requires a commitment to excellence, they do not appear just because management commits to the philosophy.

IMPLEMENTING JIT

There can be no specific set of rules or procedures offered for implementing JIT production, but the following sections will suggest some potential steps to encourage the utilization of the just-in-time/zero inventory philosophy.*

Process-Controlled Quality

- Review designs and specifications to check what is really necessary in the product as a result of experience and particularly such basics as tolerance stacks, effects of probable contaminants, and other factors that establish the requirements of a process that will produce 100 percent quality.
- Study and improve the capability of processes, tooling, and equipment so that sources of "random defects" are eliminated by keeping the range of process operation well within what is required for the product. (It is often possible to do this inexpensively by attention to maintenance and proper

---

*The following two sections are adpated from Hall, Third Quarter, 1983 *Production and Inventory Management,* Journal of the American Production and Inventory Control Society, Inc., pp. 1–9. Reprinted with permission.

standards. It is expensive if tooling has been neglected.) Not possible in *every* case. Thus control quality is achieved through the control of the production processes themselves, not through lot inspection conducted long after production is complete.

- Instrument equipment and adopt work rules to stop automatically when a defect is produced (or even when a process is out of control, but the parts are still technically acceptable). Develop people to anticipate problems so as to avoid these stops.
- Adopt fail-safe methods of production to the maximum extent. Make it difficult to unknowingly produce a defect or miss an operation.
- Develop immediate feedback methods to immediately relay the presence and nature of a defect to the point where it originated.
- Develop professionals, supervisors, and operators to ferret out the root causes of quality problems as they arise. (Except for quality professionals, only basic statistical concepts are usually necessary. What is necessary is the ability to isolate the causes of problems and to devise counter-measures for them in the context of specific production areas.)
- Insist that vendors develop the capability to meet your JIT requirements. This may require education or it may require stronger measures. An organization's just-in-time policy will not work if vendors cannot meet the requirements.

Manufacturing Flexibility

- Eliminate clutter from the plant floor. Organize it so that only necessary items are present and all have assigned locations. That in itself starts to clarify problems.
- Reduce set-up times. The usual definition of set-up time for fabrication is: last good piece to first good piece. That is, reduce the production downtime required for a specific set-up. Attention to this usually reduces labor time of set-ups also.
- Reduce lot sizes. The ideal lot size is one unit. Small lot sizes promote balance in repetitive flow operations. Strive for lot-for-lot production in job shops.
- Set up much more frequently. Make set-ups a part of the daily routine. This requires learning how to do them properly and consistently, which in turn reduces scrap and promotes quality. The ideal is for set-up to be accomplished within the allowable production time for one unit. That provides ultimate flexibility.
- Establish the range of parts or units over which production is to be able to switch flexibly. This prevents starting from an impossible situation, but it may require a review of the purposes and role of each plant and work center.
- Compact the plant layout.

- Develop material handling capability for small quantity transport. The ability to quickly move a small quantity where it is needed promotes flexibility. It also relieves the need for part storage or for long conveyors.
- Establish preventive maintenance as part of the daily routine. This is necessary to preserve the capability of the equipment for process-controlled quality and to preserve the flexibility of its use.
- Develop flexible, multipurpose workers. When the actions above are taken, an operator's job becomes more diverse. It is a hindrance to the program if parts must be stockpiled to keep specialists busy. (The problems with established work rules in some plants are obvious.)
- Maximize the use of group technology. Group parts families or similar sub-assemblies so that they can be produced in cells with piece-at-a-time transfer between machines. Keep set-up times down for flexible use.
- Extend this system to develop effective flexible manufacturing systems and completely automated plants. The definitions here are somewhat loose, but what is implied is computer-controlled, automated production. The idea is to evolve to this state so that we know exactly what we want without investing money in systems that do not have the desired end effect of flexible automation.
- Reduce throughput times as much as possible. All the above actions contribute to that. Short throughput times also allow running production exactly as intended with little disruption from "inaccurate forecasts and shifting priorities."

Planning and Control Related to the Nature of the Physical Production Process

Process-controlled quality and increasing manufacturing flexibility reduce total lead time to the customer, and they reduce throughput time. They should reduce the time required to start new models or products into production as well as reduce costs and increase productivity. To be effective, the methods of planning and control must work with process-controlled quality.

For an overview of the planning and scheduling concepts which integrate with process-controlled quality, oversimplify a bit by classifying production into two categories for the purpose:

1. Repetitive or continuous planning and control is based on production rate. Material "flows."
2. Job shop or batch planning and control is used to make specific, nonuniform amounts of each product or part, usually with a job order system.

Whenever possible, production should evolve to the repetitive/continuous mode because throughput times and total effort will be less if material moves in a direct flow. However, a great deal of production must be done by the job shop/batch mode, and that in itself should be developed to go as smoothly as possible.

[The following suggestions are offered for implementing *repetitive manufacturing planning and control:*]

- Key on final assembly schedules. Assemble at the rate to serve the market, but assemble in short runs. Assemble in mixed model sequences, if possible. Exactly what to do depends on volumes, physical sizes of units, and other factors.
- Level schedules for even use of all material. This is not done just as averages on paper, but the final operation should be developed to actually use level rates of material and maintain the level condition over the shortest intervals of time possible.
- Stabilize the schedule. This requires some form of time-fence discipline. Run a uniform daily schedule for fixed periods of time, how long depends on the time required to establish and stabilize a new flow pattern. Five to twenty working days are commonly used fixed periods.
- Establish a range of parts or materials mix which the flexibility limits of the production process can adapt to within each period of fixed schedule. This depends on set-up flexibility and material change capabilities. With expertise, it is even possible to integrate a limited number of irregular options into such a flow pattern.
- Use pull systems of material control. Users draw material as needed and directly from the source which makes the parts as much as possible.
- Limit the amount of material in the pipelines of the pull system. The pull system forces synchronization of all production operations.
- Eliminate stockrooms in the conventional sense.
- Balance fabrication operations to final assembly use rates. Each fabrication operation needs a plan based on the rate of use of material at final assembly, and which allows for expected changes in mix of material required. The plan must consider quality procedures, tooling, materials handling, manning, and so forth. Actual operation at fabrication is by signals through the pull system, not from a fixed schedule.
- Systematically reduce inventory whenever possible. This stimulates the development of further improvements which will contribute to smoother material flow—and probably to improved flexibility.
- Use high-visibility methods to synchronize flow and to signal conditions which might disrupt synchronized operations of the plant floor. Operators follow the signal system to establish flow and to perform corrective actions.

[The following suggestions are offered for *job shop planning and control:*]

- Key schedules on final assembly if possible, but this is frequently not possible because of inherent imbalance between fabrication and assembly.
- Level the master schedule for material use, labor hours, or machine time as necessary. By nature, production work having different time content cannot be made completely smooth. This is a capacity check as well as an attempt to "smooth."

- Backschedule for fabrication job order releases. If job shop operations can become highly assured, it becomes possible to do this in a more precise manner.
- Use small lot sizes, lot-for-lot as much as possible, so as not to produce what is not yet needed. If necessary, split lots to prevent consuming capacity with long runs while short runs sit in queue. This keeps overall throughput times down. A lot size of one is still the ideal.
- Systematically work on reducing the stockroom inventory and or reducing the queues on the shop floor. Identify the reasons why production is not completed at the times expected. Set up programs for corrective action.
- Use high-visibility methods to update shop floor status and to maintain current priorities. For example, develop status boards for departments that are large enough that everyone can see them. Methods may be computerized or manual. It is the result that counts.

Planning and control need to work as part of a program to stimulate excellent execution on the plant floor. Excellent execution comes from overcoming the kinds of quality and flexibility problems mentioned earlier. With better execution, scheduling and planning need to make fewer allowances for error, so they become simpler and more precise. These allowances are usually made in material planning without the planners being conscious of what they really are.

THE QUALITY ASPECTS

Just-in-time production involves a commitment to quality. Some have referred to this as *total quality control*. The small lot production enhances quality in the following six ways (Schonberger 1984b):

1. Large lots high in nonconformities are avoided. Material that does not comply with specifications can be identified quickly and corrected before it becomes a large problem. The *Wall Street Journal* (October 28, 1983) reported that Commodore International received 120,000 defective disc drives that might have been discovered with small lot production and corrected before such a significant problem developed.
2. There is rapid feedback to the source of a quality problem. Small lot production encourages the producer of defective material to be told about the problem as soon as it occurs. This encourages rapid correction of the problem.
3. The production workers, because they know the process best, often can correct the problem as soon as it occurs. Giving quality responsibility to production workers along with the authority to correct problems when they arise is necessary for JIT to work.
4. Data collection is simplified. Most production data in small lot production do not have to be maintained for extended periods of time. Only the data that are needed by quality control, that is, the production workers, are

kept. Because they are important to the production workers they are maintained accurately.

5. Involvement of staff experts in production problems is increased. Production workers cannot solve all the quality problems. Often production quality control can only identify the problem—substandard raw material has to be addressed by the purchasing department, excessive tool wear problems can be solved by the engineering department.
6. Scapegoats are not sought to blame for poor quality. Assuming that workers are doing their best, the resources are made available to help them and the organization do even better.

Attention to quality certainly pays handsome dividends. JIT emphasizes placing the attention and resources at the point in production where they will have the optimum effect.

KANBAN

Closely associated with just-in-time production, although not necessary for its implementation, is the procedure known as *Kanban*. Originally developed for use in Toyota's Japanese assembly plants, Kanban can be defined as follows:

Definition: *Kanban* is an information system designed to control production inventories at every step in the manufacturing process.

The operation of the Kanban system is relatively simple, as the following extract illustrates.*

> In Japan, Kanban means card. Kanban is a pull system, which means that work centers that need parts, subassemblies, or assemblies from other producing work centers pull them out. In this way, the materials produced exactly equal requirements. For smooth function of a Kanban system, certain plans have to be followed. The system uses a quarterly planning horizon and a monthly planning cycle. The master production schedule [MPS] is frozen for a period of 2 to 4 weeks, and the monthly requirements are broken down into daily requirements. The MPS is exploded to get a list of parts for daily production. The parts list is sent to departments in the form of Kanban. When the MPS is changed, a new set of cards is put into the system.
>
> The cards are used for two purposes: (1) to move parts from one place to another or (2) to authorize the production of parts, subassemblies, and assemblies. The former is known as *conveyance Kanban,* and the latter is known as *production Kanban.* A standard size container is used, and each card is treated like a coupon and is good for one container. The Kanban system is shown in Figure 1.
>
> As an example, suppose that a container of item X is required from work

---

*Adapted from D. W. McLeavey and S. L. Narasimham, *Production Planning and Inventory Control,* pp. 661-663. Copyright © 1985 by Allyn and Bacon, Inc. Reprinted with permission.

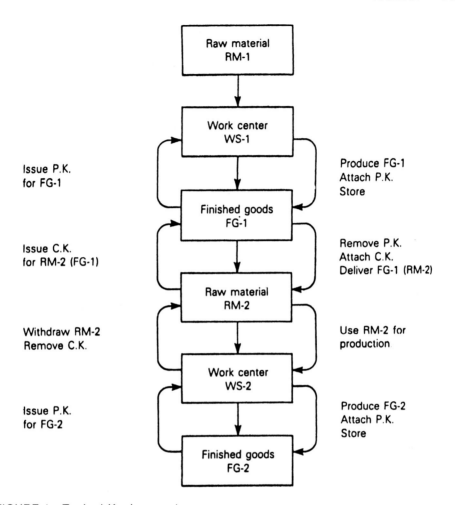

FIGURE 1 Typical Kanban system.

center WS-2. As a first step, a production Kanban is issued to work center WS-2. The work center withdraws a container of raw materials RM-2 from its inventories. The container of RM-2 also includes a move card (conveyance Kanban). Work center WS-2 removes the move card from the container and sends it to the preceding work center, WS-1. The move card serves as an authorization to pick up a container of FG-1. The container of FG-1 also includes a production Kanban for FG-1. Finished goods FG-1 serve as raw material RM-2 at work station WS-2.

When a container of FG-1 is moved to WS-2, the production Kanban is removed from the container and a move card is attached to it. The production Kanban just removed from the container of FG-1 is hung on the board or sent back to work center WS-1. It serves as an authorization to produce another container of FG-1.

148 NUMERICAL CONTROL

Then work center WS-1 withdraws a container of raw material RM-1. The entire process is repeated at work center WS-1, with its feeding work center.

There are many variations of Kanban and JIT in use. Companies such as Renault in France, and GE, Hewlett Packard, and Harley-Davidson in the United States have documented successful applications.

Example*

One of the techniques that Harley-Davidson has used to attack inventory and quality problems is just-in-time. They call their program MAN (materials as needed). It incorporates JIT and Kanban, the Japanese card system for inventory control. They give it one more interesting twist and call it a "health plan" for motorcycles. Carrying the analogy a little further, they refer to the final assembly reject area as the "hospital."

Not long ago, their hospital had over 900 patients (sick motorcycles). Of the 160 bikes built each day, 30 to 50 percent were ill. The primary cause was a severe case of "lack of parts," in spite of a $22 million component inventory.

Just-in-time is generally thought of as an outside vendor program. The problem is to get them to deliver what you need just as you need it. However, many components for assembly are produced in-house. Thus, to get the most benefit, it seemed reasonable the JIT approach should include the in-house supply departments as well as outside suppliers.

For Harley to comply with its in-house JIT program, machine set-up times had to be reduced. For example, set-up and throughput time to stamp fenders and gas tanks took 3 to 4 weeks. This definitely would defeat the program before it started. Money and mostly ideas were needed to correct the problem. The money came from Harley, and a good share of the ideas came from the quality circles. As a result, set-up and throughput time for fenders and tanks now takes only 2 days. Much of what was batch production is now a flow process. Now H-D can react quickly to market changes—a real bonus.

Smaller standard size lots makes a perfect situation to use a card system for inventory control. A card for each part number tells the number of pieces to be made, where the parts are going, and where they have been. A card lot may be as much as a week's supply or 1 hour's.

When the parts are used up, the card from that lot is returned to the previous (supply) operation. In the three-card system, returning the second card triggers a reorder. The newly ordered material will arrive just before all the parts from the third container are used. Thus, there is flow, and not storage area, for parts. The additional free floor space can now be available for more production. This is an obvious element in greater plant capacity.

Harley found that the MAN system would break down when the parts being made were not good—it stopped the flow. Quality was a problem, but was corrected for the most part by using a statistical approach to process control.

*This example describing Harley-Davidson's application of JIT and Kanban is reprinted, with adaptations, with permission from *Quality,* April, 1985, a Hitchcock Publication.

Not only in-house but outside suppliers are being encouraged to use control charts as a statistical process control [SPC] tool. The training required is not insurmountable for operators, and it provides a means of assuring good parts. Approximately 75 percent of the purchased dollar volume is on the MAN system. With the company's willingness to invest, employee ideas, and SPC, a complete program seems to be a feasible goal.

MAN has already had an impressive impact. As motorcycles come off the assembly line, over 95 percent go directly to shipping. The "hospital" now contains a meager 100 patients at most. Component inventory has dropped $11 million. Inventory turns have gone from 4 to 20. Since 1982, the average productivity per employee is up 20 percent. The MAN program has played a key role in bringing health to an ailing company that is now putting it all together.

LIMITATIONS OF JIT

Although the just-in-time, or zero inventory, approach to manufacturing has the potential for significantly increasing productivity, it is not the last word in productivity improvement. A number of limitations have been suggested regarding the application of JIT. For example, although cellular manufacturing is an important aspect of JIT, some machines cannot be included in cells. Either their size or cost or wide usage may prohibit including such equipment in a cell.

A goal of JIT implementation is reduced set-up times. Some processes simply require longer set-ups, and no amount of practice can reduce the set-up time.

JIT focuses on long term productivity growth. "Workers are judged and compensated based on overall and long-term performance and not on individual production levels. An idle time is not necessarily non-productive; it may be needed for reducing work-in-process inventory, preventive maintenance, or problem solving" (Sepehri 1985, p. 51). This may bother some elements of management because it is a change from the traditional practice. While it is a problem that has to be overcome, the resistance of first line and middle management is a very real limitation.

Another limitation is the fact that JIT's implementation takes time. Historically, management in the United States has been impatient for results.

One final limitation needs to be noted. As stated earlier in this chapter, JIT production continually evolves as it is implemented. Initial solutions to problems are tried, and, depending on the results, are either adopted, adapted, or discarded. Procedures may have to be modified or changed several times. Constant change requires constant communication and training, or retraining. This is a definite handicap in some organizations. Just-in-time is not a one-time, quick fix. Initial failures or modifications may weaken commitment to the philosophy.

CONCLUSION

Several aspects of just-in-time have to be emphasized. First, JIT is a philosophy that represents a total commitment to excellence by management. The philosophy, in order to work, requires good planning, good execution, and a good environment

("JIT and MRP II," 1984). The characteristics of JIT include flexibility, quick response to changing conditions, qualified vendors, and dependable material deliveries (Quinn 1984).

The philosophy is not a quick fix. It cannot be added to a corporate operation like a new piece of equipment. Finally, while the changeover to JIT may seem like a relatively complicated procedure, it is important to remember that JIT is really a crusade for simplicity in reducing waste and increasing productivity.

The sole purpose of reducing costs is to obtain a better market competitive edge and, thereby, to maintain the need for production in the long run. The resulting benefits are shared by all and not credited to only a few. The workers can really believe the JIT system is the ultimate solution which eliminates all waste from the manufacturing floor and places a higher value on their work. JIT depends on teamwork for continuous improvements and on a full understanding of the workers who should support and maintain it (Sepehri 1985, p. 55).

REVIEW QUESTIONS

1. What is meant by just-in-time production?
2. How does zero inventory relate to just-in-time production?
3. Why is JIT considered a commitment?
4. What are the major characteristics of JIT?
5. What is the key to making JIT work?
6. What is meant by manufacturing flexibility?
7. How does JIT relate to throughput time?
8. What are the two major divisions of production processes?
9. How does JIT enhance quality?
10. What is Kanban?
11. What are the characteristics of Kanban?
12. What are some of the limitations of JIT?

BIBLIOGRAPHY

Hall, R. 1983, 3d. quarter. Zero inventory crusade—More than materials management. *Production and Inventory Management.*

JIT and MRP II: Partners in manufacturing strategy. *Modern Materials Handling,* December 10, 1984.

Monden, Y. 1983. *Toyota production system.* Norcross, Ga.: Industrial Engineering and Management Press.

Quinn, F. J. 1984, September. No room for error. *Traffic Management,* 28–38.

Schonberger, R. J. 1984a, October. Just in time production systems: Replacing complexity with simplicity in manufacturing management. *Industrial Engineering,* 52–63.

Sepehri, M. 1985, February. How Kanban system is used in an American Toyota Motor facility. *Industrial Engineering.*

Chapter Eight

ROBOTS AND ARTIFICIAL INTELLIGENCE

After you have read this chapter, it will be clear to you that

- ❏ Robots can help with productivity, quality, and costs.
- ❏ Robot hardware is composed of a manipulator that does the work, a drive unit that powers the manipulator, and a controller that coordinates everything.
- ❏ Robots can be classified according to how their moves are controlled (i.e., nonservo- or servo-controlled).
- ❏ Programming is normally computer-assisted.
- ❏ Artificial intelligence (AI) is helping us move toward the day when computers are as easy to use as telephones.

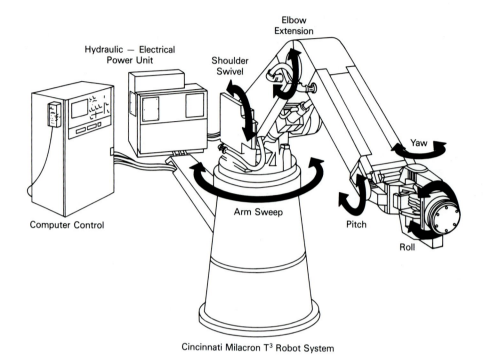

FIGURE 8-1 (Courtesy of Cincinnati Milacron.)

World War II destroyed much of the economic base of the world, except for North America. Consequently, we had little competition for a considerable period and could sell our goods almost without difficulty. We got into some bad habits, and now that others have rebuilt with newer plants, we face a much more competitive environment. Our huge international debts, our gigantic federal budget deficit, and our well-documented quality and productivity problems evidence the new situation.

Symptoms of the new business climate include shorter product life cycles, increased product customizing demands, and higher expectations about quality. Robots can help. Their versatility can assist with productivity, quality, and costs. Reprogramming and retooling a robot, for example, are relatively fast and inexpensive, which helps in short production runs and with customizing. Robots can do dangerous jobs (e.g., welding, painting), and dull, repetitive ones (e.g., stacking products in a warehouse). Robots are good at boring, hard, and dangerous work.

An *industrial robot,* as defined by the Robot Institute of America, is a programmable multifunction manipulator designed to move material, parts, tools, or specialized devices through variable programmed motions for the performance of a variety of tasks. It can be reprogrammed and so is flexible. A robot has three main components (see Figure 8-1):

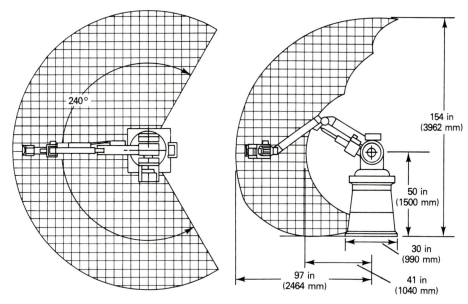

FIGURE 8-2 The work volume of a jointed-arm robot. (Courtesy of Cincinnati Milacron.)

- The manipulator, which performs the work
- The power unit, which moves the manipulator
- The computer control, which directs the manipulator.

Robots can be discussed in terms of their *work volume* (see Figure 8-2). The path of points (the locus) the robot can reach is its work volume (or space, or envelope). The axes of motion determine this, as suggested by Figure 8-3. The rectilinear example (Figure 8-3a) has a cubic work volume; Figure 8-3b has a cylindrical work volume and Figure 8-3c's is spherical. The robot's envelope is illustrated in Figure 8-2.

For robots, the term *degree of freedom,* means one variable of motion (i.e.,

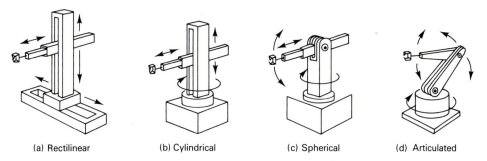

(a) Rectilinear (b) Cylindrical (c) Spherical (d) Articulated

FIGURE 8-3 Axes of motion. (Courtesy of Cincinnati Milacron.)

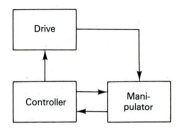

FIGURE 8-4   Robot hardware components.

axis of movement). For example, cylindrical robots have 3 degrees of freedom (i.e., one rotational and two linear). The robot in Figure 8-1 has six degree of freedom, as follows: (1) arm sweep, (2) shoulder swivel, (3) elbow extension, (4) wrist pitch, (5) yaw, (6) roll. Accordingly, this robot can place a tool in any position in its work space.

HARDWARE

Robot hardware is composed of the manipulator that does the work, the drive unit that powers the manipulator, and the controller that coordinates things. Figure 8-4 is a block diagram, and Figure 8-1 shows the actual hardware. We discuss these three elements next.

Manipulator

The *manipulator* is the arm that does the work. It is built from links and joints that can move and perform tasks. The manipulator's reach is its work volume, and its flexibility is indicated by its degrees of freedom, as discussed above.

The *end effector* (gripper or tool) is attached to the robot's arm and wrist. Figure 8-5 shows some grippers, and Figure 8-6 some tools. Grippers are analogous to the human hand and grasp objects. Examples of tools are spray guns, welding torches, and vacuum suction cups. Just as an NC machine center can change tools, so can some robots. This makes them flexible, general-purpose machines.

Controller

The *controller* directs the manipulator's moves. It may be in the robot or in a separate cabinet. Robots have nonservo controls (which are relatively simple and cheap) and servo controls (similar to NC controllers). In either case, the controller converts programming instructions into signals that direct the arm.

Nonservo robots move among predefined stops. They work without feedback, and their moves are limited to a given number of programmable positions. Relatively inexpensive and easy to program and maintain, they are fast and good at repetitive motions. Examples of their use include parts handling, machine loading, conveyor unloading, and die casting. A nonservo control loop is shown in Figure

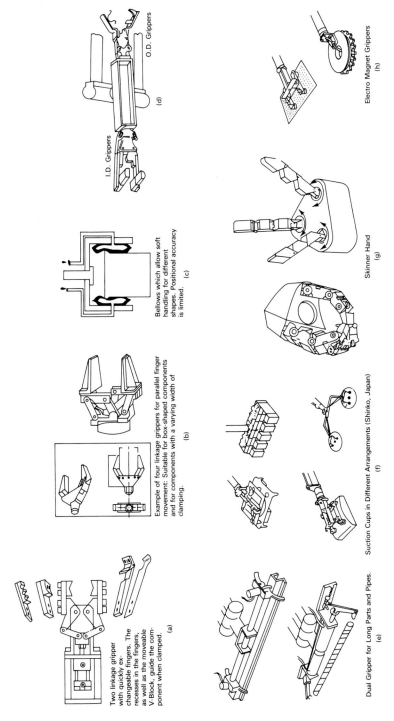

FIGURE 8-5 Grippers. [From E. L. Hall and B. C. Hall, *Robotics* (New York: CBS College Publishing, 1985), pp. 39, 40.]

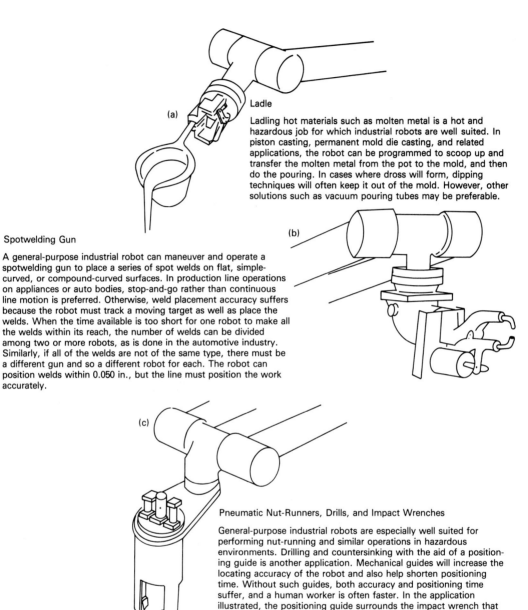

(a) **Ladle**

Ladling hot materials such as molten metal is a hot and hazardous job for which industrial robots are well suited. In piston casting, permanent mold die casting, and related applications, the robot can be programmed to scoop up and transfer the molten metal from the pot to the mold, and then do the pouring. In cases where dross will form, dipping techniques will often keep it out of the mold. However, other solutions such as vacuum pouring tubes may be preferable.

(b) **Spotwelding Gun**

A general-purpose industrial robot can maneuver and operate a spotwelding gun to place a series of spot welds on flat, simple-curved, or compound-curved surfaces. In production line operations on appliances or auto bodies, stop-and-go rather than continuous line motion is preferred. Otherwise, weld placement accuracy suffers because the robot must track a moving target as well as place the welds. When the time available is too short for one robot to make all the welds within its reach, the number of welds can be divided among two or more robots, as is done in the automotive industry. Similarly, if all of the welds are not of the same type, there must be a different gun and so a different robot for each. The robot can position welds within 0.050 in., but the line must position the work accurately.

(c) **Pneumatic Nut-Runners, Drills, and Impact Wrenches**

General-purpose industrial robots are especially well suited for performing nut-running and similar operations in hazardous environments. Drilling and countersinking with the aid of a positioning guide is another application. Mechanical guides will increase the locating accuracy of the robot and also help shorten positioning time. Without such guides, both accuracy and positioning time suffer, and a human worker is often faster. In the application illustrated, the positioning guide surrounds the impact wrench that unscrews a lifting lug from the nose of a projectile in a munitions plant.

FIGURE 8-6   Tools. From E. L. Hall and B. C. Hall, *Robotics* (New York: CBS College Publishing, 1985), pp. 41–43.

Stud-Welded Head

Equipping an industrial robot with a stud-welding head is also practical. Studs are fed to the head from a tubular feeder suspended from overhead. One caution concerns accuracy with which welded studs can be located. An industrial robot can position a stud within 0.050 in., but on-the-line work positioning must be exact. The weight of the head is rarely a significant limitation. Stud-welding heads are well within the 100-lb capacity of standard robots.

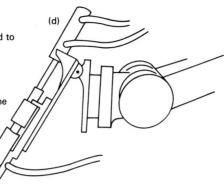

Inert Gas Arc Welding Torch

Arc welding with a robot-held torch is another application in which an industrial robot can take over from a man. The welds can be single or multiple-pass. The most effective use is for running simple-curved and compound-curved joints, as well as running multiple short welds at different angles and on various planes. Maximum workplace size is limited by the robot's reach, unless the robot is mounted on rails. Where the angle at which the gun is held must change continuously or intermittently, the industrial robot is a good solution. But long welds on large, flat plates or sheets are best handled by a welding machine designed for that purpose. In addition to welding for fabrication purposes, wear-resistant surfaces and edges can be prepared by laying down a weld bead of tough, durable alloy. And the robot will handle a flame cutting torch with equal facility.

Heating Torch

The industrial robot can also manipulate a heating torch to bake out foundry molds by playing the torch over the surface, letting the flame linger where more heat input is needed. Fuel is saved because heat is applied directly, and the bakeout is faster than it would be if the molds were conveyed through a gas-fired oven.

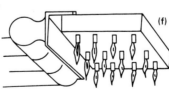

FIGURE 8-6 (Continued)

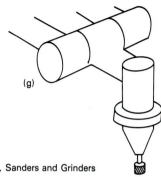

(g)

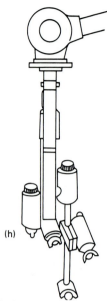

(h)

Spray Gun

Ability of the industrial robot to do multipass spraying with controlled velocity fits it for automated application of primers, paints, and ceramic or glass frits, as well as application of masking agents used before plating. For short or medium-length production runs, the industrial robot would often be a better choice than a special-purpose setup requiring a lengthy changeover procedure for each different part. Also, the robot can spray parts with compound curvatures and multiple surfaces. The initial investment in an industrial robot is higher than for most conventional automatic spraying systems. When the cost of frequent changeovers is considered, the initial investment assumes less importance. Industrial robots can be furnished to meet intrinsically safe standards for installation in solvent-laden, explosive atmospheres.

Routers, Sanders and Grinders

A routing head, grinder, belt sander, or disc sander can be mounted readily on the wrist of an industrial robot. Thus equipped, the robot can rout workpiece edges, remove flash from plastic parts, and do rough snagging of castings. For finer work, in which a specific path must be followed, the tool must be guided by a template. The template is a substitute for the visual-and sometimes tactile-control that a human worker would exercise. In such a case, the overall accuracy achieved depends upon how accurately the workpiece is positioned relative to the template. Usually, the part is automatically delivered to a holding fixture on which the template is mounted.

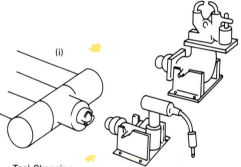

(i)

Tool Changing

A single industrial robot can also handle several tools sequentially, with an automatic tool-changing operation programmed into the robot's memory. The tools can be of different types or sizes, permitting multiple operations on the same workpiece. To remove a tool, the robot lowers the tool into a cradle that retains the snap-in tool as the robot pulls its wrist away. The process is reversed to pick up another tool.

FIGURE 8-6   (Continued)

8-7. The controller sends a move signal to the valve that drives the device which converts pneumatic, electric, or hydraulic energy into motion (the actuator). When the axis reaches the desired position, a signal is sent to close the valve.

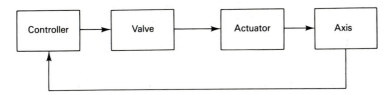

FIGURE 8-7 Nonservo robot control.

Servo-controlled robots are similar to NC machines. The controller stores the program, sends control signals to the robot, and then processes the feedback data, sending adjustments to the drive system. Figure 8-8 illustrates the servo control mechanism. The controller processes the stored program and sends the desired position instructions to the actuator, which drives the arm. The current position is fed back and compared to the desired position. If there is a difference, a signal is sent to the actuator. This system can control speed and acceleration and allows the robot to move to any point in its work volume, making for a versatile device. Servo robots tend to be more expensive than nonservo robots, but, being so flexible, they can do more.

One advantage of servo-controlled robots is their precision, which comes mostly from how their motions are controlled. Three ways the path of movement is achieved are

- *Point-to-point.* The manipulator is moved from one desired position to another without controlling its path. This is used when only the final position matters and neither the path nor velocity is important. It is a simple, frequently used control method. Programming (teaching the robot) is typically done with a control box (a teaching pendant) the operator uses to guide the robot through the desired moves. The motions are recorded in the controller for playback to later perform the task automatically.
- *Continuous path.* Both the end points and the path are defined. The robot is usually taught (programmed) by holding it and physically leading it along the path at the desired speed. Spray painting is an example of continuous-path motion control.

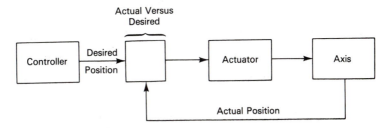

FIGURE 8-8 Servo robot control.

- *Controlled path.* The end points are specified, and the computer itself generates a controlled path for the manipulator, controlling the velocity and acceleration as well. This type of control is often used to ensure that the robot follows a straight line between programmed points.

Drive Unit

The drive unit powers the manipulator with one of three technologies:

Hydraulic drives move the manipulator with fluids, making them safe in most hazardous environments. They are characterized by few moving parts, high speed, and high load capacities.

Electric drives are widely used because they are accurate, are quiet, and require little space. But their load capacity is less than that of hydraulic drives.

Pneumatic drives (air-driven) are common for nonservo robots. Used in simple pick-and-place applications, their low payloads and limited accuracy are disadvantages.

PROGRAMMING

Manual robot programming seldom occurs and then only for elementary applications. Computer-assisted programming is normal. We next discuss three levels of computer-assisted programming.

Lead-through (teach). The robot's controller is set to programming mode, and the programmer grasps the manipulator and leads it through the task. The controller remembers and can duplicate the moves. Much programming is done in this teach mode. It is time-consuming, however, and program changes usually mean repeating the entire teaching sequence.

Teach pendant. This is also real-time programming done at the robot. The hand-held pendant has buttons that move the manipulator as required (see Figure 8-9). This creates the program. Thereafter, the robot remembers and can consistently repeat the task. But the dumb robot will repeat the exact sequence even when some unexpected change occurs. For example, it will proceed as if it's picking up a part even when the part is missing.

Off-line. Off-line programming is done at a remote computer which sends the coding to the robot's controller. VAL is a language widely used for such programming. It originated at Stanford University and was developed by Unimation, Inc., the first major US robot manufacturer. Figure 8-10 shows a robot programmed this way. It tends NC machines. Such high-level programming of robots at remote computers ties into computer-integrated manufacturing. It suggests how, via computers, the design and manufacturing processes can be part of the same automated continuum.

FIGURE 8-9 Teach pendant for the Cincinnati Milacron T³ robot. (Courtesy of Cincinnati Milacron.) Safety equipment may have been removed or opened to clearly illustrate the product and must be in place prior to operation.

FIGURE 8-10 A robot tending machines, placing work on them, removing and inspecting finished parts, and stacking them. This is a work cell. (Courtesy of Cincinnati Milacron, Inc.) Safety equipment may have been removed or opened to clearly illustrate the product and must be in place prior to operation.

Benefits

Robots are used for machine loading, assembly, arc welding, painting, material handling, and many other applications. The benefits from using robots include the following:

- *Reliability.* An uptime of about 98 percent is normal.
- *Flexibility.* Because robots are reprogrammable, tasks can be changed relatively quickly and easily.
- *Safety.* Robots can effectively do many jobs which are hazardous to people.
- *Productivity.* Robots don't tire, strike, or get sick. For certain jobs, they work faster and more consistently than people.

Return on investment Used on a two-shift basis, a return on investment of 30 percent is conservative (with a payback period of between 12 and 24 months).

ARTIFICIAL INTELLIGENCE (AI)

Since the first commercial computer was connected in the US Census Bureau in 1951, we have struggled to make them smarter. When computers can do jobs that require human characteristics, such as intelligence, imagination, and intuition, they will be much more helpful.

We are progressing. There now exist programs that are expert on particular topics. For example,

- Authorities on mineral prospecting were interviewed. By formalizing the rules these experts follow in locating underground mineral deposits, this knowledge was converted into a program and made available to others. Now novices can provide the computer with data about their geological problems and receive analyses based on the facts and rules supplied earlier by the experts.
- The Ford Motor Company uses a similar knowledge-based system to help maintenance technicians diagnose problems with their factory robots.
- There is an emergency monitoring system for power plants. It alerts the operator to any changes and provides an explanation. The system can also be used to test the consequences of changes in plant operations before the changes are actually made.

Despite such real progress, computers remain dim-witted. The machines lack both the knowledge base of a typical person and the ability to communicate in everyday language. Accordingly, natural language processing is getting much attention. It is a difficult area. "Right here, turn left" may be obvious to human drivers, but not to machines. Or, "Time flies like an arrow" is clear to you, but the computer analysis may conclude that

- Flies are being timed (for speed) by the same method used for timing arrows.
- Time flies (particular insects) enjoy consuming a certain arrow.

Computer vision is another awkward area. Connecting a TV camera to a computer is no problem. Getting it to sense and decipher what it "sees" is the challenge. We are advancing, however, so that satellite photographs, for example, can be analyzed for information about crops, weather, geology, and other matters.

Further, robots may ultimately become intelligent servants. They can now duplicate some human mechanical abilities. When they can sense the environment through their computers (e.g., sight, touch, and hearing), they will be able to adjust to the conditions registered by their sensors. Add a knowledge base plus a way to reason, and robots can begin to make intelligent decisions. Robots are now used as "night watchmen," patrolling buildings and alerting humans to fires and other security problems.

Computers remain difficult to use, despite major advances. Expert systems, natural language interfaces, computer vision, and intelligent robots (collectively termed *artificial intelligence,* AI) will help move us to the day when computers are as easy to use as telephones.

SUMMARY

1. Robots are good at boring, hard, and dangerous work.
2. A robot's reach (work volume) and flexibility (degrees of freedom) are important characteristics.
3. The hardware is composed of the manipulator that does the work, the drive unit that powers the manipulator, and the controller that coordinates everything.
4. Grippers and tools are attached to the manipulator.
5. There are two types of control: nonservo (without feedback) and servo (with feedback).
6. The drive unit is hydraulic, electric, or pneumatic (air).
7. Programming is usually computer-assisted.
8. The robot can be taught by grasping the manipulator and leading it through the task.
9. Off-line programming can be done on a remote computer (often with the VAL language) and sent to the robots' controller.
10. Robots are reliable and flexible and can offer attractive returns on investment.
11. Expert systems, natural language interfaces, computer vision, and intelligent robots are collectively termed artificial intelligence. Artificial intelligence is helping us move toward the day when computers are as easy to use as telephones.

REVIEW QUESTIONS

1. What is the "new business climate"? How does it impact on you?
2. Define: robot, work volume, degrees of freedom.
3. Explain a robot's main components.
4. Give examples of some end effectors.
5. What's the difference between a nonservo- and a servo-controlled robot?
6. Compare and contrast: point-to-point, continuous path, and controlled path.
7. What are the characteristics, advantages, and disadvantages of hydraulic, electric, and pneumatic drives.
8. Explain the three computer-assisted ways to program a robot.
9. Which are real-time and done at the robot?
10. Define: pendant, VAL, and teach mode.
11. What are some benefits robots offer? What about return on investment?
12. Based on what you have learned so far, how do robots fit into the idea of computer-integrated manufacturing?
13. How do they fit into CAD/CAM?
14. What is the relationship between robots and MAP?
15. Describe ESIE's parts and explain their functions.

Chapter Nine

PROCESS PLANNING

After you have read this chapter, it will be clear to you that

- There are certain tools manufacturers traditionally use in process planning.
- Process planning for computer-aided manufacturing has to consider added capabilities.
- Computer-aided manufacturing adds capabilities such as manufacturing cells, automated storage and retrieval, automated transportation, and flexible manufacturing systems.

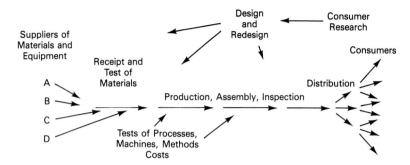

FIGURE 9-1 Production system. [Reprinted from *Out of the Crisis*, by W. Edwards Deming by permission of MIT and W. Edwards Deming. Published by MIT, Center for Advanced Engineering Study, Cambridge, MA 02139. © 1986 by W. Edwards Deming.]

"Figure out what people want and supply it" is the essence of business. Providing what people want is the key to survival. The consumer, present and future, is the most important part of the production system.

Figure 9-1 illustrates the system. Materials and equipment come in at the left, and the process flows counterclockwise back to the suppliers. It is a never-ending cycle. When your customers tell you what is good and bad about your product, you can innovate and redesign. This will modify your materials, manufacturing, and so on.

It is a continual process, but, for any one cycle, the manufacturer must know

- What to make (e.g., design specifications)
- How many to make (e.g., orders, contracts, forecasts)
- How to make them.

We assume in this chapter that the first two questions have been answered, so we are concerned only with how to make the product. That is, we have decided on its design and specifications and have estimated demand, so we already know what and how many to manufacture. Accordingly, the relevant part of Figure 9-1 is production, assembly, and inspection.

TRADITIONAL PROCESS PLANNING[1]

Traditional *process planning* generates the detailed sequence of production steps in the manufacture of a product. Figure 9-2 suggests the typical flow of activities. As noted, the input to the process is what and how many to make.

The manufacturing process is conventionally planned with some of the following tools:

- *Make or buy analyses.* If you make an item, labor, materials, and equipment, are required. Management then controls production of the item but

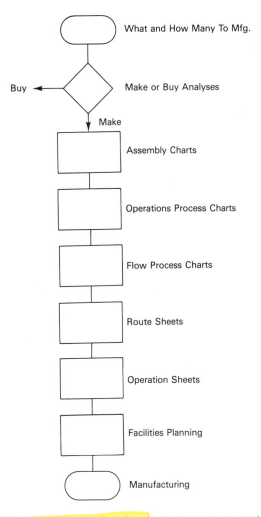

FIGURE 9-2 Traditional process planning (sequence may vary).

has to earn a return on the assets so employed. If you buy the item, you lose some control and avoid some headaches (which your supplier assumes).
- *Assembly charts*. Each assembly, such as your car's engine, has parts and a sequence in which they are assembled. Assembly charts show the relationships of parts and subassemblies to the whole, thereby depicting sequences.
- *Operations process charts.* Similar to assembly charts, operations process charts usually contain more detail, such as specifications and times for machining and for inspection.
- *Flow process charts.* These are operations process charts which include nonmanufacturing factors such as delay, transportation, and storage.

- *Route sheets.* These define the operations and their sequence, as well as the equipment and tools used in the manufacturing process. Set-up times and run times are usually given.
- *Operation sheets.* Each operation on the route sheets is detailed, giving the standard manufacturing method and specifying how that operation is accomplished.
- *Facilities planning.* Site preparation and tool design may be needed and so have to be planned.

Traditional process planning is thus what happens between making the decision as to what and how many to make and the start of actual manufacturing. Plans have to be made for converting the raw material into a valuable product. There are many techniques, skills, and operations involved, so knowledgeable individuals are needed to prepare process plans. Such people are even more necessary as the number of computer-aided processes increases on the factory floor. We discuss some aspects of computer-aided manufacturing next. (*Computer-aided manufacturing* is the use of computers to help in manufacturing.) Production planning in the CAM environment has many more capabilities available than in the traditional plant but also many more variables to deal with.

COMPUTER-AIDED PROCESS PLANNING

Computer-aided process planning depends heavily upon a system called *group technology,* which groups parts according to their shape or their operating process (see Figure 9-3). Arranging plant machinery into manufacturing cells to process particular part families helps to cut costs, too (see below). When the parts classification data are entered in the data base (where the design information is presumably already stored), design and production are tied together even more closely.

Part families can be defined using operation and route sheets which indicate common operations and routes. There are many classification and coding schemes. Generally, both manufacturing and design characteristics are considered, producing a part code of, say, 10 digits. Effective classifications, when coded, help to retrieve and to analyze parts information for manufacturing efficiency.

As a result of group technology,

- New parts can be derived from existing designs, saving time.
- Time savings can also be realized by modifying current process plans and production schedules.
- The advantages of mass production can be realized while enjoying the flexibilities of batch manufacturing.

MANUFACTURING CELLS

As computers dropped in price, shrank in size, and grew more powerful, we upgraded the idea of the machine center (a flexible NC tool). Now a few machine tools and their related equipment (e.g., inspection machines) can be grouped together into

Examples of Part Families

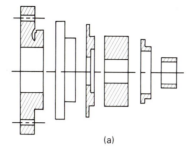

(a)

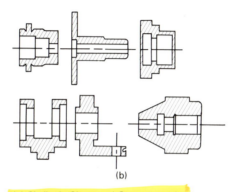

(b)

(a) Similar in Shape and Geometry and
(b) Similar in Production Operation Processes

FIGURE 9-3 Examples of part families. (a) Similar in shape and geometry and (b) similar in production operation processes. [From G. Salvendy, ed., *Handbook of Industrial Engineering* (New York: Wiley, 1982), p. 7.8.2.]

manufacturing cells to produce a limited number of part families (see Figure 9-4). When the programs are loaded and the work delivered, the cell can operate unattended until it runs out of work pieces.

These automated manufacturing cells often have laser gauges to check the accuracy of the finished piece. Similarly, they may have monitors to change dull cutting tools, to alter the feed and speed of the cutting tool, and to summon maintenance workers.

Work is delivered to the cell by a forklift or automated guided vehicle, for example, and within the cell a robot probably transfers the work. Programmable controllers usually sequence the machining, automatically redistributing work according to the load. Controllers can typically perform diagnostics, reporting the overall reliability of the manufacturing cell, pinpointing malfunctions and mistakes, and provide performance reports.

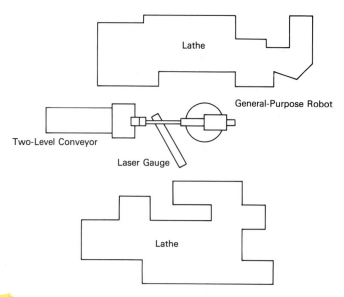

FIGURE 9-4 Manufacturing cell. The robot receives raw material from the first level of the conveyer and places it in one of the lathes where it is machined. After the machining is complete, the robot removes the finished piece and checks it for accuracy with the laser gauge. If the part is good, the robot places it on the second layer of the conveyer. If the part is not good, the laser sends a signal to the cell controller which initiates the proper corrective action. [From *CAD/CAM* (Heath Company, 1987), p. 5-24.]

Traditionally, all similar machine tools are located in the same area. Parts often require serial operations by different machines, and have to be moved around and wait in line. A part can thus spend 5 percent of the time in machining and 95 percent waiting. Machine cells do all the operations at the same location, reducing the wait between operations. There might be a robot surrounded by various machine tools, programmed to deliver parts to the correct machines at the right time. Such manufacturing cells are economical for a wide variety of parts with relatively low production volumes.

AUTOMATED STORAGE AND RETRIEVAL

Computer-controlled automated storage and retrieval systems can help with raw materials, supplies, and work in process. Figure 9-5 illustrates a typical system for storing and retrieving loads. The carriage moves vertically on the double mast, which itself moves horizontally on the support rail. It is the shuttle (on the carriage) which stores and retrieves loads on the storage rack.

Pallets of incoming material are placed on the input conveyor. Then they are

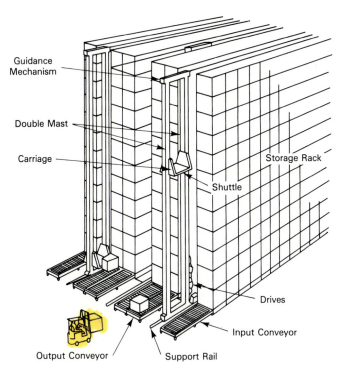

FIGURE 9-5 An automated storage and retrieval system. (Courtesy of Material Handling Institute, Charlotte, NC)

automatically put in a storage cell under computer control. When needed, the particular pallet is retrieved and placed on the output conveyor. From there, the pallet may be picked up by a forklift or by an automatic work transport vehicle. People responsible for the process planning have to consider the areas of storage and transportation, because a work piece generally spends 95 percent of the time waiting somewhere or being moved and only 5 percent of the time on a machine tool.

AUTOMATED TRANSPORTATION

Roller conveyors and forklifts are beginning to give way to *automatic guided vehicles* in some plants (see Figure 9-6). These are self-propelled units that follow a path (e.g., wire, special paint) on the factory floor. Under computer control, signals for stopping, speed, and direction come from the path. To illustrate, the vehicle picks up raw work pieces from the output conveyor of the storage rack and drops them off at the manufacturing cell, where it picks up finished work pieces and takes them to the next workstation.

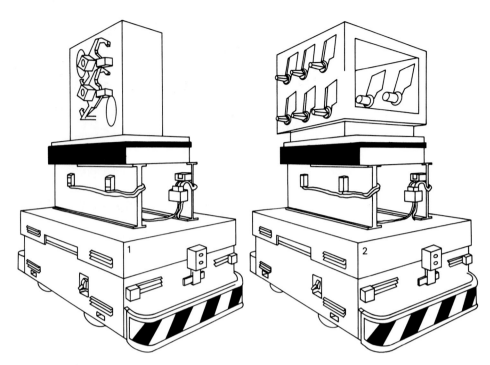

FIGURE 9-6 Automatic guided vehicle. [From *CAD/CAM* (Heath Company, 1987), p. 5-14.]

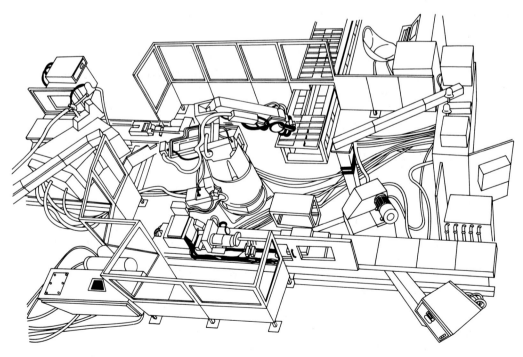

FIGURE 9-7 Typical FMC. [From *CAD/CAM,* (Heath Company, 1987), p. 5-7.]

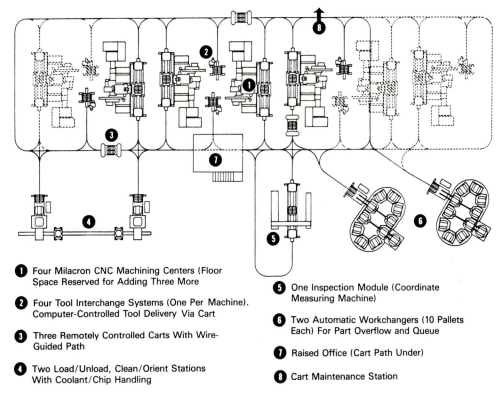

FIGURE 9-8 CIM layout at FMC corporation. (Courtesy of Cincinnati Milacron.)

FLEXIBLE MANUFACTURING SYSTEMS

When several manufacturing cells are combined with automated storage and retrieval, automated transportation, and other such computerized components, the aggregate is termed a *flexible manufacturing system* (FMS; see Figure 9-7). The FMS can, for example, machine the members of one or more part families almost without humans and all under one system of computer control. FMS thus builds on part families and manufacturing cells and moves us closer to computer-integrated manufacturing.

Process planning with flexible manufacturing systems can provide such benefits as

- Greater flexibility in meeting changing market demands
- Reduced skilled labor (i.e., the skill has been built into the harware and software)
- Shorter lead times because work can go on 24 hours a day with little human supervision.

Figure 9-8 illustrates how various types of automation can be combined into a CIM layout. This particular plant was developed by Cincinnati Milacron for the FMC Corporation. The installation produces a variety of parts for US Army equipment.

COMPUTER-AIDED MANUFACTURING

Manufacturing costs depend heavily on the number of units to be made (i.e., the volume). High-volume mass production is one extreme, and manufacturing an individual prototype is the opposite. Batch production falls in between.

The relationships among volume, costs, and price are normally that, as volume goes up, costs come down (because the relatively fixed overhead is recovered over more units, so each unit carries less). Prices can then be lowered. A lower price usually improves sales, which increases volume, so that costs fall. Prices can again be cut, and so on.

Such advantageous high-volume manufacturing becomes less likely as worldwide competition increases. Shorter product life cycles and increasing demands for customized products are now typical. This means that non-mass production is the rule (e.g., much manufacturing is in batches of less than 50 units).

NC equipment is more productive than conventional machine tools for such small-batch manufacturing. Manufacturing cells, automatically producing a limited number of part families, improved productivity again. Adding automatic materials handling and computer-controlled production management can cut the unit costs of batch manufacturing so they approach those of mass production. Accordingly, the principle of computer-aided manufacturing is that shifting to these flexible production systems with their programmable automation makes possible fast changes in the products manufactured and the processes employed.

MATERIAL REQUIREMENTS PLANNING

Material requirements planning (MRP) is a production and inventory control tool used in manufacturing to help make purchasing and production decisions. Readers who want to review MRP concepts can do so by referring to the selection at the end of this chapter.

SUMMARY

1. The consumer is the most important part of the production system.
2. Once the manufacturer has decided what and how many to make, he or she has to plan the process for making them.
3. Traditional process planning generates a detailed sequence of production steps.
4. Process planning can be partly automated with the help of group technology, which groups parts into families according to their shape or machining process.
5. Manufacturing cells are defined as a few machine tools and their related equipment which are grouped together to produce a limited number of part families under computer control.
6. Computer-controlled automated storage and retrieval systems can help with raw materials, supplies, and work in process.

7. Roller conveyors and forklifts are beginning to give way to automatic guided vehicles in some plants.
8. When several manufacturing cells are combined with automated storage and retrieval, automated transportation, and other such computerized components, the aggregate is termed a flexible manufacturing system.
9. The principle of computer-aided manufacturing is that shifting to flexible production systems with their programmable automation makes possible fast changes in the products manufactured and the processes employed.

REVIEW QUESTIONS

1. Describe the production system in Figure 9-1. What is its most important element? What part(s) does this chapter consider?
2. What is involved in most make or buy decisions?
3. Describe: assembly charts, operations process charts, flow process charts, route sheets, and operation sheets. What are they used for?
4. What is group technology and how can it help automate process planning?
5. What are some benefits of group technology?
6. Illustrate how a manufacturing cell might work.
7. Explain Figure 9-5.
8. Comment on automated transportation
9. What is a flexible manufacturing system? Why is it important?
10. What is the principle of computer-aided manufacturing? Explain.
11. "Market changes and evolving technology interrelate and compound." Discuss. (For example, the markets represented by railroads and textiles were eclipsed by such industries as cars and chemicals, and the technology of the steam engine gave way to electromechanical equipment which is being supplanted by electronics.)
12. In volume mass-production situations, what are the relationships among volume, cost, and price. Why?
13. If volume is critical to mass production's productivity, what is the key to productivity of small-batch manufacturing (e.g., runs of 50 units)?
14. Discuss the difference between production process planning in the traditional and in the CAM environments.

REFERENCE

1. See E. S. Buffa, *Operations Management* (New York: Wiley, 1972), pp. 80–89.

Appendix
MRP SYSTEMS*

INTRODUCTION

Material requirements planning, or MRP, is a production and inventory control technique used by manufacturers to determine

- What, when, and how much to buy.
- What, when, and how much to make.

The technique uses the master production schedule (MPS) to define the end products that the plant or organization is to deliver.

MRP takes this information and then calculates the materials needed to meet the master production schedule. MRP considers the completion dates of the end items, then computes the dates at which each raw material, fabricated part, subassembly, and assembly must be "ordered" to meet the completion dates in the MPS.

> **Defintion:** The *lead time,* as it is used in MRP, is the time that elapses from when a raw material or manufactured item is ordered until the time it is delivered.

By using lead times, MRP calculates not only the quantities of parts required, but also the date on which they are required.

This ability to produce a time-phased schedule of orders enables manufacturers to avoid having excess inventories and allows them to avoid stockouts of parts that will be needed in the future.

BACKGROUND

Many engineers, data processing professionals, and even top executives have had their first involvement with production and inventory control as the result of a project to install a material requirements planning system. Tackling an MRP project without a sound foundation in basic production and inventory control concepts is analogous to receiving your first introduction to a wrench while building an automobile from the ground up or learning how to use a soldering iron while sitting at a television assembly line. A sound understanding of the concepts and techniques that preceded the development of MRP will lead to an appreciation that MRP:

*This chapter was written by Don Swann, P.E., Partner, Deloitte Haskins and Sells, Atlanta, Georgia.

- Requires a significant amount of supporting detail.
- Requires strict data accuracy in these support sytems.
- Can generate dramatic improvements in a manufacturing company's inventory levels, costs, productivity, and customer service.

The search for tools to achieve the improvements that are now promised by MRP has been under way for decades.

For example, the ABC analysis, which uses Pareto's Law, was first published in 1916. The EOQ calculations were first published in 1915.

Although these procedures have been around for a long time, there are bona fide shortcomings associated with some of them. Just-in-time, Kanban, and other, newer techniques have evolved with the intent of overcoming the shortcomings of existing techniques. Although it can be argued that "failures" in inventory control are more often caused by poor execution than by poor techniques, companies with well-run inventory control programs will see improvements as they adopt more sophisticated techniques. Companies with sloppy execution will be just as disappointed with newer techniques as they were with the old ones.

The basic assumption in the remaining sections of this appendix is that MRP will be executed as designed, with the success of a production and inventory control system determined more by execution than by techniques.

STOCK REPLENISHMENT

Stock replenishment is an inventory planning technique that precedes MRP. It assumes that future usage of a part or material will be the same as historical usage. If future usage is known, then it is possible to determine when the current inventory will be used up. If the length of time it takes to receive a new order is also known, then the order can be placed at a date that will ensure that no excess inventory is carried. Figure 1 shows this.

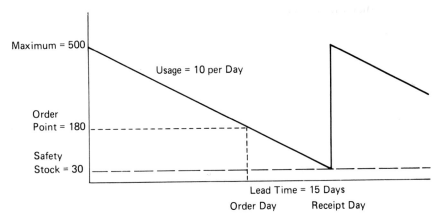

FIGURE 1 Ideal inventory replenishment model.

Stock replenishment is a valid model. Inventory does behave in a pattern generally like this. However, inventory movement rarely fits a pattern that is this regular. It is the irregularity of inventory movement that causes the stock replenishment model to fail to produce optimal inventory levels.

Usage is not regular, but comes in "bunches." The demand curve in the model is a straight line, but actual demand is often a series of spikes. For example, the usage of an item might *average* 10 units per day, but might in fact be used as a lot of 500 once very 50 days. In industry, production is often run in lots once every 2 to 6 weeks, not run in small quantities every day.

Example

Using Figure 1 as a guide, suppose that the part we are attempting to control has the following characteristics:

$$\begin{aligned}
\text{Average daily usage} &= 10 \text{ units/day} \\
\text{Lead time} &= 15 \text{ days} \\
\text{Safety stock} &= 30 \text{ units} \\
\text{Order point} &= \text{usage during lead time plus safety stock} \\
&= (10 \text{ units/day})(15 \text{ days}) + 30 \text{ units} \\
&= 180 \text{ units}
\end{aligned}$$

When the on-hand quantity of this part reaches 180 units, we will issue an order for more. The new order should arrive in 15 days, at which time our on-hand inventory will be 30 units. This technique should give us minimum average inventories, while avoiding stockouts.

But see what happens when 500 of these units are removed from inventory in 1 day for a production run. This is shown in Figure 2. The inventory immediately drops below the order point, triggering a replenishment order. It may even drop

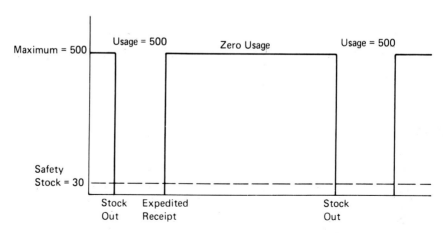

FIGURE 2 Realistic inventory usage pattern.

below the safety stock level, triggering an expedited purchase at additional cost. A new order is received in 15 days, and remains in inventory unused for 35 days, until another withdrawal of 500 units triggers a new order.

The intent in using stock replenishment was to reduce the inventory and reduce carrying costs. What has happened, in fact, is that the organization involved in this example unnecessarily carried a large inventory that was idle for 35 days. Worse, the possibility for a panic purchase existed had the inventory dropped under the safety stock level.

Note that the same logic applies to fabricated parts or subassemblies produced in house. If a machine shop within a plant is producing parts to inventory based upon stock replenishment, then the shop frequently faces situations where they are told to hurry to make a part because the part's inventory is well below order point. Then they make a large quantity, and the parts sit unused for longer than a month.

Clearly, a better model of inventory usage is needed. A better inventory planning tool would be one that recognizes the true usage pattern of each part and does not have to assume that usage will be regular over time. MRP is a tool that calculates the future usage of all parts, at the time they will be used, and in the quantities that will be used.

MRP COMPONENTS

Backscheduling

One of the key concepts in MRP is backscheduling.

Definition: *Backscheduling* is a technique that allows the determination of the starting date for a project based upon a known or targeted completion date.

The procedure for backscheduling follows these steps:

1. Define a future event that must be accomplished.
2. Define the steps that must precede the targeted future event.
3. Define the lead time for each of the support steps.
4. Set a completion date for the targeted future event.
5. Calculate the start date for the last support step by subtracting its lead time from the completion date of the project.
6. Calculate the start date of each preceding support step by subtracting the lead time of that step from the start date of the next step.

Example

A simple illustration of backscheduling is provided through the events that might lead up to a social engagement, commonly known as a date. The objective is to determine when the individual must start preparing for the date in order to arrive at the target time of 7:00 p.m. To calculate this start time, the backscheduling would begin from 7:00 p.m., as shown in Table 1. With all the events being sequential, the entire project must begin no later than 4:25 in order to be completed on time.

TABLE 1 Backscheduling for a social engagement

Event	Complete	Lead Time	Start
Arrive at date			7:00
Drive to date's house	7:00	:20	6:40
Shower/Dress	6:40	:40	6:00
Wash car	6:00	1:00	5:00
Pick up cleaning	5:00	:35	4:25

Master Production Schedule

The starting point of backscheduling in MRP is the master production schedule. The MPS is a schedule of future events, showing the dates at which the manufacturing plant must deliver its products, or end items.

While the example showed the backscheduling of a single future event, the MPS will show all of the end items that the plant has committed to produce. The MPS will show the finished goods, spare parts, or other shippable items; the dates they are needed; and the quantities of each item. Figure 9 is an example of an MPS.

The MRP model starts with these future events and their due dates, then backschedules to calculate when each manufaturing operation must be performed and when materials must be purchased in order to meet the due dates in the master production schedule.

Bill of Materials

In order for MRP to calculate the materials that must be purchased and the parts that must be made, there must be a definition of how the end items in the MPS are put together.

The following example illustrates another important piece of information required for MRP. AftTech's home appliance subsidiary, known as AftCan, produces can openers. The master production schedule shows that AftCan must complete production of 200 model X can openers 60 days from now. In order to produce these can openers, AftCan will need motors, gears, handles, wire, cabinets, and so forth. The specific gears, motors, and so on must be defined if the correct parts are to be ordered. The correct quantities must also be known.

The bill of materials is the record that specifies this information. Figure 3 shows the bill of materials or product structure for any product. The end item is called the *parent,* and the parts that make up the parent are called *components.* Note that the bill of materials can have several levels. A motor, for example, is a component of the can opener, but the motor itself has component parts. In fact, subassemblies that go into the motor may have more than one component. Each of these tiers in the bill of materials is called a *level.* Normally, each level is assigned a consecutive number. For example, the zero level is the "top" item. A "one-level bill" has a zero level plus "level one" components. Each succeeding tier of component parts is a level. Figure 3 shows a bill of materials with three levels.

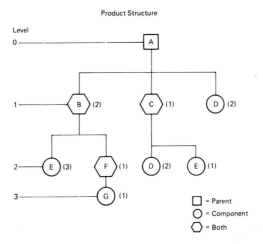

FIGURE 3 Product structure.

Standard Routings

MRP not only calculates the materials needed to support the master production schedule, it calculates the lead times, labor hours, and machine hours required to produce the items in the MPS. To perform these calculations there must be a record of the processing steps that each part and assembly goes through and the labor and machine hours needed to perform each step.

Definition: The *standard routing* is a record of the processing steps, labor standards, and machine time required for the processing of each part of component produced.

Standard routings provide lead time information to MRP by defining the time that it takes to set up equipment and the time it takes to actually produce parts. Figure 4 shows a typical routing.

PART NUMBER G   LOT 200

Work Center	Operation No.	Description	Set-up Time (Min.)	Unit Run Time (Mins.)	Queue Time (Hrs.)
10	01	Cut Strips	60	1.00	16
10	02	Cut Length	60	.50	16
20	01	Weld End	5	1.50	16
30	01	Mill Top	120	1.50	24
20	02	Weld Edge	5	1.50	16
40	01	Deburr	5	2.50	8

FIGURE 4 Standard routing.

182   PROCESS PLANNING

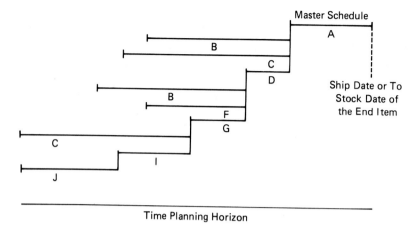

FIGURE 5   Time-phased requirements.

Note that other elements of lead time can be defined in standard routings. These are defined as follows:

Definition: *Move time* is the time parts spend in transit while they are moved from operation to operation.

Definition: *Queue time* is the time spent in line behind other parts that are also scheduled for this machine.

Definition: *Set-up time* is the time required to perform adjustments to the machine so that it can produce the needed part.

Definition: *Run time* is the time required to process each part produced by a specific operation.

Time Phasing

Given the bill of materials records and the standard routings, MRP can use back-scheduling to calculate the exact dates that parts must be purchased and the exact dates that the shop must begin fabricating parts or assembling parts. Figure 5 is an example of this. Note how important time phasing is. Just knowing that AftCan will build 6000 can openers this year and will therefore need 6000 motors, does not indicate *when* the motors will be needed. If all 6000 are purchased on the first day of the year, the finance charge for this large inventory will be significant. If they all are not ordered until day 350, then AftCan will not be able to meet the delivery dates that the customers require.

Using MRP not only lets us calculate how many parts are needed, but also tells us when we need the parts. This feature is key to the success of MRP in reducing inventories.

MANUFACTURING RESOURCE PLANNING

Material requirements planning was originally designed as an inventory planning tool. As such, it was intended only to calculate the time-phased material requirements of a manufacturer.

After using MRP for a while, companies began to expand the uses of this planning tool. If MRP could be used effectively for planning material requirements, it could also be used for planning the following requirements:

- Labor hours.
- Machine hours.
- Cash.
- Floor space.
- Other resources.

The acronym *MRP* came to represent *manufacturing resource planning,* or a technique for planning for these other resource requirements in addition to materials. To distinguish between the two versions of MRP manufacturing resource planning was given the distinction *MRP II*.

Two of the resources that are especially important to a manufacturer are labor and machine hours. Every plant has a limited number of labor hours by skill type, and a limited number of machine hours by type of machine. It is vitally important to a company to know whether or not their planned production (to support the MPS) will exceed their available labor hours or machine hours.

Capacity Requirements Planning

Capacity requirements planning, or CRP, is one of the features of MRP II. To use this tool, a company will define the available labor hours by skill and available machine hours by machine type. The MRP II logic will calculate the labor hours and the machine hours necessary to produce the items in the MPS. The CRP logic will then compare the hours required to the hours available and will produce a "load profile." An example of a load profile is shown in Figure 6. This example shows that the MPS planned calls for 50 percent more milling machine hours than are available in week 3.

WORK CENTER		MILLING MACHINES			
Week of			% of Capacity		
From	To	0%	50%	100%	150%
350	355	XXXXXXX			
355	360	XXXXXXX			
360	365	XXXXXXXXXXXXXXXXXXXXXXXXXX			
365	370	XXXXXXXXXXXXXX			
370	375	XXXXXXXXXXXXX			
375	380	XXXXXXXXXXXXXXXX			

FIGURE 6 Load profile.

Gross and Net Requirements

So far, only the gross or overall requirements of the MPS have been discussed. That is, to produce the 6000 can openers, 6000 motors were required. But what would happen if AftCan already had 500 of these in inventory? Then only 5500 motors would be needed. On the other hand, what if AftCan used the same motor in other products, for example, clocks, timers, or icemakers? Would AftCan need 5500 motors or even more?

A company's master production schedule may have several hundred or even several thousand items in it. Many of these items will have common component parts. Many of these components will have on-hand inventories. MRP will calculate the requirements for every component for each end item, and will then add all of these demands together for a total or "gross" requirement for each component. Then MRP will compare these gross requirements to on-hand inventories, and will compute the "net" requirements that on-hand inventories will not meet.

Order Parameters

Once MRP calculates the quantities of component parts required, it may have to modify these requirements for any of several reasons. For instance, MRP may have calculated that 40 motors will be needed by next week. But should 40 motors be ordered?

There are a number of factors, called *order parameters*, that modify the basic quantities of parts called for by MRP. For example, suppose the vendor sells these motors in boxes, with 12 motors per box. Or what if the minimum order the vendor will ship is 100 motors? There are other modifications that will change the order quantities that MRP will recommend. Some of these modifiers are the following:

- Minimum. The vendor will not accept an order for fewer than x units.
- Multiple. The order must be in increments of y units, because the part is produced or packaged y units at a time, e.g., 55-gallon drums, dozen, gross.
- Maximum. Due to the size of our delivery vehicle, or our forklift, or our storage rack, we cannot order more than z units of this part at one time.
- Scrap factor. Because units are damaged or lost to scrap in production, we may need n units, but have to order s percent extra to compensate for this loss.
- EOQ. Calculate the economic order quantity for this part and always order that number of parts when an order is placed.
- Coverage time. Always order the number of parts that will be used during the next w weeks.
- Lot-for-lot. Order exactly the net requirement for each period. Do not modify in any way.

Day 360

Part Number	Description	Make or Buy	Quantity	Due Date	Lead Time	Action Date	Recommended Action
C	Bracket	Make	60	370	10	360	Work Order
E	Hinge	Buy	200	370	15	355	*Rush Order
F	Hex Screw	Buy	100	365	5	360	Purch. Order
F	Hex Screw	Buy	100	370	5	365	Purch. Order

FIGURE 7   Order action report.

- Safety stock. This is an absolute minimum to keep on hand. Most MRP systems treat safety stock replenishment as a top priority function. For example, even if there are no immediate demands for a part, if the safety stock level is 5 and 4 are on hand, MRP will issue an "expedite" replenishment order to return the on-hand inventory to the safety stock level.
- Other. There are many other qualifiers that a particular MRP system may allow to "fine tune" the order recommendations made by MRP.

Work Orders/Purchase Orders

The final output of MRP is a recommendation to the company's inventory planners as to what, when, and how much to buy and what, when, and how much to make. Figure 7 shows an example of this.

Planners will react to these recommendations by issuing purchase orders or work orders. In calculating the new orders that should be released, MRP must take into account the orders that have already been released but have not yet been filled. Bear in mind that a vendor may take several months before shipping the parts that have been ordered. MRP uses purchase order and work order records to keep up with the status of open orders.

CLOSED-LOOP MRP

For MRP to produce useful and realistic instructions to inventory planners, it must have access to the most current information about on-hand inventory, open purchase and work orders, and changes to the MPS. This information changes constantly as materials are received from vendors, parts are completed by production departments, end items are shipped, and customers change their order quantities and due dates. For MRP to be a realistic tool it must use the most current information.

MRP is a *planning* tool. It predicts what should happen in the future based upon what is known in the present. To use MRP as a *control* tool, a company must constantly monitor what *actually* happens and compare this to the plan. This monitoring action is called *feedback*. Once planners receive this feedback, they can

186 PROCESS PLANNING

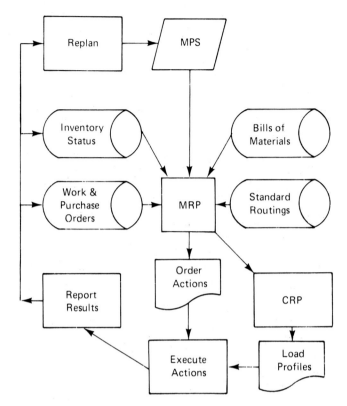

FIGURE 8 Closed-loop MRP.

change their plan, that is, issue new purchase and work orders, based upon how closely actual results met their previous plan. This cycle of plan/feedback/replan can be looked at as a *closed loop*. Figure 8 shows how feedback can be used to generate new plans.

MECHANICS OF MRP

MRP goes through hundreds of calculations to generate the recommended purchase and work orders needed to support the master production schedule. Commercial computer software for closed-loop MRP may have more than 1000 programs and over a million lines of computer code.

Because of the number and complexity of these calculations, manual MRP systems are impractical. On an ongoing basis, it would be virtually impossible to compute the needed work orders and purchase orders manually.

However, to understand the output messages that the MRP system generates, the mechanics of the MRP calculations must be understood. These computations are logical and understandable, but the following section will require careful study. The following example will illustrate the use of MRP.

Example

The starting point of MRP is the master production schedule. Figure 9 shows the demand for two end items, A and B, for five periods. As previously discussed, the bill of materials must be available to show the relationship between the end items and their components. Figure 10 shows the corresponding bills of materials for these two products.

Another bit of information that must be known is the lead time for each component part. The lead time can be calculated from the standard routings information. In this example, the total lead time by part is shown in Figure 11. Figure 11 also shows the order parameters or quantity modifiers. MRP must also have the on-hand inventory and the on-order quantities. The on-hand quantities are shown in Figure 9. On-order quantities are shown as scheduled receipts.

Given all of this information, we will now go through the computation logic of MRP. Figure 12 shows the calculation logic, based upon starting with the end item in the MPS and "exploding" down through each level of the bill of materials to find the demand at each lower level.

Figure 9 shows the specific calculations for this MRP example. The MRP worksheets show the calculated *planned order release* for each component part. The logic for components D, E, and F can be similarly applied. The calculations for component C will be described in more detail in the following paragraphs.

First, note from the bill of materials in Figure 10 that end item B does not use part C, but that end item A uses two of part C. The MPS shows that we must deliver 10 of item A in period II, 20 of item A in period III, and 15 in period V. This translates into gross requirements for part C in period II of 20 units (remembering that there are 2 units of C needed to build one of A); 40 units of C in period III; and 30 in period V.

On-hand inventory of part C is 5 units. There is a scheduled receipt (open order) for 60 units of part C that will arrive in period II. The net available inventory by period is calculated as follows:

$$
\begin{aligned}
\text{Last period's net available} &= +5 \\
+ \text{ Scheduled receipts} &= 0 \\
- \text{ Gross requirements} &= 0
\end{aligned}
$$

In period II these numbers are

$$5 + 60 - 20 = 45.$$

In period III they are

$$45 + 0 - 40 = 5.$$

Note that in period V the net available inventory is negative. That means that the gross requirements in that period exceed the on-hand plus new receipts. This

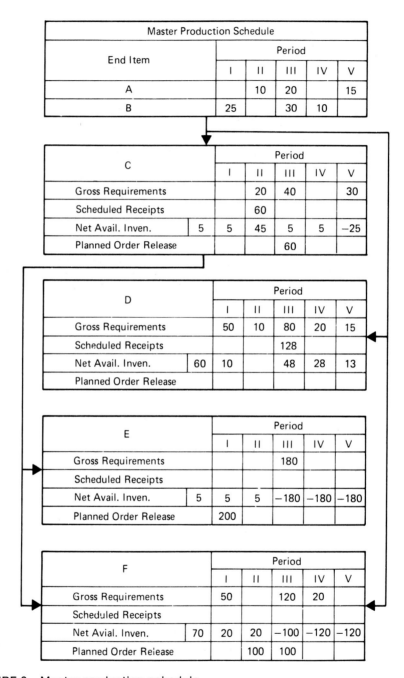

FIGURE 9   Master production schedule.

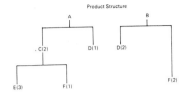

FIGURE 10   Product structure.

Component	Lead Time Period	Safety Stock	Order Quantity Modifier	Lot Sizing Rule
C	2	None	None	Quantity = 60
D	4	None	10% Scrap	3 Periods
E	3	Quantity = 5	Multiple of 50	2 Periods
F	1	None	Minimum of 100	1 Period

FIGURE 11   Planning factors.

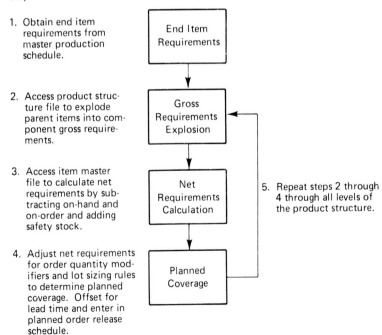

FIGURE 12   MRP processing steps.

information is needed when deciding whether to place a new order. If shortages are to be avoided, then a new order of part C must be placed to arrive during period V.

If the material is to arrive in period V, we must backschedule to determine when the order must be placed. The order parameters shown in Figure 11 indicate that part C has a lead time of two periods. Therefore, for an order to arrive in period V, the order must be placed two periods prior to then, or during period III.

This has established when to order, but not the quantity to order. This is where the order quantity modifiers are used. On the face of the problem, the obvious conclusion would be that 25 units of C should be ordered. If more than 25 are ordered, then there will be excess inventory. This order quantity logic is called "lot-for-lot." But the order parameters indicate that whenever part C is ordered 60 units must be ordered. Therefore the planned order release is for 60 units of part C in period III.

MRP performs these calculations for all parts, at all levels. Note that only one item in the MPS used part C. Consider the complexity of this exercise if 500 MPS items used part C. Also note that lower-level parts such as item F have demand from MPS items plus other assemblies. For a manufacturer with 10,000 parts and a seven-level bill of materials, these computations require automated systems.

Automated systems build a "worksheet" similar to the one shown in Figure 9 for each of the 10,000 parts. To go through each of these 10,000 worksheets would take a massive amount of time, so automated systems produce a separate report that only identifies the specific actions to be taken.

Definition: The *exception report* shows the specific situations that require management to take action.

Figure 7 is an order action report for the example discussed in this section.

WORK CENTER SCHEDULES

The above example stressed the material requirements function of MRP. There is also an important role that MRP can play in scheduling the production facility. MRP produces recommended work orders, or actions that the manufacturing facility should take to produce fabricated parts, subassemblies, and assemblies. Recall also that the MPS contains all of the end items that the plant will produce. It follows that all of the activities of all of the production departments should be directed toward on-time delivery of the items in the MPS. If that is the case, then MRP should define all of the work that the production departments are to perform.

MRP may generate several hundred work orders. The work orders will affect many different departments, or work centers. There may be dozens of different operations performed on a part. The end result of the MRP run is a very complex set of instructions for the manufacturing departments.

The order action report helps the purchasing professionals decide what, when, and how much to purchase; and it helps the production planning professionals de-

WORK ORDER #1

PART C   QTY 100

W.C.	OPERATION	QTY	START	DUE
10	01 Cut Strips	120	252	255
20	01 Weld Edge	110	255	259
30	01 Mill Top	110	259	267
40	01 Deburr Edge	100	267	269

WORK ORDER #2

PART G   QTY 200

W.C.	OPERATION	QTY	START	DUE
10	01 Cut Strips	250	235	253
10	02 Cut Length	230	253	254
20	01 Weld End	215	254	258
30	01 Mill Top	215	258	263
20	02 Weld Edge	200	263	271
40	01 Deburr	200	271	274

FIGURE 13   Work orders.

cide what, when, and how much to make. Purchasing is a one-step activity—we issue a purchase order on day X, and the material arrives on day Y. However, a work order states that we must have a quantity of "make" parts complete on a given day, but the parts may go through 20 production steps in 10 work centers, for example, cutting, welding, drilling, milling, deburring.

MRP will backschedule the make parts through all of the various operations. During this backscheduling process, MRP will note the needed start dates and end dates in each work center. The result of this backscheduling process is shown in the work order detail in Figure 13. The subject of this report is the part, and the report shows all of the steps that the part must go through.

By itself, this report is not useful to the first-line supervisor. There may be hundreds of work orders in the manufacturing plant. The supervisor needs some guidance as to which one should be used next. MRP will extract from the work orders all of the work to be performed by each work center and will re-sort all open tasks by work center.

Definition: The *dispatch list* is the MRP-generated list of tasks to be completed by a given work center, normally sorted in start date sequence.

A supervisor can use the dispatch list to indicate the next work to be performed. If each supervisor follows the schedule and meets the due dates, then all of the commitments in the MPS will be met.

To better understand how work orders and dispatch lists are tied together, look at Figures 13 and 14 together. Figure 13 shows two work orders. Figure 14

DISPATCH LIST
WORK CENTER #20

WORK ORDER	PART	OPERATION	QTY	START	DUE
2	G	01 Weld End	215	254	258
1	C	01 Weld Edge	110	255	259
2	G	02 Weld Edge	200	263	271

DISPATCH LIST
WORK CENTER #30

WORK ORDER	PART	OPERATION	QTY	START	DUE
2	G	01 Mill Top	215	258	263
1	C	01 Mill Top	110	259	267

FIGURE 14 Dispatch lists.

shows the developed dispatch lists for work centers 20 and 30. Note that the work order shows all operations required to produce a part in its final form. A dispatch list shows only the operations that a particular work center must perform. In Figure 13 it is noted that part C must go through both work center 20 and work center 30. Part G also goes from work center 20, to 30, and back to 20 again. In Figure 14, the dispatch lists for work centers 20 and 30 show only the activities each supervisor must execute. Work centers 10 and 40 would also receive similar dispatch lists.

CONCLUSION

MRP is an extremely powerful and useful planning and control tool. You can see from the prior examples how MRP is an improvement over stock replenishment and manual shop floor scheduling techniques.

MRP does have some weaknesses, however. For example, MRP assumes infinite capacity. As was illustrated in Figure 6, work center 30 has more work to do in period III than capacity available to do the work. Since MRP backschedules, it determines start dates and due dates needed to meet the MPS, and does not consider the impact on each work center. MRP will load a work center at 10 times capacity and never be aware that it has created an impossible schedule. To fix the schedule requires manual manipulations. Because of the complexity of all the interwoven work center schedules, set-up times, lot sizes, and other variables, it is extremely difficult to schedule away overloads manually.

Production and inventory control professionals have long recognized the need for a scheduling tool that recognizes that capacity is finite. The techniques that recognize that no work center can be loaded at more than 100 percent of capacity utilize forward scheduling. Recall that backscheduling starts with a future date, then subtracts lead times to calculate a start date. Forward scheduling starts today, assigns the first operation in a work center, then will schedule the second operation only when the first operation is completed.

Had forward scheduling and finite capacity been considered in generating the work schedules shown in Figure 14 and the work loads of Figure 6, then there would not have been a 150 percent load in period III. Jobs would have started sooner in work center 30 and would have taken advantage of available capacity in earlier weeks.

Many of the early attempts at forward scheduling/finite loading were unsuccessful. The complexity of the technique led to inflexible and unrealistic schedules. In the late 1970s, a technique called *optimized production technology* (OPT) was developed by an Israeli physicist, Dr. Eliyahu Goldratt. OPT works in conjunction with MRP to identify overloaded work centers. The OPT software will forward schedule/finite load the bottlenecked work centers, then backschedule the work centers that have available capacity. The result is work center schedules that are realistic and maintainable.

The logic used by OPT is a proprietary product of Dr. Goldratt's company. The scheduling process requires a sizeable mainframe computer to calculate all of the complexities mentioned above. To date, OPT is unique in its ability to develop optimal shop floor schedules, and it is being used by manufacturers throughout the world.

Proper production control and inventory management and control are intertwined and potentially complicated matters. As advances continue in computerized applications, more sophisticated systems can be developed that will help management to maintain even better control.

REVIEW QUESTIONS

1. What does MRP stand for?
2. What information does MRP provide for management?
3. What is stock replenishment?
4. Why does the stock replenishment model sometimes fail?
5. What is backscheduling?
6. What is meant by the term *product structure?*
7. What is a level in a bill of materials?
8. What is a standard routing?
9. What are the factors that should be included in a standard routing?
10. What is time phasing?
11. What is the difference between MRP and MRP II?
12. Differentiate between gross and net requirements.
13. What are order parameters?
14. What are some examples of order parameters?
15. Why is MRP considered a closed-loop system?
16. What is an exception report?
17. What is a dispatch list?
18. What is the main limitation of MRP?
19. What is forward scheduling?
20. What is meant by OPT?

PRACTICE PROBLEMS

1. For Table 2, use backscheduling to determine when operation 20 must begin.
2. A truck manufacturer has the following daily demand for the last 250 days for a particular fastener: average = 15,000 and standard deviation = 1000. Would stock replenishment or MRP be better for controlling inventory on this part?
3. Dependent demand parts are items whose demand depends on the usage of some other item. Independent demand parts are items whose demand cannot be calculated readily, but must be forecasted or predicted. Which of these categories of parts would go in the MPS?

Refer to Figures 9, 10, and 11 for the next four questions.

4. Why are there no order recommendations for part D?
5. Why are 200 parts E ordered instead of 180?
6. Why is the net available of part E in period III 180 and not 175?
7. Why was part F ordered as shown instead of 120 in period II? Why weren't 200 ordered in period II and none in III?

Refer to Figures 13 and 14 for the next two questions.

8. What work order, part, and operation will the foreman in work center 10 run first? Next?
9. What is the first work order, part, and operation on the work center 40 dispatch list? Next?

TABLE 2 Data for Problem 1

Operation	Must Follow	Lead Time (Days)	Due Date	Start Date
20	10	4		
50	40	6		
30	20	5		
10	Start	4		
40	30	2		
60 (End)	50	3	6/30	

Chapter Ten

FACTORY MANAGEMENT

After you have read this chapter, it will be clear to you that

- ❏ Purchased materials represent 55% of manufacturing costs in an average American plant.
- ❏ Manufacturing problems are often caused by changing markets and by how people think.
- ❏ Manufacturing technology is not an automatic cure-all.
- ❏ Factory managers who shift to flexible production systems having programmable automation can begin to realize fast changes in the products manufactured and the processes employed.
- ❏ Managing change is usually the crucial element in determining the success of a CIM project.

196 FACTORY MANAGEMENT

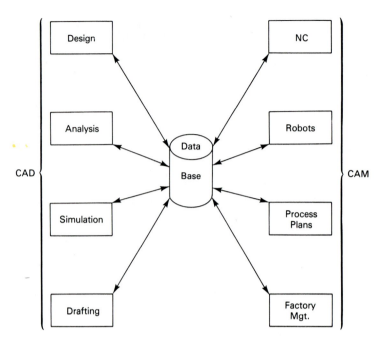

FIGURE 10-1 Factory management ties together the CAM areas.

Factory management ties together the CAM areas, coordinating manufacturing (see Figure 10-1). The entire cycle from raw materials to finished goods is managed, for example, using group technology data bases so individual manufacturing cells can specialize in certain part families and using computers to help with inventory control and scheduling. We begin with a review of some business basics.

MANUFACTURING COSTS

Costs in an average American plant are about as follows:

Purchased materials (raw materials to purchase subassemblies)	55%
Manufacturing overhead (burden)	35%
Direct labor	10%
	100%

One look at Figure 10-2 and you will know what to concentrate on if you want to be more competitive.

MATERIALS

Responsibility for about half of our costs is thus split among:

- Product engineering, determining what and how much to make, with input from the sales department

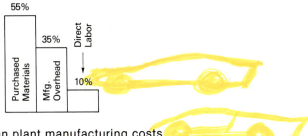

FIGURE 10-2 Typical American plant manufacturing costs.

- Purchasing, negotiating deliveries and prices
- Manufacturing, producing (often with unsatisfactory equipment).

If these functions work together effectively (as one department?), they can strive jointly to constantly improve. Costs can be lowered while quality is raised by such improvements as fewer parts, lighter materials, and simpler manufacturing. For example, a different shape might mean another raw material and a better manufacturing process.

With 55 percent of our costs spent on materials, you can see why Deming advises: "Stop awarding business on price alone" (see Chapter 2). That is, the initial cost of a product may be only a fraction of its final total cost if it lacks quality. This is why he advises working with a few chosen suppliers, building your relationships based on trust and statistical process control.

This kind of thinking explains why people from the customer's factory often visit a supplier's plant to learn firsthand how process improvements are achieved. What is usually of interest is whether the environment encourages everyone to strive continually to improve. Therefore, one thing they usually look for is whether a proper statistical process control system is in place throughout the supplier's facility (see Chapter 4).

The idea is to help your suppliers to improve quality while lowering costs. This increases the profit margins so that the prices you pay can be lowered.

OVERHEAD

Manufacturing overhead (burden) represents about 35 percent of costs in an average American plant. Symptoms of overhead include big inventories of work in process, too much handling of parts, lost and damaged parts, workstations idle waiting for parts, shipping dates unmet, back orders, excessive scrap and rework and poor quality. Carrying charges on the work-in-process inventory are often greater than any direct labor costs they might save.

Many plants grew and were modified to adjust to market changes. Machines were added (justified at the time) and put wherever there was room. The usual result is poor quality, scrap, and rework. What is needed now is a system (process) where raw materials become finished products quickly and nonstop, eliminating non-value-added activities.

DIRECT LABOR

Direct labor is usually only about 10 percent of total manufacturing costs. Material and overhead together are about 90 percent so our efforts are not normally aimed at cutting direct labor costs.

TYPICAL MANUFACTURING PROBLEMS

Symptoms of competitiveness problems include

- Low productivity (despite larger plant facilities and sales volumes)
- High work-in-process inventories
- Low profit margins (even with price increases)
- Slow deliveries.

This listing of typical manufacturing problems implies that shifting to flexible production systems having programmable automation makes possible fast changes in products manufactured and in processes employed. We need to consider shifting to manufacturing technology to remain competitive.

MANUFACTURING TECHNOLOGY

One aspect of technology was illustrated in Chapter 1 when we discussed the Fremont, California, plant that GM now owns as a joint venture with Toyota. When GM ran the plant, there were about 5000 workers assembling about 240,000 cars a year. Absenteeism was about 20 percent, wildcat strikes occurred and there were thousands of outstanding grievances.

Japanese managers now use the same plant, the same labor force, and dated technology to assemble Chevrolet Novas. The same number of cars is built with half the original number of employees—in other words, the same workers, the same building, the same technology, and the same volume, but different management with a different production system. How the Japanese-managed plant (Nummi) outpaces GM is shown in the table below.

	Nummi	*General Motors*
PRODUCTIVITY		
Hours of labor to assemble car.	20 hours	28 hours
ABSENTEEISM		
Unexcused absences, as a percent of work force.	2%	9%
QUALITY		
Survey of new car owners in the first 90 days after purchase.	Chevy Nova ranked No. 2 of cars sold in the U.S.	No GM car in the top 15

(Source: *NY Times,* 1/29/89, p. 3-1.)

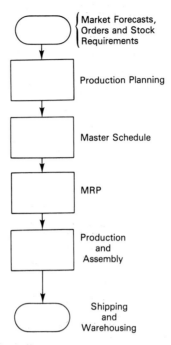

FIGURE 10-3 Factory management.

What made the difference? It is in the managerial—in contrast to the technological—approach. For example, our competitors are committed to thorough training and to participative management. They have few management layers and they place decision making at as low a level as possible.

Manufacturing technology is not necessarily the most essential element in competitiveness. Expensive technological blunders are understandably downplayed. People want to brag about their technological accomplishments, not to confess failures. Therefore, supporting data is scarce, but the message is that manufacturing technology is not a cure-all.

FACTORY MANAGEMENT

Factory management is the coordination of the different processes illustrated in Figure 10-3:

- Market forecasts, orders, and stock requirements are the usual inputs to production planning, which determines what products will be manufactured, and where.
- The master schedule follows from this, defining the production of products over the planning horizon. Process planning is part of this (giving the materials required, the machines needed and the operation sequences), as is capacity planning (which outlines the labor and equipment needs).

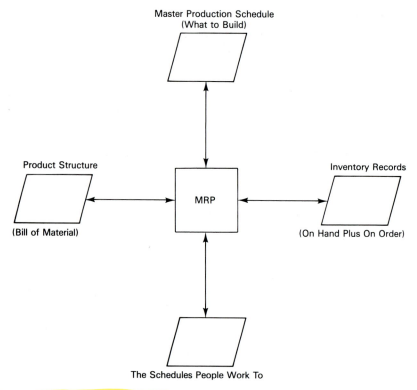

FIGURE 10-4 The logic of MRP.

- Material requirements planning is based on estimated demand for a product, which generates the requirements for raw materials and purchased parts, thereby helping economically to execute the production plan. MRP uses the bill of materials, inventory information and the master schedule to control incoming material and inventories, ensuring that finished products are available as needed (see Figure 10-4). Appendices thoroughly discuss MRP and Just-in-Time manufacturing.
- Production and assembly is the actual manufacturing of the product, according to the master schedule. It includes these functions: assigns priorities, monitors work-in-process, and provides status data for management.

Computers can help with all these processes. Computer-aided process planning, for example, generates a standard process plan for each family of parts (the group technology of Chapter 9). Process planning for a new part involves modifying the standard in the data base. MRP is often computerized, too, producing reports on, for instance, inventory and production status.

All of these processes are related. The information has to pass among them quickly. When it does, the manufacturer can rapidly adjust to the market demand.

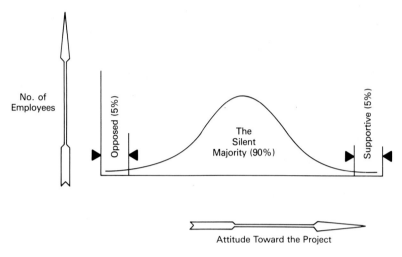

FIGURE 10-5

Again, our principle of computer-aided manufacturing is that shifting to flexible production systems having programmable automation makes possible fast changes in the products manufactured and the processes employed. In implementing this principle, however, the reader will want to heed the warning that technology is not an easy solution to all business problems.

MANAGING CHANGE

To become a high-quality, low-cost producer, you must deal with resistance to change. It doesn't matter whether your strategy is Manufacturing Resource Planning, Just-in-Time, Statistical Process Control, or Computer-Integrated Manufacturing. The factor determining success is how you manage change.

The Silent Majority

Whatever your new program, those who prospered under your old system oppose it. You will also have a few dedicated supporters. Ninety percent of your people, however, will be in the "silent majority" (see Figure 10-5).

This silent majority is fearful. For example:

- "I doubt if this program will work any better than the last one."
- "If this one survives, can I handle it?"
- "Will it erode my stature and job?"

There is little confidence among these people: "At least the old system works; I don't see any benefits from this new one." Misunderstandings abound. The rumor mill is like the parlor game where people get in line and the first whispers something to her neighbor, and so on. The last person then says what he heard. What began as: "My husband is a cross I bear" soon becomes "George is a cross-eyed bear."

"We're unique" is a common attitude. It supports the argument that "it doesn't matter if this project cut costs and raised quality at a competitor's shop, because we're different." Doubts about managements' support are also typical. Old-timers will think: "I've seen a lot of these projects. Most died and their champions moved on, but I'm still here. I'll give this one six months." Further, the silent majority is unconvinced of the importance of CIM (or JIT, or SPC, etc.).

Let's say you decide the path to higher productivity is to have everyone strive to improve things all the time. This won't happen unless you push decision making down to the operator so authority matches this new responsibility. A supervisor of the old school implements these ideas by telling an operator: "Lori, I want you to use your head and improve things around here. But check with me first." When Lori presents her first idea, the supervisor says: "Later. I've got to move my car now." The unspoken message is clear to Lori: "Don't change anything without my OK, which you're not gonna get!" This illustrates the mindsets that have to be changed.

Change

You are dealing with attitudes, feelings and habits. You have to get people to change the way they:

- Perceive how your organization works
- Think about their jobs
- Do their work.

This is a big order. Thankfully, there is a tested procedure for managing change (which the Oliver Wight Companies developed over three decades—see their book: Wallace, *MRPII: Making It Happen,* 1985, pages 19-22). This proven path to transforming your company's culture has eight stepping stones (see Figure 10-6):

1. *Preparatory education.* Your most influential executives and operating managers have to understand the program. This basic training explains the concepts, teaches the facts and presents the benefits. A consensus emerges:
   — Is this the way we want to run our business?
   — Is this the correct approach?
   If there is general agreement, you proceed to the next step.
2. *Cost justification and commitment.* These managers now have to decide if the tangible and intangible benefits justify the costs. If the numbers support the project and, if the key executives believe them, you get a decision to do it right.
3. *Executive steering committee.* The steering committee is the means by which the general manager (GM) leads the process of change. It includes the GM and senior people from all the business functions. Meeting monthly, or as needed, the committee oversees the project team, helping with resources, bottlenecks, schedules, and the like.

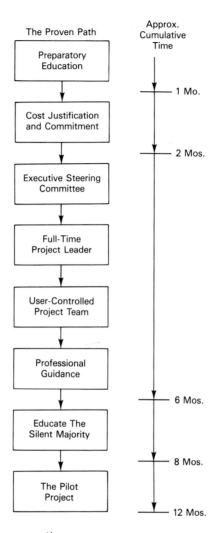

FIGURE 10-6 The proven path.

4. *Full-time project leader.* A part-time project leader has to give attention to operating responsibilities. You need someone to manage the change full time. This individual should know your company and its people and needs to be able to get things done through others.
5. *User-controlled project team.* The project team should be the same people who will be responsible for operations when the project "goes live." Typically composed of department heads, it reports to the steering committee (see Figure 10-7). The team members lead project meetings in their own departments.

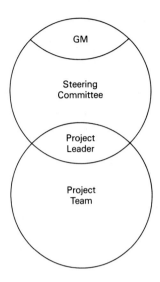

FIGURE 10-7 Leadership chain.

6. *Professional guidance.* Since the project encompasses a whole new way to run the company (and not an extension of past experience), your steering committee and project team need to be able to call on broad-based experience to avoid pitfalls. This individual does not do your work, make your decisions, or control your project.
7. *Educate the silent majority.* At least 80 percent of all the employees need training in your project before implementation (and the rest need it immediately after). They need to know what will change for them, and to learn the benefits to them and to the company. New techniques and terms should be covered, as should the reasons for the changes.
8. *The pilot project.* You don't need to "bet your company" on the project. Prove that it works in a receptive pilot group before cutting over all products and parts.

Machiavelli was a master of politics. He wrote *The Prince* in 1513, describing how to maintain power. In that book, he comments on managing change as follows:

> There is nothing more difficult to carry out, nor more doubtful of success, nor more dangerous to handle, than to initiate a new order of things. For the reformer has enemies in all who profit by the older order, and only luke-warm defenders in all those who would profit by the new order. This luke-warmness arises partly from fear of their adversaries, who have the law in their favour; and partly from the incredulity of mankind, who do not truly believe in anything new until they have had actual experience of it.

Thus, the difficulties of managing change have been recognized for over 400 years.

Changing a company's culture is indeed a major task. The change is managed with this proven path. It is a tested way to implement your program with very little risk.

CASE STUDY

After reading "Preparing for the Factory of the Future," at the end of this chapter, write a brief explanation of the single most important factor in getting ready for the future.

SUMMARY

1. Factory management ties together the computer-assisted manufacturing areas, coordinating the whole.
2. Purchased materials represent 55 percent of manufacturing costs in a typical American plant. Overhead accounts for 35 percent and direct labor only 10 percent.
3. Many manufacturing problems stem from market changes which impact on manufacturing processes. People's attitudes also cause problems.
4. If a manufacturing system were designed from scratch today, it would probably not resemble the present plant in many cases.
5. Manufacturing technology is not necessarily the crucial element in competitiveness. The essential factor is probably good management.
6. Factory management coordinates the manufacturing processes, such as the master schedule and material requirements planning.
7. Computers can help with all these processes, assisting the manufacturer rapidly in adjusting to market demand.
8. The principle is that shifting to flexible production systems having programmable automation makes possible fast changes in the products manufactured and the processes employed.
9. When implementing this principle one should heed the warnings implicit in this chapter (e.g., manufacturing technology is not an automatic cure-all).
10. There is a tested procedure for managing change involving eight steps.

REVIEW QUESTIONS

1. Reducing the direct labor component of manufacturing costs is the key to American competitiveness. Comment.
2. If you supply a manufacturer, you can expect him or her to visit your plant. Why? What is he or she looking for?
3. A competitive firm awards business on price alone. Comment.
4. What is burden? Why is it important?
5. Explain Figure 10-1.

6. Why is growing unit volume sometimes a problem?
7. What principles support the idea of shifting to manufacturing technology?
8. Manufacturing technology is a sure route to competitiveness. Comment.
9. Choose (and explain): good management (and little technology) versus much technology (and weak management).
10. Review the processes of factory management (i.e., explain Figure 10-3).
11. How can computers help with factory management?
12. As a consultant, what would you advise a client about changing her company's culture and managing this change?

Case Study
PREPARING FOR THE FACTORY OF THE FUTURE*

Prologue

Powerful changes, affecting both our personal and business lives, are sweeping across America and the world. *Modern Machine Shop* has shown its readers the impacts of numerical control, computer-aided manufacturing and design, group technology, material requirements planning, and so on.

For these technological advancements to be implemented in America's factories of the future, changes in management styles are essential. Without them, the new technologies simply will not work as they should.

The following article addresses the challenges management faces with these technological changes. The reading is not always easy. The dialogue style departs from our traditional editorial format, and some of the terms and expressions are new. Those who read this article and comprehend the ideas expressed will gain new insights in management philosophies. They will have new resources to utilize in becoming successful managers of their factories. These concepts are that important.

We hope you find the article interesting, informative and important enough that you will want to share it with others in your company. You may even want to use it to help launch the development of a Dynamic Information Strategy Plan for your company, as mentioned at the conclusion of the article.

Charles M. Savage, PhD., Organizational Consultant,
Digital Equipment Corporation

Confusion among middle managers . . . unfocused engineers . . . work that is difficult to get out on time . . . unreliable vendors . . . mounds of work-in-process beside idle machines . . . apathetic employees—all these problems and no time to address them because fires must be put out!

A whole new host of computer-based solutions are offered as a cure to these ailments. Yet, more often then not, the new information-age solutions are simply

*Reprinted with permission of *Modern Machine Shop,* © 1983.

shoved into traditional industrial organizations. The patterns of the past clash with the new answers. Good technical solutions drown in political turf battles!

How does a manufacturing company prepare to use the new system effectively—the CADs, the CAMs, the MRPs, the CNCs, the FMSs, the DBMSs, the PCs, the DSSs, the CIMs,* the robots, and the text-processing and electronic-mail systems?

This question is especially critical as pressure builds to integrate and network these systems across functional boundaries. Top managers know the resulting highly interactive systems are like new wine in old wine skins. The familiar and traditional industrial era management approaches will burst asunder!

Should the new solutions be avoided? No. Competitive pressures are forcing many managers to take the plunge. More and more companies are introducing these new systems out of pure necessity. But along with the new hardware and software, we need new *managementware:* new attitudes, systems, procedures, and ways of dealing with people and data; in short, new organizational cultures.

Towards Information-Intense Businesses

In each era the managerial problem changes. In the agricultural period, it was to maximize the use of human labor. The industrial age forced managers to devise ways to use labor and capital efficiently. The information era is placing a premium on the effective utilization of information.

The new managerial challenge is to integrate the business strategy with the evolving information infrastructure. Unfortunately, many companies are finding this easier said than done.

The following narrative concerns Precision Materials and Components, Inc. (PMC), a hypothetical components supplier. In our story, Henry Pierce, President of PMC, Frank Baker, VP Engineering and Bill Cooper, Operations VP, struggle with many of the same issues that *Modern Machine Shop's* readers are facing.

Pierce senses the enormity of the challenge. At age 47, his career is peaking in the midst of this major transition into the information era. He is determined to give quality leadership to PMC, but he is not always sure exactly what he is up against.

WIP and DIP

Exasperated beyond belief, Henry Pierce knows it has been more than just another long day at the office. "I might have been upset by the high level of work-in-process (WIP), but what really kills us are overly abundant decisions-in-process

---

*CAD, Computer-aided design; CAM, computer-aided manufacturing; MRP, material resource planning; CNC, computer numerical control; FMS, flexible manufacturing sytsems; DBMS, data base management systems; PC, personal computer; DSS, decision support systems; and CIM, computer-integrated manufacturing.

(DIP). These decisions-in-process are the normal daily decisions which must be made to change priorities, adjust to changing customer demands, plan for the next series and so forth. They never get made, or if they do, their timeliness and quality leave much to be desired. I'll bet that if our DIP rate were quantifiable, it would be costing us 20 to 40 percent of our operation efficiency."

Pierce continues his thoughts, "Marketing cannot determine what it wants for the next generation of products. Engineering is of little help because it is so buried in change orders. Manufacturing engineering is constantly behind in preparing operations sheets and determining the necessary tooling. Finance complains about the slow inventory turnover, but offers little help. True, there is more than enough activity at PMC, but too often it is of the fire-fighting variety.

"In the growth years of the 1960s and early 1970s, companies survived and even prospered in spite of managerial sloppiness and high DIP rates. But those days are over.

"New management approaches are needed for the 1980s and 1990s. The signs of change abound: industrial growth is slower, product life cycles are shorter, international competition is more fierce and the cost of money, inventory and assets is higher."

A New Competitive Factor: Flexibility

In the past, competitive strength was achieved through cost, service, quality and reliability, usually within a well defined industry. The industry life cycle and learning curve were critical concepts. Now industry boundaries are blurring so the learning curve does not give the advantage it once did. Instead, market and production *flexibility* are fast becoming the critical competitive factors.

PMC's inability to adapt to change, exemplified in the DIP problem, is caused not only because its internal systems and procedures are out of date, but also because its management style fits an era which is passing. To achieve flexibility, it must pay more attention to the quality and timeliness of its decisions.

Pierce realizes his challenge is not trivial, so he decides to take Friday off and think the problem through with two of his vice presidents.

FIRST OFF-SITE DISCUSSION

Let's Automate Everything

"Let's computerize the company to the gills to get rid of the DIP problem," suggests Baker. Cooper nods support, as they and Pierce begin their Friday off-site session.

Cooper continues, "What we ought to do is develop a network with computerized marketing, design, production and inventory control. Managers should have their own PCs which should be linked to our mainframe. Once we achieved computer-integrated manufacturing (CIM) we would be on easy street."

"Do you have any idea how difficult a task this is? Our existing data files are a mess. Who knows how to access them? I commend you on your eagerness, but wonder about your naivety," responds Pierce. He continues his thought, "Haphazard attempts to link stand-alone systems in the different functional departments will get everyone upset. These systems have been built on the unique assumptions of the particular departments. Some companies have had to throw out their old systems and start afresh. We may have to consider this approach."

"Those are a lot of fancy words, Pierce, but what are you really saying?" asks Cooper.

"It is hard to get there from here." Pierce responds, "If we just automate everything, it is easy to see how we could get indigestion from too much hardware and software. In fact, if we simply added systems as they became available from the vendors, we would probably rival the Tower of Babel. CIM could turn out to be a disaster instead of a dream.

"The more I think of it, the more I become convinced we should start by scooping out those three or four critical success factors which give us our strength in the marketplace, then buy systems which can increase our market leverage. The new systems should give us flexibility, while also lowering our costs, increasing quality and product reliability. This is a tall order, but the stakes are high."

Automatic Pilot or Real-Time Management?

"Wait," interrupts Cooper, "If we were able to integrate our manufacturing process via computers to achieve CIM status, couldn't we put our operation on automatic pilot and relax?"

Baker jumps in, "Cooper, think of the ways we presently make decisions. We make them by not making them or by failing to recognize they need to be made. So much of what happens at PMC happens by default. Opportunities are overlooked because we don't know where to get the necessary information. Risk is assumed without our even realizing it. And there is often a major gap between our assumptions about the market and what is actually going on."

"I'm beginning to wonder," reflects Pierce, "if we shouldn't turn our thinking around 180 degrees. Instead of CIM on automatic pilot, I suspect the 1990s will demand a new kind of involvement of us managers. Instead of stepping out of the loop, we are going to have to be involved in a more intense and demanding manner.

"No, there is not going to be much relaxing. Instead, we as managers will have to be more *interactive*—not only externally with the marketplace and our vendor base, but also internally. We will need to be *integrative* across functions and between levels, and we must learn to be *interrogative* in our ability to ask the right 'what if' questions in a timely manner and act upon the information obtained. Yes, we are going to need an operating system or approach to which we can effectively leverage the information infrastructure we will carefully put in place. In short, we are going to have to master *real-time management*."

"And just what is real-time management?" asks Cooper skeptically.

"It is still not quite clear to me either," responds Baker, "but let me try to define it. Real-time management is not just working against plan, the guestimations we put together once a year, but against the continually changing reality of our internal capabilities and the external market. It is managing in both short- and long-term time horizons simultaneously."

"That makes some sense," Cooper admits. "As things now stand we are slow to respond to changes in the market. There seems to be built-in inertia to change. We're not well coordinated across functions and we seldom know how to ask the right questions in a timely fashion. And when some do, it is hard to communicate the information to the right people."

"These are all real problems," agrees Baker, "but we can never achieve real-time management unless we become more interactive, integrative and interrogative."

Computer Integrative, Interactive and Interrogative Management

Baker's face has a grin from ear to ear. "What we are talking about . . . wait, let me use the flip chart." He jots down the following:

<pre>
            Computer
Interactive, Integrative and Interrogative
          Management,
               or
             CIIIM.
</pre>

Cooper groans, "You engineers can't operate without acronyms! But CIIIM (C triple I M) does capture much of what we have been reaching for. Our problem has been that we have had to wait a week, month or quarter before we know how we're doing. By speeding up the feedback, we can take more timely corrective actions. If we achieve that, then we can manage in real time."

Pierce agrees, "CIIIM is a mouthful. But we are already used to saying 'I triple E' (IEEE) and 'CIM.' To date, the emphasis has been on the linking or integrating of the hardware and software. For the most part, the managementware aspects are still missing. Baker, aren't we trying to redefine the challenge from a broader perspective?"

"You're right," responds Baker. "Without attention to managementware issues, a CIM is likely to flounder in a marsh of glitches."

Cooper, intrigued but still skeptical, challenges Pierce and Baker, "If our manufacturing organization is likely to be built around an integrated information infrastructure, how can we characterize our present organization? I must know where I am before I can begin to reach for a CIIIM."

"Fair enough," answers Pierce. "Even though we have a data processing department supporting our financial functions with batch runs, we're still essentially in a manual mode. We are in a manual mode not only in the way we transfer information between departments but also in the way we manage our policies, systems and procedures. Our operating approach is haphazard at best, which means many people are working at cross purposes. It is a small wonder, as I think about it, that so many decisions get shunted off the track.

"Come to think of it, it's our informal network of old timers which really saves us. They have learned to take the necessary shortcuts and bypasses through our often rigid and inconsistent maze of policies, systems and procedures. They get the work out on schedule, but we pay a price. Our cost-tracking system is shaky at best, and our warranty costs are too high.

"Given our manual system, these are not easy problems to fix because our people are too busy putting out fires. And I am aware that the third-generation computer software packages have not always been the solution because of their own inflexibility."

Traditional Industrial Organizations

"I am convinced," interrupts Baker, "that our general approach to policies, systems and procedures is due to the way we understand traditional industrial organizations. Consider the assumptions which have shaped our industrial environment. Remember how Adam Smith's pin-making factory became the prototype model for dividing work on the shop floor? His notion of the division and subdivision of labor also laid the stage for the separation of functional departments. In the U.S., it actually came with the creating of large national corporations in the latter part of the 1800s and early 1900s. The functional structures developed by the railroads, telephone, automobile and chemical industries with their horizontal division of functions and vertical division of levels, has become the norm, even for many component suppliers and job shops.

"Smith's reasoning was perfect for a relatively stable environment. By achieving specialization between levels and across functions, overall productivity could be greatly increased. Smith, however, was also aware that such an approach had a human and organizational price. An individual (or function) who performs a few simple operations has no occasion to exert his understanding over the whole process.

"Some division of labor and division of functions makes sense, but when carried to an extreme, it becomes *divisive*."

Cooper breaks in, "Could that be why we suffer from poor vertical and horizontal communications? Come to think of it, poor communications significantly adds to our costs, although our cost-tracking system cannot capture its significance. If we could increase the decision turnover like we are trying to increase our inventory turnover, we could achieve substantial savings. As long as we tolerate a divisiveness in our organization, we will carry a hidden burden. Some people think we have five companies working at cross purposes, rather than one where everyone is pulling together."

"You have a point," responds Baker. "I must admit that many of my engineers have little idea about the produceability or maintainability of the products they design. They design with little regard for the downstream consequences."

"I appreciate your candor," says Cooper. "Could this be why my manufacturing engineers are always playing a catch-up game with the operations sheets and tooling requirements? It's amazing how decision sensitive our whole process is! Earlier I had thought that these problems were a natural part of a hierarchical organization, but now I'm beginning to wonder."

The Hierarchical Model

"That's a good point," replies Pierce. "The hierarchical model seems so ingrained in our industrial era that even though it's criticized, it is hardly questioned. Most of our employees feel the implied levels of command signified by boxes for managers and slots for workers on our organizational chart are necessary for running PMC. But there is a more subtle, significant consequence in that a protective envelope is assumed to encompass our organization. Mini-envelopes tend to surround the functions. This causes our people to look inward, shielding them from many important messages, from other functions, and more especially from the external environment. As a consequence, our managers and workers tend to become *disengaged* from the process as a whole. The envelopes are like one-way mirrors, those within them are unable to see out. This envelope around us is sustained by the way we communicate."

"It certainly is," responds Cooper in an excited voice. "If I may speak frankly, we have too much top/down communications. Messages are *declarative* in nature. Interrogative responses upward and across functions are hardly tolerated by anyone. As a consequence, one often hears one-line expletives off-line!"

"Touche," admits Pierce. "I've been guilty of perpetuating this top/down approach, in spite of all my lip service for creating a participatory environment. I guess I took too seriously the old idea of the chain of command where direction and control were the critical elements. I now see a mismatch between our existing approach and the organization toward which we want to move."

Manual, Divisive, Disengaging, Declarative Management

"Cooper, earlier you asked if we could characterize our present organization," Baker reminds Cooper. "In the terms we have been using, let me caricature PMC." Again Baker moves toward the flip chart and slowly writes:

Manual,
Divisive, Disengaging, Declarative
Management,
or
MDDDM.

"Baker, that is more than I expected" complains Cooper. "The terms M triple D M seem more negative than descriptive."

"Yes, they do carry a negative connotation," responds Baker. "If we honestly look at PMC from the perspective of what we ought to become, I feel the same

FIGURE 1 Contrast of PMC's present and future organizations.

Present Industrial Era Organization	Future Information Era Organization
Manual	**Computer-Aided Systems**
Outdated policies, systems and procedures supplemented by informal organization	CAD, CAM, FMS, MRP, text processing, electronic mail, etc., supported by flexible policies, systems and procedures
Divisive	
Overly divided in work tasks and between functions and layers	**Integrative**
	Integrating information network, relying on some functional expertise, but in a more open and cooperative context
Disengaging	
Hierarchical approach which narrows and restricts effective problem solving, causing people to retreat into their own worlds	**Interactive**
	Active interaction both internally and externally with vendor base and client system
Declarative	
Top/down commands with little listening or feedback	**Interrogative**
	Active use of "what if" scenarios, with heavy graphic support
Off-Line Management	**Real-Time Management**

frustration Pierce expressed when he first talked about the DIP problem. Let's sharpen up the contrast between our industrial age organization and the information era company toward which we want to move."

Baker remains at the flip chart, summarizing with the help of Pierce and Cooper the essential contrasts between their present and future organizations (see Figure 1).

They become inventive as they fill in the flip charts. The contrast between offline and real-time management strikes them.

Pierce sums up the thinking, "In the past I gave orders and expected them to be carried out; but frankly, I did not really know their consequences. I could have been going off on the wrong tangent. Yet, I would hardly have known it, but there's a more serious problem.

"Our yearly budgets are built on a lot of guestimations and simple trend extrapolations. Once in place, we essentially manage by exception, noting the significant variances over the course of the year. I see now that this approach could easily put us out of phase with changes in the market or in competitors' activities. We're often in a catch-up mode for this very reason. It is unbelievably expensive to be running after the competition, trying to adjust to major, significant long-term trends."

Baker chimes in, "I see that with our present management approach, we'd gain little benefit from a CIM system, were we to have one. At this point, we cannot make quality decisions in real time."

Looking at each other with a sense of accomplishment, they agree to pick up their discussion in two weeks when they have had a chance to mull over the implications of the day's reflections.

SECOND OFF-SITE DISCUSSION

The Information Era Goes Critical

Two weeks later, Cooper opens the discussion. "I am not at all convinced that were are involved in any major shift, in spite of our last discussion. What justification do we have for drawing such a sharp contrast between the industrial and information eras?"

"Remember Thomas Kuhn's *The Structure of Scientific Revolutions*?" asks Baker. "He explored the ways science goes through major transitions in its constellation of beliefs, values and techniques. Why shouldn't the art of management undergo quantum leaps also? Cooper, your question is crucial. Let's see what evidence there is which might address your honest skepticism."

"I agree," says Pierce, "AT&T's advertising the coming of the information age doesn't make it happen. But I suspect historians will pick January 8, 1982 as the day the information era began in earnest. In unleashing AT&T and IBM to compete in a common arena, the Justice Department triggered the explosive fusion of computers and telecommunications: the information era is going critical. Our deliberations about PMC's future are only a small example of the kind of intellectual struggle which is going to be required to set ourselves in a new constellation of beliefs, values and approaches."

"Since our last meeting, I have been reviewing other voices," says Baker. "Alvin Toffler attempts to show how the third wave (the computer era) is sweeping in over the first and second—the agricultural and industrial—periods, respectively. John Naisbitt, a futurist, points to the megashift from an industrial- to an information-based society. And Paul Strassman of Xerox argues that we are shifting to an information orbit. Let me try to graphically illustrate the shifts." Baker again takes his place at the flip chart (see Figure 2).

Baker steps back and turns to Pierce and Cooper, "Human history passed through various major epochs, each with its dominant culture, set of values and modes of organization. The transitions from one era to another have often been turbulent and have occurred over extended periods of time. It took close to a hundred years for the industrial era to become well established, and it will inevitably take a couple of decades for the information age to solidly set in.

"I should add that the shift in orbits does not mean the abandonment of the activities of a previous era. Quite the contrary, for as agriculture learned to apply various industrial techniques, it began to prosper in a new way. This suggests many industrial-based companies may find a new vigor if they learn to master the new hardware, software and managementware of the information era."

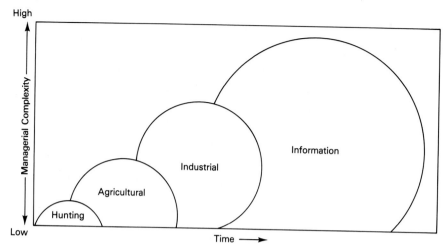

FIGURE 2 Dominant historical eras—each semicircle is a major era with its operating set of values, assumptions, logic, norms and way of doing things. These operating systems influence the way people work together in organizations.

"This makes me feel a little better," Cooper says with a sigh of relief. "Somehow, I felt our days were numbered. But you are saying just the opposite—by learning to live in the information era we can become more effective manufacturers!"

"Absolutely!" exclaims Pierce. "And there is another way to look at this transition. Consider the proportional mix of key elements used in the different eras: labor, raw materials, capital and knowledge. Considering the four elements, the relative mix has changed over the years (he draws Figure 3 on the flip chart). The agriculture era was very labor intense, used the land (raw materials) extensively, but used relatively little capital or scientific knowledge. The industrial era has been capital-intense while still using masses of low-skilled labor. It extended the range of raw materials used. The information era is more knowledge-intense. The professional is to the information era what the blue collar worker has been to the industrial era. The relative proportions in the diagram are purely subjective, but they convey the magnitude of the transition under way."

Less Direct Labor, More Mid-Level Professionals

Bill Cooper's face lights up, "For some time I have been resentful about having to make do with less direct labor per sales dollar, while engineering's professional staff has been increasing. I guess no one is out to get me. Instead, it seems as if I've only been seeing the symptoms!"

"I remember," says Pierce, "reading a recent article about the relative shift of resources at IBM. It has been rather dramatic. Between 1957 and 1979 the cost of goods sold (material, direct labor, rental and service equipment) decreased from

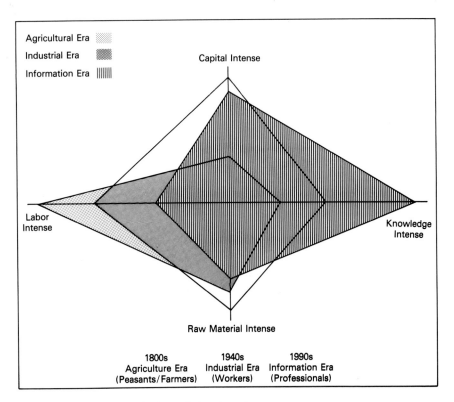

FIGURE 3 Historical evolution of dominant eras.

54 percent to 37 percent, while the cost of marketing, engineering (professional and other) and G and A has risen from 25 percent to 40 percent (profits and interest expenses round the figures out).

"IBM is quite different from PMC, but I have noticed the same hiring trends as Cooper. We have been adding post-processor technicians, manufacturing engineers and quality engineers faster than traditional direct labor. But this is what Figure 3 suggests, doesn't it?"

Baker is already back at his flip charts. "Absolutely, what you have been saying confirms my last diagram. We have always thought of our company as being an enveloped pyramid; that is, the traditional fuctional hierarchy. But we're in transition. As we use more robots and CNC controls in the manufacturing and assembly operations, the direct labor content diminishes. At the same time, we experience a professional bulge in the middle of the organization.

"As these changes take place, I suspect we will find it possible to operate with a flatter hierarchy, especially at the top." Baker steps back and sketches Figure 4.

"You mean," wonders Cooper "that instead of a pyramid, we will soon become a *spade*. That's what the information organization is beginning to look like."

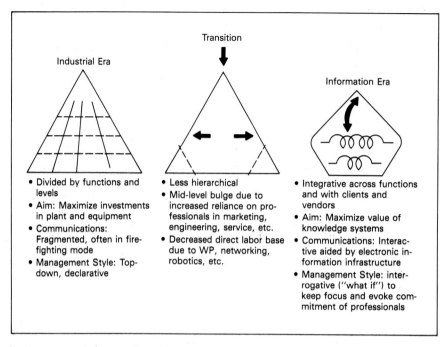

FIGURE 4 Organizations in transition.

Pierce is bothered. He senses a clash between the assumptions and implicit values he learned in business school, exemplified in the pyramid. "When working on my MBA we reviewed Henri Fayol's principles of management. There was general agreement in my class that his concepts are still current. The unity of command suggested every subordinate should have a single superior.

"The scalar chain described the direct line of this command from the chief executive through successive superiors and subordinates to the workers. And the span of control dealt with the number of subordinates reporting to a single superior. These are the major assumptions underlying the operating system, or management approach to the industrial era."

"Pierce, you are sounding more like a professor than a president," complains Cooper.

Pierce, ignoring Cooper, exclaims: "Fayol's notions are hopelessly out of date! In Fayol's era, the companies could be hard wired, the routines set, and the people trained. Mangement's role was to control and monitor and to do some kicking when things got out of line. Today, the fixed logic of the industrial era is giving way to a variable logic made possible by the information revolution. The flexibility of software routines is opening up new vistas in what are being called decision support systems (DSS). Our management style, our values and our manufacturing culture need more than a major overhaul—they need some fundamental retooling."

With a smile on his face Cooper suggests, "Perhaps you can use the spade to plant some new notions. For some time I have wondered why manufacturing companies have not been quicker to get involved in flexible manufacturing systems, but the answer is becoming clearer."

Baker continues, "Their traditional fixed logic management systems cannot handle the variable decisions which have to be made to justify an FMS or even CIM. Frankly, I doubt if flexible manufacturing systems belong in a pyramid type organization."

"I am beginning to see," chimes in Cooper, "what it means to shift from a fixed to a variable logic setting. If we have not done our homework as a group, if we cannot interact well across functional lines, if we cannot grasp the changing intricacies of the market, and if our department charters, systems and procedures are out of date, we can hardly hope to make the required transition into the twenty-first century."

Pierce smiles, "Aren't you the two guys who wanted to simply computerize PMC? We have a bit more of a job ahead of us than I first imagined!"

Knowledge Management

"Ouch!" grunts Baker. "The more I think of it, the more I realize knowledge management represents a radically new challenge. The various computer-aided systems will make massive amounts of information available in easily digestable forms with computer graphics and spread sheets. The process of thinking through the information, analyzing the trends and understanding the implications will be the real test of information-age management."

"None of our old ways are sacred any longer," adds Pierce. "Your last statement got me thinking about the word '*management*.' It is derived from the Latin manus which means '*hand*.' Managing is handling or training something. But knowledge and information involve the mind far more than the hands. Forgive the expression, but maybe we should be talking in terms of *mindagement*."

"Please let up," pleads Cooper. "You've been introducing new concepts faster than my mind can assimilate them. And what a silly term—mindagement. Who are you trying to kid?"

"Cooper, it may sound silly at first, but part of our problem is that we have only industrial-era words and they are not very good for describing the information revolution. Remember how the industrial era had to invent a whole new set of concepts because the agricultural era's terms were hardly adequate," responds Pierce.

Before Cooper can really holler uncle, Baker wants his chance to add still another concept. "If there is a shift in managing from the hand to the mind, then the power of shared ideas, concepts and understandings increases in importance. It will be these ideas which will hold the company together more so than a fixed and rigid set of policies, systems and procedures. Paul Strassman has pointed out that while assets depreciate with usage, shared ideas appreciate with usage. One of the key tasks to top management in the information age is to take seriously the ideas

220 FACTORY MANAGEMENT

and norms which will provide the glue to hold the organization together in a rapidly moving environment. Managing a variable logic is mind boggling, and to be able to do it in real time is more than a challenge."

"And I thought my problems would be over once we put in a good MRP system together with a shop floor control system and some robots, but I see the fun is just beginning," moans Cooper.

"Possibly you were thinking of the promises of automation, weren't you, Cooper?" Pierce asks. "Automation seemed to hold out the promise of removing the human element, but everything we have said argues for putting the human back at the center of the process. I am convinced that the word automation is a terribly misleading term. It really confuses the issues. The movement toward decision-support systems is taking us in a more realistic direction. True, direct labor tasks on our factory floor and in our offices may be automated, but the real significance of computer-aided systems is elsewhere."

"I have just thought of an example," Baker volunteers. "In the industrial era, it was relatively easy to relate time and output. But in the future, clock time will be more difficult to relate to the quality of the knowledge of professionals. Some professionals may see an essential relationship in an instant while others will dwell for weeks on the same problem. Instead of using control, often it will be necessary to cajole our professionals. Instead of narrow and specific task definitions, there must remain some grayness in task assignments. And instead of building an organization to facilitate the interchangeability of people, we had probably better build a long-term sense of community held together by a shared vision, which can endure together over time."

Small Stripped-Down Units

"I wonder," responds Pierce, "if the U.S. Army has not understood something which we in the business community have overlooked. In their 'AirLand Battle' concept, they are now emphasizing small, stripped-down units that can move swiftly. Battlefield commanders will have a rare degree of freedom to exploit enemy weaknesses. No longer will the outcome of battle be decided by attrition between lines drawn up as in a football game. Picture instead a soccer game where each element is maneuvering in what appears to be an independent, uncoordinated way. In reality, it is a highly coordinated plan of action built on a shared knowledge base."

Baker notices Coopers skepticism again, "The old Army system of sticking strangers into combat slots may look just dandy to business school graduates, but it can often be a disaster on the battlefield. It is no longer possible to manage people to their death. They must be led."

Cooper replies, "This suggests our practice of moving people around like interchangeable parts is outdated. What is the alternative?"

Baker continues, "Permanent regiments are being formed. The recruits will remain with one regiment through his or her hitch. The Army has plans for an initial set of 87 regiments. The intent is to foster the cohesion and team spirit that the

Army realizes is essential for combat success. Eventually, the whole U.S. Army will be organized into a regimental system, like Great Britain's, but with Israel's mobility."

"More pieces are beginning to fall in place," Pierce says thoughtfully and carefully. "We got going in these discussions because I was so bothered by the DIP problem. Now I see why timely decisions are so hard. Our impersonal and mechanical atmosphere puts people on guard, rather than bringing their entrepreneurial energies to the surface. Earlier, we realized the organization in our future must be interactive, integrative and interrogative. This really calls for a group of key managers and professionals who are open minded and committed to one another, who are adaptive like a soccer team, and who can problem solve on the run. It is going to require a new management etiquette. In short, we're going to have to feel as much at home with the thorns of variety, complexity, quality and flexibility as Br'er Rabbit did in the briar patch."

"Pure bunk," retorts Cooper. "Next you'll be telling me about the importance of PMC's values, culture, traditions and shared visions. What's all this got to do with the running of a business?"

Baker and Pierce both laugh. "Cooper, you're so perceptive . . . it's not bunk!" responds Pierce. "We've already pointed out that our values, manufacturing culture, traditions and shared visions are the glue which will hold us together. They are part and parcel of an operating system. They add excitement, a sense of accomplishment and accumulated wisdom. A group's ability to be interactive, integrative and interrogative depends on its internal cohesion, like the newly conceived U.S. Army regiments, and its sense of history and mission. These attributes were not really that important in the industrial era, but I am convinced that in the emerging information era they will be crucial."

The three conclude the day by briefly reviewing their discussion. Pierce adds some parting words, "What we see points to the centrality of the human element as a decision maker in the organization in our future. Computer-aided systems will have us thinking more, rather than less. We have come a long way in our thinking about our future, but still I feel another day is going to be necessary to help our ideas mature. I don't think Cooper can take any more today."

THIRD OFF-SITE DISCUSSION

Managementware

"It is fortunate we are back together again," Pierce says as they begin their third off-site meeting. "General Motors has just announced a new approach to its suppliers. It wants fewer, but more reliable, suppliers of higher quality components. It seems that GM wants the inventory burden to rest with the vendors and the program seems to be modeled after Toyota's kanban (just-in-time) system. If we want to stay in the market, we will have to supply the required parts almost on the exact day they are needed, or just-in time (JIT) for them to be bolted into the car as it

222 FACTORY MANAGEMENT

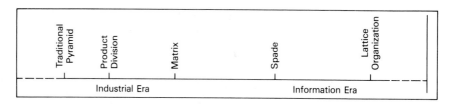

FIGURE 5   Range of possible organizational models.

moves down the assembly line. To participate, we will have to provide quality parts based on very short delivery cycles. But for all our talk, I don't feel we're ready. What do you guys think?"

Cooper sighs, "Do the rules of the game ever change fast! We've been an OEM supplier job shop for a long time, but with this new twist we'll probably become a hop shop—hopping to the short production schedules we are sent via electronic mail. How can we change and adapt priorities on a continual basis? Frankly, we do a lousy job of coordinating our present business. How can we ever meet JIT requirements? Just think how long it takes us to change our tooling and dies!"

"How ironic," says Baker pensively. "Is our rhetoric catching up with us? In our previous two sessions we were describing an ideal organization of the future, but now faced with a situation where we need it today, what do we do but panic!"

Cooper says sarcastically to Baker, "Are you going to draw us out of this one?"

"Maybe you had better get back up to a flip chart, Baker. We are going to have to think of a way of developing our operating systems and philosophy so we can interact more dynamically both internally and with our clients," Pierce says in a sober tone. "It is going to be a while before we have many of our computer-aided systems in place, but we might as well learn to become more integrative, interactive and interrogative, even if we remain in a manual mode. Even our present MIS system shows little flexibility for the emerging needs. Baker, could you draw a line on the flip chart and let's develop on a continuum a range of options."

Baker draws the line and together they begin to fill it in with a possible range of options they may choose from. Intuitively, they want to place themselves at the spade. Pierce promises to explain the various options shown in Figure 5.

Organizational Options

"We have already explored some limitations of the traditional functional hierarchy; that is, the pyramid," says Pierce. "A long-standing problem of the traditional model has been its inability to develop good product/market focus. Therefore, beginning in the 1950s, many Fortune 500 companies shifted to product divisions. In essence, they kept their old functional organizations and overlaid them with a product responsible administration. Next came the matrixing organization. The matrixing of both large and small organizations has been to try to correct the bad communication between functions. It's worked in some places, but in many others the people cannot adapt to having two bosses. And there is always a power struggle, subtle or open, because either the functions or the product groups are assigned more power."

Pierce continues, "The spade represents the situation when an organization's direct labor base shrinks and its professional staff increases. The lattice organization is intriguing and I would like to tell you more about it, even though it is something in the far distance as far as we are concerned."

"Please do, Professor Pierce," retorts Cooper.

"I have recently come across a company," Pierce says with a smile, "which in the words of its president, William Gore, has a system of un-management. It is based upon a lattice organization, a cross-hatching of horizontal and vertical lines. There are no titles, no orders and no bosses. The associates (the name for all employees, managers and hourly alike) are allowed to identify an area they feel they will be able to make their best contribution. Then they are encouraged to maximize their individual accomplishments. The $125 million producer of wire, cable, Goretex fabrics and fibers and industrial filter bags doesn't manage people, they manage themselves. They are organized around voluntary commitments, because it was realized early on that there is a major difference between commitment and command."

"This sounds like some self-indulgent commune rather than a serious business," mumbles Cooper, unflagging in his skepticism.

"They are as committed to profits as we are," responds Pierce. "I only wish we could match their sales and earnings which have been growing at a compounded annual rate of nearly 40 percent per year. They have grown to 20 plants worldwide and have over 2,000 associates."

"In some ways, they sound like they have achieved what the U.S. Army is aspiring to in its new AirLand Battle concept. Their model is more like the soccer team than the football team," summarizes Baker.

"We are not anywhere near ready for a cross-hatched lattice organization; in fact, we are still close to the traditional pyramid," says Pierce.

Pierce moves his hands in front of him, thinking over their past discussions and searching for just the right words. "We will need an organization built around a clearer business vision and shared data bases. We will need to pay some attention to the functions and product groupings, but our top staff is going to have to work extremely well together. Will we need the traditional boxes and slots? There has to be room for people to grow into the situation, to complement one another's strengths and support one another's weaknesses. For example, even though you are an engineer, Baker, you also have a natural talent for marketing. This talent should not be a threat to our marketing vice president, but a resource instead. And Cooper, you have a way with conceptual designs and should be a greater resource to Baker's operation. . . . And we have to learn to manage our external relations with our own suppliers and our clients as vigorously as we do our internal resources. We therefore have to design a management approach which looks outward as effectively as it looks inward. The opaque envelope around our organization must be peeled off. Baker, can you help me by sketching out some of these ideas?"

224 FACTORY MANAGEMENT

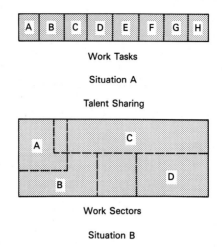

FIGURE 6 Contrasting approaches to ways of dividing work.

Talent Sharing

"As you have been talking, a number of images have been running through my head," responds Baker. "First I thought of the way we traditionally divide up work and then, as shown in Figure 6, contrasted it to what you seem to be saying."

Baker explains his sketches, "In Situation A each task is scoped out by an industrial engineer. Most often, a large portion of a person's abilities are never really used. In Situation B, a work sector is scoped out. Those assigned are expected to complement and reinforce one another. They are expected to grow into the areas which none of them naturally covers, and it is expected that some of their overlapping talents, as with A and C, will be mutually reinforcing. Situation A is regulated by commands of the supervisor, whereas Situation B is more self-regulating. It is the human side of group technology."

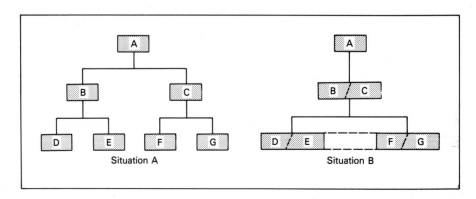

FIGURE 7 Industrial organization versus talent-sharing organization.

"That is most intriguing," comments Pierce, "because Situation B reminds me in some ways of what some people are trying to accomplish with quality circles, employee involvement or quality of work life approaches."

Baker picks up his thread of thought, "While you were talking I was also thinking of ways to redefine the managerial boxes. Look at Figure 7. In Situation B, functional accountability is maintained but, by design, B and C are expected to come up with innovative solutions between themselves, rather than involving person A as a mediator as is common in Situation A. Likewise, D, E, F and G are expected to interact laterally in Situation B, more so than what is expected in Situation A. This allows room for them to overlap in their abilities and reinforce one another's talents. They are supported in their efforts by a shared information base. In Situation A, each unit's information is usually jealously guarded."

Pierce breaks in, "Are you not pointing out that Situation A exemplifies the traditional scalar principle? Although the line of command is clear, there are two drawbacks. First, the superior gets dragged into settling disputes between B and C, and second, cooperation between the two persons is not assumed. Situation B exemplifies a different tone. It recognizes a degree of specialization, but also structure, in a more cooperative approach. It takes the divisive sting out of the traditional organization."

"I am not impressed with your art work," adds Cooper, "but your ideas have merit. I was assigned to an interdisciplinary team to flow diagram the routing of products through our facility. None of us on the team were rookies, but did we ever struggle to map out the flow. We'd worked so often in the vertical dimension that thinking horizontally was a new experience."

Modifying the Matrix

"Matrix organizations represent an operating system designed to cut across the vertical commuications channels in our traditional functional organizations," adds Pierce. "Implicitly, the matrix is designed to address what we are calling the DIP problem. Unfortunately, matrix setups are often considered an intruder in an already well established power constellation. They have worked well where there are able people, but otherwise they usually fail because they change nothing fundamental."

Baker then wonders out loud, "Pierce, you suggest the problem is that the traditional power balance is disturbed because the product integrators are short circuiting the traditional lines of authority. What if we could devise a form which balances the power of the functions with the product groups, so neither group is on top? Suppose we shift the traditional matrix 45 degrees as shown in Figure 8?"

The Wedge

"Baker, do you realize what you have done?" asks Pierce excitedly. "We can combine your last two diagrams. By redefining the performance measurements of

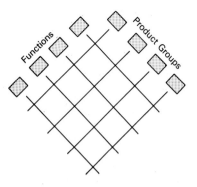

FIGURE 8 A 45-degree matrix.   FIGURE 9 The wedge.

the top staff, both functional and product, we could define in talent and competence sharing. No longer will our vice presidents be measured solely by the way they administer their departments, but also in terms of how they interact in a positive manner with one another. We might draw the organization like this (see Figure 9.)"

Pierce takes command of the magic marker from Baker and says, "Look, we can build in an information infrastructure within the new management configuration, the *wedge*." Pierce sketches in a linked system containing CAD, CAM, MRP, CNC, FMS, DSS, DBMS, PC, and automated inventory storage. He steps back as a puzzled look comes over his face.

"There is something missing, what is it?" he asks.

After some silence, Pierce senses what he is looking for. "There's an abundance of conferences, articles, books, brochures and eager consultants ready to explain the hardware and software of these systems, but there is hardly a word about what attitudes are going to be necessary to link us as persons in these new operating systems. We are going to have to learn to work together in a new way, as we suggested in the CIIIM model."

"That is really welcome news," exclaims Cooper, "because I am tired of the garbage coming out of engineering. We set up our operation sheets and test procedures based on the initial set of engineering drawings. Then what. We get drowned in an avalanche of change orders. We cannot do our jobs amidst constant turmoil, unless we develop a more efficient and effective system of anticipating the downstream impact of various changes."

"I have to admit you are right," responds Baker sheepishly. "But there is hope. Our experience with CAD already shows us that we can make a number of iterations of the prototype design and stress test it before we finally commit it to paper. But what you are suggesting is that operations gives us an additional set of parameters to test it against produceability."

"Yes, and you can expect that the service department would like to have you build in maintainability parameters, and inventory will want some say about the family of parts," adds Cooper.

Pierce smiles, "Our discussions may help us to learn to communicate in a

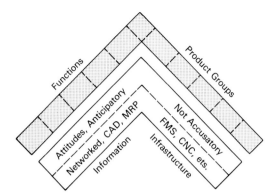

FIGURE 10 The wedge built around an information infrastructure.

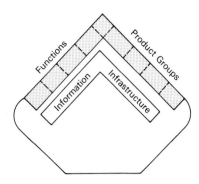

FIGURE 11 The spade—a prototype information-era organization.

anticipatory manner, rather than in the usual accusatory mode. I hate to think of how much emotion is burned up in our cursing the other guys. It is like sand in the machinery of our organization. But with a shared information base, the divisions between functions will become more transparent. Mistakes will show up more rapidly, and we can take corrective action more swiftly as a team. In short, we will be able to move from a reactive to a proactive management style.'' Pierce finishes sketching his ideas as shown in Figure 10.

Baker's face lights up. ''Do you suppose that we could fit the wedge into the spade? The spade is really built around an active information infrastructure, managed in real time by the top group which shares its talents.'' Baker combines the two ideas in Figure 11.

Where Is the Power?

Baker studies the spade model and says, ''We must move beyond thinking in terms of proprietary functional data bases. The information infrastructure needs a shared common data base if it is to work. We will need to develop a whole new etiquette in interacting with one another. We must become more respectful and helpful to one another, rather than using access to data to become picky and demeaning. Respect, trust and mutual support are essential. In the past it was assumed that information is power, but will it be true when all top managers have access to essentially the same information?''

''I never thought about the significance of the spread of personal computers,'' says Baker. ''Sales have really been stimulated by the availability of the spread sheet, which makes it possible to ask a wide range of 'what if' questions and to get answers in real time. It is awakening many managers to a new way of thinking. It's becoming possible to see cross impacts of various decisions on the viability of product lines. It is no longer simply having control over the data which gives power, but power will be in our ability to ask the right questions of the data. *It's analytical power that counts in the information era.*''

Cooper adds, "This can really be threatening to old line managers. So many of them are used to having control and giving orders, but when decisions can be questioned because the projected consequences can be readily seen on a spread sheet, it is a whole new era. No wonder various efforts to introduce networked computer-aided systems are being quietly sabotaged. The Luddites of the 1990s will probably be managers rather than workers because most managers will find it difficult to transition into an information- and knowledge-intense era. It may be necessary to develop some Quality of Management Life effort to address these needs, similar to the Quality of Work Life movement for employees."

"Cooper, you have a point," responds Pierce. "We are going to need some way to introduce managers to an interactive, integrative and interrogative atmosphere exemplified by the spade. But at this point I feel a need to know how a company like ours will fit into the larger competitive environment. We have still not quite understood how we will respond to General Motor's Just-in-Time approach."

Baker, seizing the opportunity to return to the flip chart, says "While we have been talking, I have been thinking of a way to sketch out the larger picture. It is becoming clear that we as top managers must manage our external operations. Traditionally, managers have assumed the primary task is to manage within the envelope of the pyramid. This has to change."

"Are you suggesting there are strategic implications in our purchasing policy, yet we often leave purchasing to some clerk?" asks Pierce. He continues, "There are strategic implications in the choice of new process technologies, but often engineering or operations makes the decision based on narrow interests. There are strategic implications in the way we manage deliveries, yet a shipping clerk often assumes full responsibility."

"Yes," responds Baker. "With a more interactive information infrastructure, we can quickly spot the policy issues and make the appropriate strategic decisions. When the data is not adequate, we can tie into a wide variety of external data bases. In short, our interactive, integrative and especially our interrogative approach is not only focused inside the company, it must also be focused on the external environment." Turning to the flip chart, he outlines PMC's situation as shown in Figure 12.

Cooper looks over the diagram and wonders, "Let me see if I understand our evolving model. The functions must also discover ways to leverage more effectively our external resources. Make/buy decisions take strategic importance. Quality assurance must be extended to our suppliers. We must choose carefully supporting microprocessor technologies to embody in our enhanced products. In summary, we are going to have to get a much better picture of the ecology of our supplier base and know where the leverage points are."

Baker agrees, picking up the discussion. "Yes, and similarly, we need to understand our customer base ecology to know the leverage points there. For example, we may get to one group of customers through consulting engineers. Rather than just focusing on product quality, we need to examine the quality of our interaction with our clients. Do we need to build electronic mail capabilities so that our clients

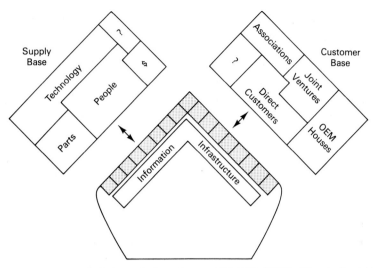

FIGURE 12 The spade—managing the external environment from an enterprise perspective.

can send their CAD designs directly to our CNC equipment? Our competitive advantage will come not only from our product quality, but also our ability to manage information effectively so that we can produce just-in-time."

Just-in-Time

"With your helpful diagram," says Pierce, "let us focus on our changing relationship with GM. As I am coming to understand it, GM realizes the whole components production and delivery system has become very fragmented, with little overall coordination. Unnecessary buffer stock is accumulating within companies and at many points along the chain of delivery. Our whole generation of managers has grown up with the notions of trying to lengthen the production cycle to get economies of scale by building buffer stocks in the process. These buffers have hid many of the problems in our production processes. By removing them we can more quickly see where the problems are and correct them. We need a simpler and more direct interaction between ourselves and our workforce.

"Part of our problem has been that it takes an incredibly long time to change the tooling and dies on our equipment. In contrast, the Japanese are designing integrated but flexible production processes which can handle tight schedules and allow for quick changes. Problems are out in the open. Quality is designed into both the product and production process. In their tightly managed systems, defects are not tolerated. This is naturally giving them a competitive edge. GM sees no reason why we cannot build our own systems to get the same results.

"The Japanese have established a planning system which operates on a combination of monthly and ten-day cycles, allowing suppliers to adjust their production runs to deliver the components just when they are needed. This requires a good tracking system which pulls the material through the pipeline and well-oiled transportation system. This is one additional reason why we will need a good information infrastructure."

Cooper sees his chance, "So far our discussion has focused on a new information, infrastructure, but if I read you right, we are going to have to take a hard look at our machinery and equipment also. We are going to need tool and die changes which take not hours, but minutes, are we not?"

Pierce answers, "Yes, you are right. Earlier we spoke of integration, I now see that is an integration of our people, information systems and our plant and equipment."

"But isn't it even more?" asks Baker. "Are we not going to have to integrate ourselves more effectively in the market through more active management of our relationships with our supplier and our customer base? We will have to leverage the new technology, be it in terms of computer-aided systems or new flexible manufacturing systems. And we are going to have to pay much more attention to major shifts in the business ecology which a company like GM is proposing. From what little I know of their new approach, they want companies like ourselves to cut down on our WIP through more careful management of our own supplier base. This is different from what we first thought. We thought they were trying to sluff off their inventory on companies like ourselves. But this is not the case."

What Business Are We Really In?

"I have a very uneasy feeling about the nature of our business," confides Pierce. "We started out this discussion because I was so upset about our DIP problem. We have come a long way in our understanding of the requirements of an information-age company. Our suggested changes will certainly aid the DIP situation, and may also reduce WIP significantly. But there is one question we have not asked: What is our real business?"

"What are you getting at, Pierce?" asks Cooper. "Isn't it clear that we are a metalworking job shop which has a reputation for excellence in components?"

"That is just it, we have always thought of ourselves as a component house," answers Pierce. "Our management focus has been on getting our components out the door on schedule, but . . . *I believe our business is to sell predictability, flexibility, quality and reliability.* We must focus as much, if not more so, on our systems and procedures, our managementware, so that we can build a reputation in the market of excellence in these attributes. This is how we will increase our gross margins. A well developed information system can give us a competitive edge."

Baker lights up, "I was recently at a meeting in Detroit where Robert Stone, a GM VP discussed their new Just-in-Time program. I did not really understand what he was getting at then, especially when he said there is a tremendous opportunity for growth for those suppliers who can improve their quality, control costs and provide Just-in-Time delivery. Now it makes sense! He should have added that the real key is a well working information infrastructure combined with perceptive and decisive managers.

"As I think about it, Stone did not really address the managementware side of the problem. He is asking for a whole new relationship with a smaller vendor base, but he does not seem cognizant of the hidden problems."

"That is interesting," adds Pierce, "because I have also felt an uneasiness about GE's promotion of the Factory With a Future. GE has been looking so hard at the hardware and the software, but is it doing an adequate job to address the managementware needs of the companies which might use its offerings? They will need new operating systems."

"These are GM and GE's problems," says Baker. "We have our own problems to address, especially because I believe you are right, our business is undergoing a qualitative transformation. We are in need of a new set of beliefs, values and techniques, especially if we are going to manage our plants in an interactive, integrative and interrogative manner. Pierce, you are going to have to set new performance criteria by which to evaluate PMC's top managers."

"Your suggestion makes sense. I haven't given it much thought," comments Pierce, "but it seems we will need to have four areas of review: (1) the way managers handle internal resources (the traditional criterion), (2) the way managers cooperate and complement one another's talents (talent and competence sharing), (3) the way managers handle external resources (supplier and customer), and (4) the way we all manage our organizational culture, the sytems and procedures which will give us quality, predictability, reliability and flexibility."

Cooper's skepticism begins to fade, "Pierce, earlier you called Baker and myself naive for wanting to computerize PMC. I guess we were seduced by the idea of automation. In the future, some things will be automated, but I see now that the real challenge is to put human decision making back into the company. We chose words beginning with 'i' to illustrate the type of organization we would like. Our evolving organization will be *information* intensive, especially to tie into GM's Just-in-Time system. It will take a lot of maturity and *integrity* on the part of all, management and employees (associates). It will use the *intellect* in a new and challenging manner, require *initiative,* rely on *intuition* at times, use *iterations* to solve problems before they happen and strive for analytic *insights*. In so many ways, these 'i's are the new 'eyes' of our organization."

"Cooper, that sounds like something we would say, but not you. It sounds like you have been infected by our way of thinking," Pierce says kiddingly. "We have had three intense days, and developed a lot of new ideas. We will have to let them mellow a bit. But our next task is to turn these ideas into a process of transforming PMC from a producer of individual components to providing quality, flexibility and reliability, no matter what components we manufacture. At the outset, I thought we would be able to take four or six years to accomplish our goals, but I now feel a greater sense of urgency. We need to begin right away with a carefully prepared situation analysis to determine where we are in our internal and external systems and procedures. We will need to devise a participative and supportive process so everyone feels comfortable in growing into a new mode of operations. I feel we are ready to put our decisions in progress, as we learn to manage in an interactive, integrative and interrogative approach, even before we build in our computer-aided systems."

BACK AT THE PLANT

A New Beginning

Following their third session, Pierce decides to give his five vice presidents—marketing, engineering, operations, finance and human resources—their own personal computers. After two months at home, the computers began to appear on office desks. Their spread sheets address all sorts of conditions. Excitement increases as they realize their power to work quickly and effectively with large amounts of data.

Without talking about it, Pierce notices the vice presidents are becoming more openly interrogative rather than subjectively declarative in their styles. The quality of interaction among four of the VPs improves. However, the financial VP cannot cope with the fact that others can play with the financials. He accepts a job with another company because of a better offer. The remaining VPs suspect that it is really his inability to see himself as being anything but the custodian of the numbers.

All is not easy sailing. They are frustrated at the haphazard shape of their company's existing data base. It has been built up to handle specific applications such as invoicing, accounts receivable and purchasing rather than subjects such as products and customers and parts. Gradually they re-architecture their files around a planned interactive relational data base system. They are still not sure how to handle the growing conflict between DP and the more powerful stand-alone microsystems seeping into various departments. A top level interfunctional committee, the Dynamic Information Strategy Committee (DISC) is created to tackle this and related issues.

The DISC first decides that PMC's information infrastructure development cannot continue in a haphazard manner. Traditionally, the individual departments have been putting in requests based on traditional payback schemes. Instead, the DISC (with some outside consulting help) decides to develop a Dynamic Information Strategy Plan (DISP) to guide PMC's acquisition of hardware and software as well as the evolution of its managementware.

Their first step is to list the five key critical success factors which give PMC strength in the market. The Committee's task then becomes one of developing a way to leverage these critical success factors with the appropriate information system, such as CAD, CAM, WP, DBMS, DSS or a combination of these and other possibilities.

As top management is involved in the formulation of the DISP, it is able to take a much broader approach to investments in hardware, software and managementware. It bases the choices on strategic business considerations as much as the traditional return-on-investments criterion.

As the process gets rolling, they soon put in place a relational data base management system (DBMS/R) so data can be shared, a decision support system (DSS) so they can sift through the data to see meaningful patterns, and a computer-aided communications system (CACS) so they can better tap into the best thinking of the people in the company. These and other steps are a part of the implementation phase of their DISP.

Over time, they map out the ecology of their supplier and customer bases, looking for points to leverage new technology, suppliers and other companies. They tie into an external data base to better analyze the changes in their markets. A new understanding is reached between GM and their other OEM houses, which allows electronic data to pass back and forth. Their Just-in-Time strategy takes shape. As they relate their supplier and client strategies to their overall business and productivity approaches, they find their efforts are more focused, decisions come more quickly and investment pay-backs are faster. They set their sights not just on market share, but on selling flexible and adaptive capacity.

Gradually, they are able to manage and process more information faster. They find themselves becoming anticipatory rather than reactive. Their DIP turnover rate increases just as WIP decreases.

They do not achieve their CIIIM organization without some painful experiences along the way. It takes a lot of thrashing around to realize that their computers are being used to monitor and control. This is because the values and assumptions of the industrial era die hard. But in shifting from a declarative to an interrogative stance, they reached a new level of ability to know, anticipate and act.

Best of all, their work becomes truly exciting. Their minds are constantly challenged. Their commitment to one another deepens. They gradually begin to emphasize the importance of the intellect at all levels within the company. New challenges are given to the direct labor force. Fewer levels of management made it possible for everyone to interact more directly and solve problems and develop a shared vision. Shirt sleeve management becomes a way of life at PMC as they learn to anticipate opportunities and manage in real time rather than get bogged down in putting out fires. Their flexibility gives them a competitive edge.

In short, Pierce, over a two-year period, is able to transfer PMC from a capital-intense industrial-age company to a knowledge-intense information-era enterprise. The CADs, CAMs, FMS and robots fit together. PMC is no longer a 4-bit organization. It is fast becoming a 16-bit company with ambition to achieve 32-bit status within three more years.

Chapter Eleven

COMPUTER-INTEGRATED MANUFACTURING

After you have read this chapter, it will be clear to you that

- ❏ The golden years for American manufacturers are long gone, replaced by tough global competition.
- ❏ To compete, many managers have to change their ways.
- ❏ Deming's ideas plus statistical process control can help constantly to improve our processes (systems).
- ❏ Ineffective, outdated management practices cannot be made competitive with an overlay of CIM.
- ❏ CIM is a system for the whole enterprise: product design, manufacturing, production, management, and all other business functions.

Many American executives got their early training after World War II (as much of the world's economy was rebuilding). We could then sell virtually anything we made. Now, business has changed drastically, and the main difference is that many US manufacturers now have to compete internationally.

Foreign competitors have introduced stricter standards, and many produce for about 30 percent less cost than domestic firms. Their quality is so high that some have almost no rejects, and delivery and service are much tighter.

Americans can move production offshore, thereby losing the ability to compete in the technologies involved. Government protection just postpones reality. The only viable long-term response is to do whatever it takes to compete.

The most important factor required is a willingness to change our ways. We learned our traditional approaches in the golden days, which are long gone. Now the world market is characterized by

- Shorter product life cycles
- More complex products and manufacturing processes
- A demand for more customized products
- Container ships, making it economical to manufacture goods with cheap labor in efficient factories for assembly at their final market.

In this new world market, traditional US manufacturers have costs which are 20 to 40 percent too high, plus quality, delivery, and service records that are equally unfavorable. Hajime Karatsu, former managing director of Matsushita Communication Industries, expresses the matter well: "If Japanese industry can make money manufacturing in the United States and American industry cannot, something is wrong with American management." He adds that America allowed too many manufacturing companies to disintegrate or move offshore—weakening our economic base. Japanese products cost less, he argues, not because of dumping or government support but because of greater attention to quality. Further, Karatsu[1] observes

> There is no major difference in the type of equipment used in Japanese and American factories, whether for the production of cars or semiconductors. Nor do Japanese workers perform any better than American workers. The products made in the two countries are identical in principle. So what, one might ask, is the source of the differences in productivity, in quality, and in cost?
>
> Think about it this way. When Japanese firms move to the American market they are able to adjust their costs accordingly, but the only way that many American firms see fit to survive is to move to overseas production. This leads to one inescapable conclusion—the problem is with American management practices.
>
> Japanese plant management centers around the employee. Products are ultimately made by human beings and success is determined by how individual employees think and act. It's the one-by-one accumulation and utilization of seemingly minor techniques that finally leads to success. The machines that do nothing more than perform the manufacturing processes are secondary. This is not exactly logical in Western terms but it is truly the secret of our success. For example, it is often the case in factories built by Japanese firms that plant managers will eat their meals in the plant cafeteria alongside the workers. This practice is almost never seen in Western factories, and observers are inevitably surprised by it.

For example, for many years Americans built a manufacturing culture that traded hourly wages against tighter work rules and restrictive job classifications in the labor contract. Now, work rules and job classifications control most US plants. Japanese-owned car plants (e.g., Honda in Marysville, Ohio, and Toyota in Fremont, California) have only 3 to 5 job classifications versus some 60 classifications for GM, Ford, and Chrysler. The time it takes the individual to do any one operation is about the same in all plants, but the Japanese-owned plants turn out 30 to 50 percent more per worker per day. Sixty classifications restrict people to narrow, repetitive tasks, and work rules and job restrictions are the main cause of the productivity difference.[2] Where management has abandoned its antiquated business traditions, sales per employee have doubled and trebled, as have sales per square foot.

WHAT TO DO

Management practices is the first priority for manufacturing firms to address if they want to reverse things and compete. W. Edwards Deming's 14 points (Figure 11-1) and his deadly diseases (Figure 11-2) show the way. When management creates the proper climate, most of us do the best we can most of the time. Deming's ideas show the path to a favorable environment.

FIGURE 11-1 Deming's 14 points for management. W. Edwards Deming is the internationally known consultant whose work has resulted in a worldwide practice of statistical techniques for the improvement of quality and productivity. This summarizes Deming's management philosophy. (Reprinted from *Quality, Productivity and Competitive Position* by W. Edwards Deming by permission of MIT and W. Edwards Deming. Published by MIT, Center for Advanced Engineering Study, Cambridge, MA 02139. Copyright 1982 by W. Edwards Deming.)

1. *Create constancy of purpose to improve the product and service.* Plan for long-term business growth by investing in resources, research and development, maintenance of equipment, and aids to production.
2. *Adopt the new philosophy.* The American industry can no longer live with mistakes, defects, and delays. The statistical portion of the new philosophy is quite simple and extremely accurate.
3. *Cease dependence on inspections.* Quality cannot be inspected into products. Processes must be brought under control statistically and inspected continually by all personnel.
4. *Stop awarding business on price alone.* The initial cost of a product may be only a fraction of its total cost if it lacks quality. Aim to work with one chosen supplier and build your relationship based on trust and statistical process control.
5. *Constantly improve your process.* Use statistics to identify the problems and work to eliminate them. Remember though, once management chooses to begin statistical process control, they must not choose to ignore the results.
6. *Train and retrain employees.* The work force is generally your single largest investment and greatest resource. Invest in education to improve all employees' abilities.
7. *Overhaul and modernize supervision.* The aim of management should be to help people and machines do a better job. Train your supervisors to act on reports of defect, maintenance requirements, poor tools, or other conditions undermining quality.

FIGURE 11-4 The chain reaction. [Reprinted from *Out of the Crisis*, by W. Edwards Deming by permission of MIT and W. Edwards Deming. Published by MIT, Center for

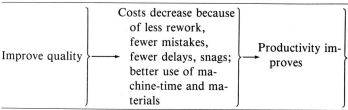

COMPUTER-INTEGRATED MANUFACTURING

Computer-integrated manufacturing is a business philosophy aiming to integrate the company's operations (from design, production, and distribution through to field service and support) by the use of computers and information technologies. CIM can help manufacture complex, customized, higher-quality products faster and cheaper, while making better use of scarce, trained people. America has some advanced factories (e.g., Apple, Deere, and IBM) where people do only the more complex assembly jobs. Scheduling, material flow, and many manufacturing processes are automated. CIM's three main benefits are higher, more consistent quality, greater flexibility, and lower labor costs. See Figure 11-5 for some information about gains across the entire product cycle.

Earlier, physical labor was reduced with water power, then by steam and, more recently, by electrical energy. Now, computers increasingly automate intellectual effort and physical work. In factories, they work 24 hours a day, freeing people from hazardous tasks and from unpleasant, undesirable jobs.

FIGURE 11-5 The benefits of CIM. The companies studied expect further benefits as full integration is approached. (From Computer Integration of Engineering Design and Production Manufacturing Studies Board, National Research Council, Washington, D.C.)

Reduction in engineering design cost	15–30%
Reduction in overall lead time	30–60%
Increased product quality as measured by yield of acceptable product	2–5 times previous level
Increased capability of engineers as measured by extent and depth of analysis in same or less time	3–35 times
Increased productivity of production operations (complete assemblies)	40–70%
Increased productivity (operating time) of capital equipment	2–3 times
Reduction of work in process	30–60%
Reduction of personnel costs	5–20%

Advanced Engineering Study,
Cambridge, MA 02139. Copyright 1982
by W. Edwards Deming.]

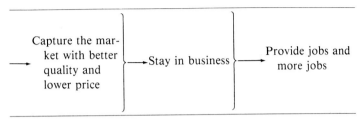

Computers have shrunk in size and fallen in price, while increasing in power. They are becoming the agents of integration for manufacturing. Assisted by two technologies, data base management systems and telecommunications, computers unite what used to be independent factory functions. Product design, manufacturing, and production management each benefit from computers as individual functions and also as one integrated system (discussed below).

Again, CIM is a system design. The system is the whole manufacturing enterprise: from computer-aided design to the finished product, from the factory floor to the administrative offices, and from the manufacturer's suppliers all the way to its customers. Creating such an integrated manufacturing system is so difficult that no one has done it yet. The technology is there and the methodology exists, but attitudes have to change. CIM is not a set of technologies; it is a corporate philosophy and strategy. Unless this philosophy is widely embraced, implementation is unlikely, because it is a new way of doing business.

Question: If CIM is such a tough nut to crack, why bother with it? Before answering, let's review how we lost our competitiveness in global markets.[3]

Our competitors sought to penetrate selected product categories, that is, products actually manufactured, such as TV sets and cameras. They looked for products with entrenched production practices, with firm, high-level demands, and limited options. These products usually employed no advanced technologies. There was no single, glaring weakness in the manufacturing, but some weaknesses at various points across all areas of activity. Remember, factory operations were not usually a high priority with America's top managers and their technical people. Generally, short-term paybacks were emphasized, and long-term investments were neglected. Our competitors pinpointed the weaknesses and made improvements in many parts of the production process. These tactical production improvements and their associated tactical investments captured the market share for them.

Ideally, CIM is a strategic counterattack on these tactics which rebuilds for strength and focuses on manufacturing. It moves to a new level of competitiveness across the whole product cycle. To illustrate: A product is selected as the vehicle for developing a CIM strategy, and then that product becomes the means of building new working relationships across the entire product cycle.

Figure 11-6 shows the traditional functions that generate marketable products

Group technology can also help with plant layout because given part families (e.g., parts with similar raw materials, processes and finishes) can often be made by certain manufacturing cells.

MANUFACTURING

In manufacturing, computers help in fabrication, materials handling, and assembly, as discussed next.

FABRICATION

Numerical control machines are often directed by computers to turn, extrude, or drill, for example. Such computerized numerical control can refer to the CAD data base for the information needed to create the programming that guides the NC equipment. This code can be edited automatically, too.

MATERIALS HANDLING

Automatic guided vehicles (AGVs) can be steered around the plant by chain drives, magnetic floor stripes, or wires. They can deliver raw materials and pick up finished parts, for instance. AGVs can service flexible manufacturing systems (which combine several manufacturing cells with automated storage and retrieval, automated transportation, and other such computerized components). Automatic storage and retrieval automates materials handling. Programmable controllers can run smart conveyors that recognize parts and route them accordingly.

A central computer thus can control material storage and retrieval and can direct AGVs delivering and fetching. Programming for the FMS can be downloaded from the central CPU for the appropriate family of parts for drilling, boring, grinding, or whatever. The central computer can monitor tool wear, replacing tools as needed, and can alert maintenance workers and reroute work in case of trouble, for example.

ASSEMBLY

Robots can help by picking and placing parts, welding, and painting, for instance. They can have a rudimentary form of vision for assembly, inspection, or navigation. Robots can remove parts from AGVs and route them through assembly, testing, and marking operations. Then they can load the finished pieces onto the AGV.

Manufacturing in a CIM plant would typically involve a MAP network, a centralized data base, and such data activities as downloading NC and robot programs, monitoring machine tools and work centers, and collecting order status information. Production processes would rely on technologies such as numerical control, work cells based on group technology, computer-assisted testing, AGVs, and automated material handling.

FIGURE 11-8 Typical production management functions.

>Inventory planning and control
>Quality
>Capacity planning
>Job scheduling (routing)
>Plant layout
>Work center design
>Assembly-line balancing

PRODUCTION MANAGEMENT

The management of production assets usually includes the functions listed in Figure 11-8. For example, one of the considerations for inventories is just-in-time, a philosophy of eliminating waste by producing only what is needed, when it is required, and in just the amount then necessary (see Chapter 7). Another aspect of inventories is automatic storage/automatic retrieval (AS/AR), which can help with raw materials, supplies, and work in process (see Chapter 9). A third area related to inventories is material requirements planning, which is based on estimated product demand and which generates requirements for raw materials and purchased parts (see Chapter 9).

Concerning quality, sensors in the equipment, for instance, can automatically inspect the work and report by voice, in print or visually, via a screen. Further, there are software packages that help to automate production management functions such as job scheduling (a simulation determines the optimal route) and assembly line balancing (interactive software helps to plan how to keep the workstations busy but not overloaded).

OTHER BUSINESS FUNCTIONS

Manufacturing is part of a business entity which typically also includes purchasing, accounting, personnel, marketing, and administration. The computer is the agent of integration. Together with data base management systems and telecommunications, computers coordinate these functions. To illustrate: The nodes of the communication network could be machine centers, AGVs, or robots, but they might also be terminals used by designers, engineers, accountants, or managers. That is, individual functions all use the same data and network, thereby integrating the tasks.

CASE STUDY

Read "Making CIM Work," at the end of this chapter, and then briefly paraphrase it, explaining how.

SUMMARY

1. Unless the managers of American manufacturing firms change their ways to adjust to the tougher global competition, their survival will be threatened (personal and corporate).
2. There are impressive benefits when management abandons antiquated business traditions.
3. Deming's ideas, along with statistical process control, can begin to improve factory and office processes (systems).
4. Ineffective, outdated management practices cannot be made competitive by using an overlay of CIM.
5. Computer-integrated manufacturing is a business philosophy aimed at integrating the company's operations (from design, production, and distribution to field service and support) with the use of computers, networks, and data bases.
6. CIM is not a set of technologies; it is a corporate philosophy and strategy which means a new way of doing business.
7. By sharing information technologies, data bases, and communications, the organization achieves higher efficiencies, greater flexibilities, and faster cycle times across the range of manufacturing and administrative functions.

REVIEW QUESTIONS

1. Global competition is tough. Explain.
2. We'll handle international competition by closing the US plant and manufacturing overseas instead. Comment.
3. We'll get Congress to raise barriers so the competition can't beat us in America. Comment.
4. What is the most important ingredient in the recipe for competing globally?
5. What does Hajime Karatsu say about the secret of Japan's success?
6. What do work rules and classifications have to do with your standard of living?
7. How can we reverse things and compete again?
8. Review Deming's 14 points and deadly diseases and process improvements.
9. CIM is the antidote for a manufacturer's problems. Explain your views.
10. Define CIM. What are its benefits?
11. CIM is a set of technologies. Comment.
12. What tactics captured shares in American markets?
13. Explain Figures 11-6 and 11-7.
14. Give examples of CIM in product design, manufacturing, production management, and other business functions.

REFERENCES

1. From Hajime Karatsu, *Tough Words for American Industry* (Boston, MA: Productivity Press, 1987), pp. 50, 67.
2. P. F. Drucker, "Workers' Hands Bound by Tradition," *The Wall Street Journal,* August 2, 1988.
3. See N. A. Chiantella, "A CIM Business Strategy for Industrial Leadership," *Management Guide for CIM* (Dearborn, MI: SME, 1986), p. 3.
4. See G. H. Schaeffer, "Implementing CIM," *American Machinist,* August 1981, pp. 151–174.

Case Study
MAKING CIM WORK*

by Willie Schatz

If a company's computer-integrated manufacturing strategy isn't of the people, by the people, and for the people, there is little chance that it'll increase productivity, lower costs, add efficiency, or deliver any of the other promises associated with factory-floor technology investments.

"CIM is really a cultural change," says Bob Ratcliff, a lead analyst for CIM services at farm machinery maker Deere & Co., which has spent a lot of time working on how to manufacture tractors more efficiently using systems. "It's really a way of life. You're not just changing your computer configuration, you're changing your methodology. You're changing the way you do business. You're changing mind-sets."

Or, as Arthur Andersen & Co. says: simplify, automate, integrate. But that's far easier said than done. CIM doesn't happen overnight. Even when it's properly conceived, a strategy that automates a significant portion of a company's manufacturing operations take years to implement. "A lot of people are going for the big win," comments Vincent Jones, author of *MAP/TOP Networking* (McGraw Hill Book Co., New York, 1988). "People are always in a rush. Management wants to see the whole problem solved today." Manufacturing companies worldwide are pouring vast sums of money into automating their operations. Boston-based Harbor Research Inc. estimates CIM investments will nearly double to $91 billion in 1992 from this year's $52 billion, with transportation companies leading the way.

But before those investments produce the kinds of returns manufacturing executives and their IS counterparts are banking on, companies have to thoroughly examine the entire manufaturing process. "Too many people automate [without thinking about what they're doing]," Jones asserts. "Step one is [for] the company to change its way of thinking. Understand the process, document the process, simplify the process, then automate. Automation is the last step, not the first."

Users agree. "CIM is a journey," says David Rea, director of the manufacturing systems division of Weyerhaeuser Information Systems Div., Tacoma, Wash. "It's a means to an end, not an end in itself. It's not something that you do in a year."

Or maybe even in a decade. Weyerhaeuser has been playing the CIM game since 1978. After an initial skirmish in 1978 and a second round in 1982—both of

---

*Reprinted with permission from *Datamation*. Copyright, 1988.

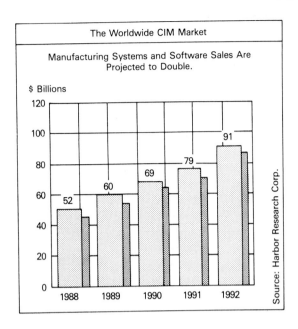

which were limited by the available technology—the company finally solved its CIM problem in July 1985 with an in-house system called ProSmart. ProSmart, a set of VAX-based software tools (including a database), furnishes real-time production information, as well as considerable savings. In fact, ProSmart has been so effective for Weyerhaeuser, saving more than $1 million annually at its Longview, Wash., pulp and paper mill, that the firm is marketing it commercially. "We made the tool rather than buy it, because we looked at the marketplace solutions and there weren't any [for us]," Rea says.

Today, manufacturers have a much broader choice of commercially available software to use as a base for their CIM efforts, especially in the MRP (material resource planning) II arena. "CIM programs are more readily available than five years ago," agrees Kreg Brown, vice president, Oriole Software, a CIM software manufacturer in Towson, Md. "Users are saying to vendors, 'Get me the functionality to do my job and we'll worry about the platform later. What software will give me the best benefit for my money? What will it take for me to get and stay competitive?'"

As with everything else in business, investment in manufacturing is driven by competitiveness. But competitiveness means different things for different industries, and that makes for a variety of CIM applications. So it's a question of how, not whether, companies gain a manufacturing advantage. Most still approach CIM with the chief objective of improving the quality of their plant processes and the products they manufacture, according to the 1988 North American Manufacturing Futures Survey conducted by the Boston University School of Management. Also among the top CIM goals of those companies surveyed is the speeding up of development and production, and increasing the flexibility of manufacturing operations.

But none of the companies surveyed is going anywhere in CIM without some serious soul-searching. "Companies have to break old habits so they can take advantage of the new environment," says Jeffrey Miller, professor of operations management at Boston University and director of the survey. "CIM is a process of discovering how to simplify the entire manufacturing process. The best firms aren't even doing MRP any more. Since MRP is really an IT reflection of the entire physical process, they've simplified the environment that MRP controls. A factory that MRP controls is automatically a better factory. It's a question of attacking root causes."

While some companies are able to identify manufacturing problems before they begin to hurt profits, others don't begin to seriously seek CIM solutions until their businesses begin to suffer—either due to external market conditions, internal inefficiencies, or a combination of both.

The farm crisis, for example, motivated the $4.1 billion manufacturer Deere to plow into factory automation, albeit late. "We became real lethargic during the '70s," remarks Ratcliff, CIM analyst at Deere's tractor factory in Waterloo, Iowa. "For so long the attitude had been that whatever we did was right, and the marketplace reflected that. So we saw no reason to change it. We were Deere the institution, not Deere the business."

The severity and length of the downturn in U.S. agriculture in the early 1980s forced Deere to focus on its core business. Tractor production had dropped to as low as 10% of the previous level, resulting in layoffs, salary reductions, early retirements, and all the other signs of a business on the brink.

"We took a crash course in CIM," Deere chairman and CEO Robert Hanson said at the recent AUTOFACT conference in Chicago. "That's 'crash' as in when the bottom falls out. We were lucky in a perverse sort of way. Other companies see the drip-drip of slowly eroding market share and put off dealing with the inevitable. When you get hit like we did, you can't do that."

Many of the early retirees were succeeded by younger, more aggressive managers who were not afraid to confront Deere's problems. They formed the nucleus of a computer-integrated manufacturing task force, whose sweeping recommendations in 1986 included the formation of a CIM services group comprised of seven members from different quarters at Deere's Waterloo works. The chief suggestion of the task force, which emphasized the merits of decentralized operations, was that the plant's middle managers should find new ways to make their individual departments more productive. Implicit in the task force's thinking was the conviction that there was a need to reform the ways those plant managers obtained information.

"We were taking on a large, powerful centralized mainframe IBM IT shop," says Ratcliff, describing Waterloo's IS dependence on relatively meaningless data generated by IBM mainframes at Deere's headquarters in Moline, Ill. With the CIM initiatives, "we were going to have to redirect the emphasis on how to collect and manage data. Everything in DP was going to have to be by and for the end user,

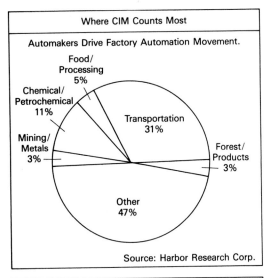

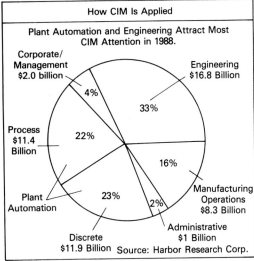

not the systems organization. We had to drive computer ownership, design, and use to the lowest possible level. That meant distributed, localized computing with a great deal of flexibility."

That also meant a totally different approach. "Any change means a fundamental and terrifying attitudinal adjustment," Hanson asserts, "but if your company's going to be competitive, it's got to change its corporate will so it has the gumption to make timely and difficult decisions. We changed not because we were forward looking, but because of the big [competitive] bang.

"Now we're not afraid of change, we can see the forest for the trees and now we know that in manufacturing integration you have to emphasize the people, not the technology. However dazzling the hardware, the 'software' between the ears must be updated first.''

And that's not easy. Despite this absolutely top-level support, Deere's progress to date has been slow. "We've spent the last 15 months just getting to the point where some people are listening to us," Ratcliff says. "Classic CIM is our end goal, but a lot has to happen before we put in massive amounts of hardware. . . . The frustration comes because we want to run, not walk. But at least we're moving."

ROLLING OUT THE CIM CARPET

Monsanto Chemical Co.'s journey down the CIM path was faster. Challenged by corporate management in 1984 to increase productivity by 50% in three years, the company's largest manufacturing plant responded by forming three "Plant of the '90s" operating committees that involved every department in the plant—accounting, data processing, research and development, engineering, finance, and operations. Management asked the committees to develop one CIM plan for the site, located on 2,000 acres in Pensacola, Fla., so the costs of implementing it could be factored into capital planning for the next decade.

The committees generated 800 ideas for how to achieve productivity breakthroughs at the plant, which primarily makes nylon carpet yarn. Those ideas were eventually reduced to three key CIM projects, all of which are intended to improve access to systems by any of the plant's 2,500 employees:

- A local area network to integrate the plant's current IBM, DEC, and HP systems, including some 300 PCs. Monsanto so far has invested about $1 million in Ethernet- and broadband-based networks to do so.
- Separate database management systems for its yarn and chemical product lines. The company has decided to implement Oracle DBMS software as a result.
- A partnership with DEC and Fisher Controls to develop a prototype architecture and application for optimization of all resources at the site.

Monsanto Chemical's plant must be doing something right, because productivity has increased 47% as measured by a complex CIM formula that includes the following variables: raw materials, capital, energy, labor, supplies, and maintenance. Moreover, the company has already recouped some of its CIM investment costs, although the average payout is two or three years.

"The most important part is planning how you're going to be doing business in the '90s," declared Carol Holmes, supervisor of information and systems technology at the Monsanto plant. "Without that cross-functional, visionary plan, we wouldn't have done anything. There were no territorial turf wars and [there was] no jealousy from the DP group . . . [which was] not in a position to set priorities. Those have to be determined by the user groups. If we [had] waited for DP to do it, we'd still be waiting."

So would Bentley Nevada, an industrial instrumentation maker in Minden, Nev. The company realized there had to be a better way to fly when an audit showed that it took 3,500 blueprints to produce one product—that's about three times too many—and the blueprints took about five times longer than they should have to translate into the product. Trying to get a product to market was like trying to swim through quicksand.

"We'd made a corporate decision that it [automation] was absolutely necessary for us to be competitive in the '90s," says Dave Biggs, Bentley's vice president of product development. "It was becoming pretty obvious that our information system wasn't going to cut it," he continues, referring to the company's $65 million hodgepodge of equipment and software that had been designed for specific functions but that was unable to work together.

"So we decided to analyze what information we really needed [for production]. We discovered that there were real good gains to be made by providing a manufacturing database [developed in-house] that could offer flexibility to other parts of the organization. We never set out to use CIM. We were just looking at improving our production process."

COMMITTING TO A SINGLE, UNIFIED DATABASE

Bentley didn't start out with CIM, but by the time it had invested millions of dollars in Compaq 386s, AutoCAD, and CADNETIX software, it had certainly finished with it. The process was hardly painless. Bentley restricted its initial database investments to its engineering departments, which alienated other departments from the CIM cause and yielded little improvement to overall productivity. The company realized its mistake and made a commitment to create a single, unified database that would serve all departments, not just engineering.

"It's absolutely essential that you have one database," Biggs stresses. "If you've got multiple databases, it's a lock that one's wrong. We did an awful lot of grinding on each other until we got the system down. You've got to have an active methodology that promotes the involvement and coordination of all the parties concerned."

Database technology has also keyed Weyerhaeuser's success in CIM, although it experienced two failures in automating its 1,300-worker Longview factory before hitting on its ProSmart solution. "We missed the mark in '78 and '82 because we thought data was the problem," Weyerhaeuser manufacturing director Rea confesses. "With ProSmart we took a people-focused approach, not just a [technological] one. The main business driver was still global competitive pressure, just as [before]. But it was easier the third time because we took the lessons learned and carried them forward."

Unfortunately, a significant number of manufacturers aren't even experimenting enough with CIM to be learning any lessons from it. Many are reluctant to change their ways, especially when some plant capacities in the U.S. are approaching 85%. The old "if it ain't broke, don't fix it" philosophy could be a costly one, however. "Those who pay CIM lip service will continue to be less competitive," networking author Jones warns. "The Japanese don't pay CIM lip service, and they're beating the pants off [U.S. manufacturers].

"Sure CIM is a lot of work," Jones continues, "and it's not a panacea. It's just another manufaturing tool. But the essence of CIM is really very simple. It's a mechanical way of putting people 10 feet away from each other so they can communicate."

Chapter Twelve

IMPLEMENTING CIM[1]

After you have read this chapter, it will be clear to you that

- Manufacturing and CIM both embrace all the activities from product concept through to aftersale service.
- CIM has a massive organizational impact.
- Implementing CIM involves four stages.

"Confusion among middle managers . . . unfocused engineers . . . work that is difficult to get out on time . . . unreliable vendors . . . mounds of work-in-process beside idle machines . . . apathetic employees—all these problems and no time to address them because fires must be put out!"[2]

These are symptoms of the environment in which American manufacturers are facing their greatest competitive challenge. Japanese and other offshore competitors are rapidly increasing their share of world markets formerly dominated by United States products. To some degree, this is also happening in our North American home markets which have long provided United States manufacturers with the formidable advantage of a large volume base and corresponding economy scale.

One aspect of the changes that brought this new, highly competitive world is our traditional mass production. The application of large-scale resources to the moving Model T assembly line illustrates where we came from. About 1900, Frederick W. Taylor defined our industrial organization in his *Theory of Scientific Management*. He introduced time-and-motion study and argued that careful analysis of every man and machine operation was necessary for operational efficiency.

Taylor believed the increasing complexity of manufacturing could be managed only by dividing operations into small elements within the specialties making up the manufacturing process. His key assumption was that by independently optimizing the individual small worker tasks, the entire process would be optimized. That is, he defined the manufacturing process as a collection of individual activities associated with the transformation process itself.

We now understand that the manufacturing process is, rather, a continuum, embracing all the activities from product concept through design, manufacturing, and aftersale service. Joseph Harrington, a well-known manufacturing consultant and member of the Academy of Engineering, defines manufacturing in this way:[3] "Manufacturing begins with the product concept and continues through support of the product in the field. Although incredibly complex in all of its fine detail, all elements are so intricately connected that no part can be addressed successfully in isolation from all the other parts."

We defined computer-integrated manufacturing as a business philosophy aimed at integrating the company's operations (from design, production, and distribution through to field service and support) with the use of computers and information technologies. The definitions of manufacturing and of CIM are thus congruent, so they coincide. In other words, the concept of manufacturing being confined to the mass production of goods on moving assembly lines is as outdated as the Model T (now being only about 20 to 30 percent of output and the balance being small and medium batches).

The new view is that we are dealing with the whole business: from computer-aided design to the finished product, from the factory floor to the administrative offices, and from the manufacturer's suppliers all the way to its customers. Consequently, to compete we must constantly work to improve the entire system—from product concept to aftersale service. Quality, flexibility, and cost are important criteria.

CIM is potentially an excellent tool for this process improvement because it is the system design of the entire manufacturing enterprise. Ultimately, the flow of information would look something like Figure 12-1 (which illustrates why it is called computer-integrated manufacturing). Some of the functions linked in such an integrated manufacturing system are

- Engineering
    Design
    Analysis
    Documentation
- Planning
    Parts planning
    Production and inventory planning
- Control
    Process, shop, and materials control
    Inspection, testing, and quality
- Production
    Parts and tool production
    Assembly
    Handling and storage
- Support
    Facilities engineering and maintenance
    Personnel management
    Data processing
    Order processing
    Accounting

This partial list suggests CIM's massive organizational impact. One way to put dimensions on its impact is to say that all aspects of the organization have to plan changes: the manufacturing system, the information system, and the human system (see Figure 12-2). The real test is integrating all these changes.

Another way to look at the changes CIM compels is to note that three infrastructures have to be integrated (see Figure 12-3):

- The technological structure that connects the various working units
- The referential structure that ensures the same meaning for the data in the data base(s) regardless of which function is using the information
- The attitudinal structure that means everyone shares the same concept of where the organization is going and how.

CIM affects the entire enterprise from original recognition of market need to the sale, delivery, and service of the final product. It uses high-speed digital computers, data bases, and telecommunications networks to integrate the entire enterprise. Constant migration toward an automated factory is typical of most successful

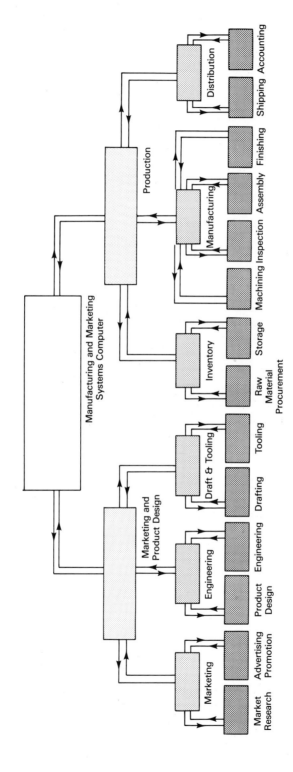

FIGURE 12–1 [From *1988 NC/CIM Guidebook* (Cincinnati, OH: Modern Machine Shop, 1988), pp. 210, 211.

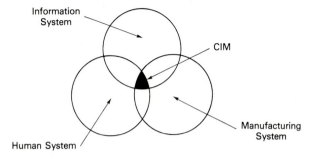

FIGURE 12-2 Integrating the organizational subsystems. (From S. Stylck, "Human Systems Demand Equal Time in CIM Effort," *Computerworld,* July 6, 1987, p. S7, courtesy ITP—Boston, adapted.)

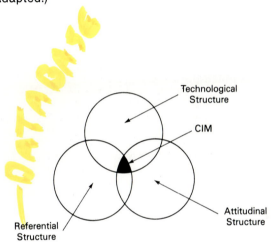

FIGURE 12-3 Integrating the organizational infrastructure. (From M. Williamson, "In Pursuit of Integration," *Computerworld,* July 6, 1987, p. S2.)

manufacturers. CIM springs from many sources which are converging (see Figure 12-4). In sum, CIM involves everyone in the organization. All must strive constantly to improve their factory and office processes as these are integrated by computers, networks, and data bases.

The changes required are immense. So are the stakes. Our manufacturing base may depend on CIM: $300 billion a year and 20 million jobs.[4] Implementing CIM is critical and complex. We will consider it in four stages (see Figure 12-5) as discussed below.

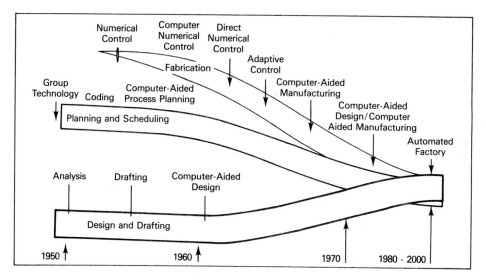

FIGURE 12-4 Computer-assisted technologies are converging on CIM. (Courtesy of Metcut Research Associates.)

FIGURE 12-5 CIM implementation cycle. [From N. A. Chiantella, "A CIM Business Strategy for Industrial Leadership," *Management Guide for CIM* (Dearborn, MI: SME, 1986), p. 11.]

Stage 1: Introduction
    a. Concepts of a CIM business strategy
    b. Managers' roles
    c. Creating interest in CIM
    d. Developing the climate

Stage 2: Preparation
    a. Forming a study team for CIM
    b. CIM opportunity candidates
    c. Conceptualizing CIM way of operating

Stage 3: Program Plan
    a. Proposal development
    b. Selling proposal
    c. Program commitment

Stage 4: Implementation
    a. Managing the implementation
    b. Measure and evaluate results
    c. Moving to next opportunity
    d. Sharing experience and expertise

STAGE 1: INTRODUCTION

Factories around the world are changing from high-volume, low-flexibility manufacturing to low-volume, high-flexibility plants so they can be responsive to consumer tastes. Variety, high quality, and low unit costs are the new watchwords. The change is achieved by planning from the top down and by implementing from the bottom up.

Accordingly, top management's personal commitment and understanding are vital. Senior management communicates CIM's objective (which is to survive as a profitable enterprise) and the need for simplicity and collaboration. The first goal might be to have a project team determine how the plant actually operates (versus how it's supposed to run). Then, a team could simplify all the procedures down to their essentials, concentrating on the functions that add value. From this could be estimated the information needed by humans and machines performing the value-added tasks. Knowing the information that is absolutely essential reveals what's not needed (which can help cut overhead without automation).

Top management's role is to see that some kind of strategy or plan has been agreed on by those who have to implement it. These workers must be involved and convinced. Retraining is part of this, as are constant persuasion and working with people on the changes.

Functional managers are the experts in their particular specialties. They advise on what to automate and how it relates to other functions. If these executives do not accept the strategy, success is unlikely. Resistance to change is normal. Those living with the existing system have learned to tolerate it. The proposed system has yet to benefit anyone and so lacks supporters. Yet, middle-management support is essential.

Creating the climate and developing an interest in CIM are part of top management's selling job. People have little interest in what you want but have a keen interest in what they want. Therefore, how they will benefit is the key. One approach is to learn what they like about the present system (plus what gives them the most trouble) and what they want but don't have. The benefits are probably in the area defined by the difference between what they want and what they have. Explaining how CIM will benefit people helps win their support.

STAGE 2: PREPARATION

As noted, implementing CIM is both critical and complex, requiring many changes. A project team is often a good device for executing such a transformation, because it brings together the right people with the necessary problem-solving tools so they can concentrate on the correct problem(s). For CIM, it should be cross-functional, multilevel, and interdisciplinary. Such a team's varied perceptions are its main strength. Problem definition normally goes through several cycles and often changes as it gets closer to the true problem and away from the symptoms. Figure 12-6 lists some characteristics of project teams.

FIGURE 12-6 Project teams. [From *How to Become a Quality Supplier,* Instructor's Manual (Methuen, MA: GOAL/QPC, 1987), p. 8-3.]

- Project teams aren't new, but the tools that are used to solve problems are sometimes unfamiliar.
- Project teams are the most widely used method for breaking down barriers between departments.
- Not every problem requires a project team.
- Project teams are most effective when they are part of a planned improvement program rather than a shotgun approach.
- Project teams are designed to be efficient but also to slow down the process at times in order to prevent members from jumping to conclusions and missing the heart of the problem.
- Project teams often force managers to involve people or functions in solving a problem that they wouldn't have considered in the past. For example, in the past, a product problem would have been tackled only by production people, but a project team might involve designing, purchasing, and customer service people as well.
- Documentation of project team progress is critical.
- The problem must define the people to be invovled in the project team.
- The composition of project teams must be seen as being fluid. Resource people come and go as needed.
- Project teams dissolve when the problem is solved, improved or stabilized. The project team must therefore define when it will know its work is finished.

The CIM team, for example, might be the present management team, with the general manager as chairperson and with the functional managers as members (e.g., materials, engineering, accounting). Using the normal chain of command demonstrates commitment and allows multifunctional decisions while minimizing turf battles. Also, decisions are made and executed without second guessing.

Identifying CIM opportunity candidates depends on customer demand and competitive pressures. Typical CIM benefit areas include:[5]

1. *Increased Productivity*—Companies usually experience manufacturing intervals shortened by 50 percent or more. Computer-aided manufacturing (CAM) shortens the elapsed time for the manufacturing cycle. Numerically controlled (NC) tools and Flexible Manufacturing Systems (FMS) give the capability to have unmanned operations. Industrial robots have experienced productivity gains of 300–400%.
2. *Engineering and Design Cost*—Computer-aided design (CAD) reduces lead time and cost of introducing new products into production. Also, changes to existing products are easier to control and introduce into production without disrupting the manufacturing process. Group technology (GT) allows for standardization of routing and computer control files, eliminating manual entry of data. This reduces errors, redundancy, and lead time.
3. *Product Quality*—Computer-aided manufacturing (CAM) makes the work force more reliable by taking the guesswork out of manufacturing. Industrial robots relieve people of monotonous and often dangerous jobs. Numerically controlled

machines increase quality because less skill is required by the operator. CIM will reduce scrap and rework, especially in an environment where one has to adhere to strict tolerances. When there is scrap or rework, CIM gives one the ability to discover the reason for the problem and allows one to take remedial action more quickly and with a greater degree of success.

4. *Production Control*—A computer-aided manufacturing system will have an integrated data base. All data needed by production control to interface with manufacturing, engineering, purchasing, and the customer is readily accessible. Production schedules are computerized, allowing the computer to become the expediter. This frees the production analyst to solve problems that were ignored in the pre-CIM era. Also, with CAM, less paperwork is required and this increases the efficiency of all parties involved.

5. *Capacity Utilization*—An integrated base provides the capability of performing facility studies helping in development of capacity plans. Also, "what if" capability prevents surprises in the future. Numerically controlled tools have less downtime due to offline programming; and they require less floor space.

6. *Customer Satisfaction*—All companies thrive on repeat business. If the customers are satisfied, they will continue to give your company their business. Along with all the advantages already listed, CIM will give your company the capability to provide shorter service intervals at lower cost. CIM's flexibility will provide a better planning tool and the capability of being more responsive to the customer. The simple capability of giving the customer an accurate answer to questions is great for customer relations.

7. *Social Factors*—Some benefits of CIM are hard to measure. One of these is the social benefit. Employees will have a higher morale because of more challenging jobs, less overtime, and in some cases, less dangerous jobs. Also, the additional training usually leads to an upgrade, builds self-esteem, and results in the employee becoming a contributing member of the overall process. An improved working environment is one of the many intangible benefits of CIM.

Besides identifying CIM opportunities, the project team needs to conceptualize how CIM operates. What you have is machines, robots, test equipment, material handling devices, and the like, which have some level of "smarts," are reprogrammable, and can communicate with each other. This implies, for example, the following types of technologies: data base management systems, telecommunications, CAD/CAM, numerical control, robots, and flexible manufacturing systems.

CIM characteristics include processing of digital signals by computers, and digital information is stored in computerized data base(s). Digital signals and data travel over the network. CAD provides computer assistance in design and analysis. Computer numerical control uses a computer to control an NC machine tool. The NC program is stored in a computer and passed down to the machine tool in digital form. A flexible manufacturing system is a set of computerized production resources usually combining machine tools, robots to load and unload them, and an automated material-handling system to move material, work pieces, and tools among them. This, then, is the flavor of the CIM environment.

STAGE 3: PROGRAM PLAN

Long-range planning is important for reasons such as the following. It helps ensure survival of the company; it is necessary for control; it provides lead time to meet future events; and it supplies a basis for current decisions. But, tomorrow's problems are in a different realm than today's operating problems and require conceptual skills not possessed by all line executives, so developing a CIM plan is not trivial. What you are planning is how to move an organization from an environment wherein computer technology plays a limited role to one in which all the firm's functions are integrated through the technology.

We will assume that the CIM project team is the present management hierarchy (i.e., general manager and department heads), so they will prepare the plan. It begins with the justification for CIM: What are the specific needs of the competitive environment that require CIM (e.g., inventory costs, inconsistent quality)? Next, the current manual and automated systems are described (sales through aftersales customer support). Then, the CIM concept is defined (e.g., islands of automation versus CIM).

Then the CIM plan is presented, including

- Dollar estimates of costs and benefits; for example, fast response and accurate, consistent on-line information are common advantages
- A concise description of the proposed system, with details on each subsystem:[6]
    1. A description of the required functionality, including what systems and functions provide input and what systems and functions use the output
    2. Explication of the available technologies that can be brought to bear
    3. Anticipated new developments in the technology in the foreseeable future
    4. How the technologies can be applied within the specific business setting
    5. Typical benefits generated by the technology
    6. How the subsystem will be integrated with the business' other systems.
- A description of the changes that must occur in the firm if the benefits are to be achieved, and some information about the risks attendant in making the changes.
- Recommended priorities, scheduling implementation of the subsystems and showing the major milestones.

CIM is a commitment to the system design for the whole enterprise, which requires the formal approval of the chief executive officer. Then, the separate CIM subsystems have to be approved (so that they appear in the budget), which requires, for example, approval from the executive committee. This means two approvals and probably two sets of justifications.

Comparing costs under the present system to costs under the proposed system is usually helpful. Reduced cycle time, inventory savings, better quality, and lower costs are often among the competitive gains mentioned in the justifications. While

CIM has to follow the company's traditional justifications procedures, many CIM benefits are not anticipated during approval, so strict return-on-investment and payback criteria may not be entirely applicable when deciding whether to commit to the recommended program.

STAGE 4: IMPLEMENTATION

There are three predominant reasons that CIM programs fail:

1. Not involving and retraining everyone
2. Moving too far, too fast
3. Lack of a long-range plan into which CIM is integrated.

Clearly, these mistakes are to be avoided. They begin long before implementation, however, and once committed cannot be corrected by the implementation process itself.

CIM implementation seldom fails for technical reasons. When it does flop, it is because of poor management. The key to implementing CIM is the management of people. The usual technical skills in manufacturing, engineering, or accounting are needed: but technical problems are seldom critical. The quality of management is decisive.

CIM involves the whole organization, so the individual responsible for the entire firm should also be responsible for computer-integrated manufacturing. The chief executive officer won't have time for the implementation details, though, so will delegate the responsibility to a CIM project manager. Again, the project manager must be able to get work done through people.

> Equally important to having the right person responsible for the project is the establishment of a good communication system. When implementing a CIM program, change is a required ingredient. In order to have change accepted, it is usually mandatory that all people or departments affected by the change "buy into" the new idea, establishing a sense of ownership in the project and the eventual outcome. An effective communication system provides an atmosphere that when a change in one functional area affects the work environment of other areas, the benefits are communicated first to the other affected areas.
>
> It is also crucial that the basic concepts of the total CIM plan be communicated to all employees involved. Regular progress meetings should be held to review progress made-to-date, to identify potential problems, and to assign responsibility to individuals for accomplishing new tasks. An important task of the project leader at these meetings is to be certain that everyone knows what new decisions have been made and how each department will be affected by these decisions.
>
> To ensure the success of a CIM project, a written milestone plan is required. When implementing this plan one must develop and maintain an attitude that says delays are considered unacceptable. Don't accept excuses and reasons for not meeting the schedule. Find out what is required to reach your objectives and make sure it gets done. Developing this attitude within everyone involved is critical if you want to reach your goals. Even if only one or two individuals begin to fall behind in their areas of responsibility, the CIM program could be in peril.[7]

To implement CIM, control of the program is absolutely vital; every single business function is involved in some facet of the project. To keep track of the myriad of activities, several levels of planning and control are necessary.

At the highest level is the "master plan." Here, philosophy, operating principles, programs, broad timetables, and resource requirements are spelled out to provide a specific yet flexible road map to get from "what is" to "what will be." Whether the master plan is for a 3, 5, or 10 year effort, the broad overview is important. This master plan needs to be updated regularly through the life of the project to reflect changing technologies and business needs.

At the more operational level, however, detailed schedules and resource allocations need to be determined. On an annual basis, management from all functions must sit down and work out monthly milestones and assignment of specific responsibilities for all facets of the project, including commitments for manpower support from each function for each project. These detailed plans provide the basis for top management's monthly review of progress. Although this process of achieving consensus among the different business functions on resources can be quite difficult, it must be done to achieve the synergy that is the power of computer-integrated manufacturing.[8]

CIM is a continuing project. It links all areas of the organization into an automated manufacturing firm. When deciding on the next CIM opportunity, the needs of the business dictate. All other things being equal, how receptive the people are in alternative areas implies where you have the greatest probability of a successful implementation.

CASE STUDY

Read "The Impact of Computer Integrated Manufacturing" at the end of this chapter. Then, write your brief recommendations about how to deal with the human aspects of implementing CIM.

SUMMARY

1. Manufacturing and CIM both begin with the product concept and continue through support of the product in the field.
2. CIM has a massive organizational impact.
3. Implementing CIM is critical and complex. It is discussed in four stages.
4. Stage 1: Introduction—Senior management's commitment and understanding are vital, as is persuading those who will be affected.
5. Stage 2: Preparation—A CIM project team is suggested, which draws up a list of CIM opportunities.
6. Stage 3: Program Plan—A long-range CIM plan is approved.
7. Stage 4: Implementation—The key to implementing CIM is the management of people.

REVIEW QUESTIONS

1. Summarize Frederick W. Taylor's ideas.
2. Compare the definitions of CIM and of manufacturing.

3. The mass production of goods on a moving assembly line is the way to compete today. Comment.
4. Explain Figures 12–2 and 12–3.
5. What's the point of Figure 12–4?
6. Factories are changing from high-volume, low-flexibility to low-volume, high-flexibility plants. Explain.
7. Recommend how to "sell" CIM to a functional manager.
8. Discuss project teams.
9. Review a half-dozen CIM benefits.
10. How does CIM operate? What are its characteristics?
11. What are some reasons for long-range planning?
12. Outline a CIM program plan.
13. Discuss three predominant reasons that CIM programs fail.
14. Implementing CIM is really a technical problem. Comment.
15. Recommend how to implement CIM. Outline the planning and controls.

REFERENCES

1. This chapter draws heavily on *Management Guide for CIM* (Dearborn, MI: SME, 1986).
2. C. M. Savage, *Modern Machine Shop,* October 1983, p. 17.
3. See G. H. Millar, "CIM and Its Impact on Engineering," paper SP-631, Earthmoving Industry Conference, Peoria, Ill., April 15–17, 1985, p. 2.
4. N. Valéry, "Factory of the Future," *The Economist,* May 30, 1987, p. 4.
5. From W. L. Ogburn, "Executive Perspective on CIM," *Management Guide for CIM* (Dearborn, MI: SME, 1986), pp. 24–26.
6. From J. F. Snyder, "Key Elements of a CIM Master Plan," *Management Guide for CIM* (Dearborn, MI: SME, 1986), p. 51.
7. P. W. Branninger, "Managing Implementation Phases of CIM," *Management Guide for CIM* (Dearborn, MI: SME, 1986), p. 70.
8. From J. F. Snyder, "Who Should Run the CIM Show?" *Management Guide for CIM* (Dearborn, MI: SME, 1986), p. 75.

Case Study
THE IMPACT OF COMPUTER INTEGRATED MANUFACTURING*

Dan Ciampa
Executive Vice President
Rath & Strong, Inc.

THE CHANGES ON THE PEOPLE SIDE

We have developed our technology to the point where we already have many of the pieces needed for the Factory of the Future. There are tool wear monitoring systems that automatically change tools exactly at the point that they start to become dull. There are vibration analysis systems that detect worn out bearings and shaft misalignment and other causes of machine failure before they occur and shut down the machine automatically. Manufacturing cells now have controls that coordinate the operation of all the machine tools and robots in the cell. CNCs incorporate on-line diagnostic systems, and productivity monitoring systems give real time information that can tell a manufacturing manager what is happening at that instant with every injection press in his plant.

There are over 6,300 robot installations in this country today, and they are at the center of the flexible manufacturing cell, which in turn has been labeled as the first step up the CIM ladder. The auto industry alone will buy 6,300 new robots in the next two years, and as of mid-1982, there were about 12 full Flexible Manufacturing Systems in this country and many more partial applications. Some experts have promised a 45 percent reduction in production time and a 25 percent reduction in manufacturing costs by using flexible manufacturing systems compared to traditional manufacturing using stand-alone, numerically controlled machine tools. The point is that enormous advances have been made over the last 10 years in bringing increased automation to the workplace, and judging from the development going on in many firms, there is much more on the way. The overall result should be increased flexibility in manufacturing, leading to an increase in efficiency and effectiveness, and that should lead to better quality.

The more options like these that we have, the more manufacturing companies will try out these options and learn how to use them effectively and the more commonplace they will become. But just having a lot of sophisticated, state-of-the-art options is not going to ensure the effectiveness or efficiency we need to achieve

---

*Originally published as "The Impact of Computer Integrated Manufacturing," by Dan Ciampa. Productivity Brief 39. American Productivity & Quality Center, August 1984.

higher quality. Increasingly, companies are recognizing the need for Computer Integrated Manufacturing (CIM) to secure that greater effectiveness and efficiency in information transfer and planning among the computerized elements of their operations. Too often CIM is looked at only in terms of integration of machines, computers and software. In reality, the planning and implementation of CIM must go far beyond these technical considerations to encompass the departments that control and use these resources.

And that integration must encompass people so that there can be unity of purpose and a common vision that people at all levels in the organization can share.

This task is more formidable than has been the task of developing the computers, software and machinery of automation, for this task must be accomplished in spite of the management philosophy and climate still found within many firms in this country. The traditional manufacturing climate discourages integration, rather than encourages it. It works against a common vision by treating people at different organization levels in different ways. It blocks a unity of purpose by encouraging outdated management philosophies and approaches.

THE CHALLENGES OF CHANGE

As we move toward CIM, more and more automation options (in the form of computers, software and manufacturing equipment or machinery) are becoming available. As companies experiment with them, more and more changes are likely on the people side of the scale. Here are at least five of those changes, some of which have already started to take place (Figure 1).

1. More jobs will change in content requiring workers to develop and use new areas of competence. This brings the chance for more growth opportunities for workers. It also carries the danger of more people being displaced and unemployed if we don't respond well with the right job training programs.

    I talked to one foreman who decided to downgrade himself to a member of the hourly work force because his company was requiring him to use personal computers, and it scared him. This change will require that jobs be redefined in such a way that the people who occupy them will understand the new areas of competence that are needed. It also means incumbents must be trained in new areas of knowledge, skills and behavior.

2. The need for better interpersonal communication will increase as we move toward CIM. This will bring the opportunity for more face-to-face contact between people and for better communication. It also increases the chance that communications could get worse because of more face-to-face contact. How organization structures are redefined will affect communications as well. If new organization structures make it more difficult to communicate, it is less likely that CIM will be a reality.

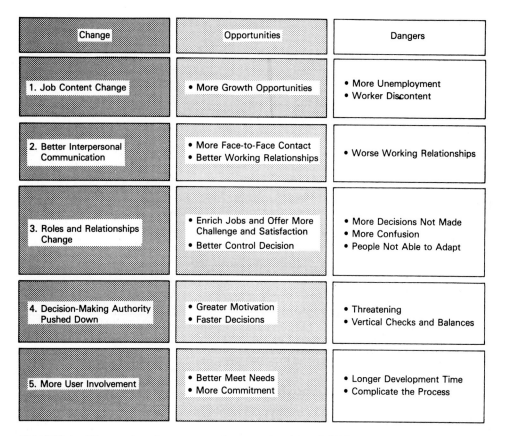

FIGURE 1   Five major changes on the people side of CIM.

3. Roles and relationships will change requiring people occupying certain jobs to behave differently and to perform different tasks in those same jobs. One opportunity of this change is to enrich and give more meaning and more challenge to jobs in the workplace. Another is to better control the decision-making process by clarifying roles and limits of authority. The dangers include more decisions falling through the cracks, more confusion as to who is to do what and poor performance by people not able to adapt to new roles.

We've often seen this happen as MRP systems are installed. In order to work well, the MRP system should be driven by the Master Scheduler who in turn needs to communicate the requirements of the master schedule to the foreman in manufacturing. Often, it is the foreman who has historically decided what to run and at what speeds, especially in firms which are manufacturing driven.

In one case a large manufacturing firm in the midwest decided to install an MRP in their three plants. After the installation had taken place and the various modules had been brought up and used, the people in Materials started to see the plant run at levels in variance with the Master Schedule. After spending weeks checking the software and procedures for some conceptual glitch, it was discovered that the foremen were making decisions about shop loading based on their areas of judgment and on a form of the manual system that the MRP system had replaced. What had happened was that the relationship between the schedulers and the foremen had never been developed; there was very little communication and the attitude of the foremen was that no scheduler was going to tell them how to run their line.

The personnel department had defined the scheduler's new role but they were never trained to fulfill it. The responsibility had been delegated and the roles had changed but no one had thought about how to make sure the schedulers would be able to exercise their new authority or whether they would be accepted.

4. Decision-making authority will be pushed to lower levels as equipment and systems that do more are made available on the shop floor. This could bring higher levels of satisfaction, greater motivation and faster decisions. On the other hand, it carries the danger of being threatening to middle management who see this as being an infringement on their power. There is also the danger of creating vertical checks and balances that will actually *slow down* the process.

In one case, the CEO of a drilling equipment firm in the south put in place a program to push down responsibility to the first line foremen as part of a plan to automate one of his plants. The foremen were trained well this time, but in giving the foremen more responsibility, he took away the responsibility for making certain decisions from the mid-level people—the superintendents—much to their displeasure. The CEO said he wanted to "raise the level of decisions" made by the superintendents so that they didn't have to deal with all the small, nitty-gritty issues.

The problem is he didn't make it clear what the superintendents were supposed to do at that different level and there was never any "contracting" that took place between them and their foremen. As the new equipment was put in place, the superintendents began to demand detailed, written reports from the foremen citing the president's directive that while the foremen had the decision-making responsibility, the superintendents were to "stay on top of things." Many of the foremen were not facile at writing reports, and if the reports weren't detailed enough, the superintendents would send them back to get more detail. The foremen became discouraged and swamped, and soon important deadlines were missed on getting this expensive equipment into operation. The superintendents complained to the president that the foremen just weren't up to the task of assuming more responsibility and pointed to the large investment made in machines that were lying unused. Quietly, the decision-making responsibility moved back to the superintendents.

This change not only threatens the decision-making power of mid-management but, indeed, its very existence in some cases. There will be opportunities for retraining as mid-managers' jobs change, and there will be displacement for those who cannot or will not be retrained. How top management approaches this issue will determine how much of a problem it will be in any one particular firm, and its resolution will go a long way toward making CIM happen.

5. More involvement of the users of new equipment and systems will be necessary in determining what will be designed, and how it is to be used. The opportunity here is that new systems will better meet the needs of the people who are to use them and that those people will be more committed to making them succeed. The danger is that development time will be longer and the process more complicated if some basic rules of power-sharing and communication aren't observed.

One MIS group we know of developed a new system for the company's warehouse and distribution network. As the new system became operational, it ran into a whole host of problems. The users in the warehouses were confused, and the MIS people were working 80-hour weeks to try to find and solve the problem with their system. What is came down to was that the users didn't understand the system and how to use it and didn't believe that it met their needs and solved the problems they faced anyway.

The reason for this was that the MIS group had never surveyed the users enough to fully understand the issues they believed were of most importance and to understand the level of sophistication of the people who had to use the system. The MIS group had gathered some data by talking with upper level people and MIS people from other companies and then made a number of assumptions about what was needed in their company.

Underneath all this was the concept that the MIS director had regarding what the charter of the group was. In her mind, the group was to respond to the needs of upper management by developing systems and then passing them off to the user—and that's where the responsibility and ownership ended. It was up to the user to pick it up from there. This attitude set the tone for the way most of the MIS people acted, and it led to a lack of user orientation, little follow-up to ensure that people understood what was needed, arrogance in dealing with user questions, and ultimately, to the near failure of an expensive system.

What is it that can be done about these sorts of barriers? Like any complicated and multifaceted problem, there is no one thing that will bring resolution; and because we're talking about behavior and habits people have developed over years, it is not realistic to expect resolution to come about quickly or easily either. These barriers can be overcome, though, by following some relatively simple principles.

ROLE OF LEADERSHIP

Organizational change is a "top-down" matter. There is no getting away from the fact that top management must spearhead any change effort—especially one which is of such great strategic significance as Computer Integrated Manufacturing. This means that the CEO must lead the way into the era of integrated manufacturing. To do that, the CEO needs to do more than support CIM; he/she must become intimately involved in it, jump into this new world aggressively and visibly and manage the transition with vigor and imagination. To do so the CEO must describe how the company can be under CIM and in so doing paint an image of the future that is exciting and compelling. The job of creating a common vision cannot be delegated.

There are four ways the CEO can create a common vision:

1. Have a clear picture himself of what CIM is and what it can do and cannot do.
2. Learn skills of creating a common vision, an exciting image of the future including:
   — Using the words that evoke emotions
   — Conveying a conviction that will respond to common needs
   — Conveying conviction with excitement.
3. Get involved in it—attend training sessions along with managers and workers, be visible on the shop floor, learn to use a personal computer.
4. Make sure vice presidents and department heads support it—talk to them about CIM, ask questions about it, stress it and make sure they understand CIM's importance to the CEO.

I do not believe that the way to make this kind of transition is to create a special effort. Some companies have created special programs to bring about CIM. They have people at the vice president level who are charged with bringing about these programs with titles like Vice President, Innovation or Director, Automation Strategy. One problem with doing this is that it sets up another structure that often clouds the fact that making CIM a reality is the responsibility of everyone and each employee should have a part in making it happen as part of his/her job. This doesn't mean that task forces or action teams can't be useful; such ad hoc groups are usually very important vehicles for positive change. The point is that the organization should see management at all levels actively working to create a more effective, efficient company as a part of running the business day to day.

We are talking about changing cultures—and that is iterative, it goes one step at a time, and it takes a long time. It means that old assumptions about the business must be replaced with new ones and then new behaviors must be put in place. One problem with many special programs is that they raise expectations that a culture will change faster than it really can. One way to look at this is to consider the emotional cycle of implementing a new effort such as CIM.

The cycle of implementation goes through some natural stages once a new effort such as Computer Integrated Manufacturing starts (Figure 2). The first is optimism that is often uninformed because people don't have any experience with this new effort or innovation. Expectations are high in this stage—often unrealistic. This is especially true when the leader or champion of the new effort or program is charismatic and creates a compelling vision of the future that captures peoples' imagination.

The second stage is a certain degree of doubt once people realize that this new effort or innovation is not going to do all they imagined, at least not as fast as they believed. As this happens, pessimism grows. This seems to be the most dangerous stage for it is here that many people allow their doubt to turn to frustration, especially if expectations were brought to a very high, unrealistic level during the first stage. The other option for people in the second stage is to stick with the effort and move on with a more wise and realistic perspective.

It is here that individual effort, inventiveness and ingenuity seem to be greatest as people share a hopeful realism. The major task of the leader is to ensure that people make the transition to Stage 3, and make it smoothly. As this takes place new, informal leaders often emerge. These are people who exercise a certain degree of courage in helping others who are frustrated. Change efforts succeed or fail based on the influence of the formal leader and/or informal leaders in this stage.

Stage 4 takes place as people become confident and share an informed optimism about success. Often by this time the original specifications of the innovation or change being implemented have been altered by people involved. They have put their stamp on this effort and have begun to share ownership for it, something the wise leader will encourage. As the innovation becomes part of the accepted way of doing things and becomes integrated into the norms of the organization, satisfaction and a rewarding sense of completion result.

RESOURCES FOR CHANGE

These stages are normal and they happen in sequence. They are to be expected. The leaders (formal and informal) can shorten the time that it takes to go through these stages and can lessen the pessimism to minimize dysfunctional effects.

In addition to various departments being integrated in this effort, there needs to be a new partnership between salaried and hourly workers. We all recognize that CIM means enormous changes on the shop floor—and those changes cannot be successful unless the direct labor work force is committed to success. They must feel

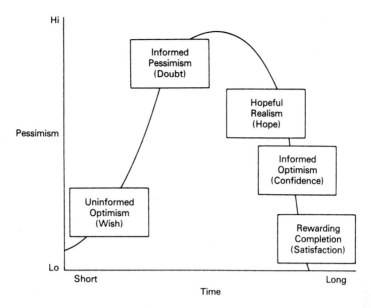

FIGURE 2 Emotional cycle of implementation.

involved and that means that they must participate in determining how CIM will take shape in their company. In order for this to happen, the traditional adversary relationship between management and labor must change—it is dysfunctional and wasteful. The energy and time devoted to skirmishes between the direct labor force and management can be put to much more productive use. Both sides have to reassess their positions and learn to negotiate in such a way that both come out winners.

What is in it for management is to know that labor is aiming for the same goal—for without labor it can't be reached. What is in it for labor is a piece of the action—emotionally through influencing outcomes and financially through plans such as gainsharing.

One of the biggest challenges will be to find and to develop managers and supervisors who can make the most of the technology that is being made available. This will require defining the areas of competence that are needed of managers and supervisors in the era of CIM and developing training programs geared to raising people's knowledge, skills and behavior so that they can perform at that level.

We should look to a new breed of human resources professionals to help in this regard. I believe that most personnel or human resource management departments are not up to this task yet. Many are generally unprepared to meet the challenge, and as a result, there is a woeful lack of creativity in resolving problems associated with the five changes on the people side of the scale described earlier. Many of those departments which are able to meet the challenge often do not have the *influence* to implement new programs. The quality of the human resources department is a reflection of the wants and needs of the CEO. If it is not meeting the needs, it is probably because the CEO doesn't know how a competent HR group can contribute or doesn't care.

The companies who will do best in the era of integrated manufacturing will be those who have state-of-the-art human resources functions providing the programs and counsel necessary on the people side of the scale. What this means is having a human resource function that meets conditions such as these:

- One that is a true service organization with a manager who does not care about building an empire.
- One that includes a personnel administration function that is state-of-the-art in terms of compensation, wage, salary policies, communication to employees and recruiting and hiring.
- One that includes a training and development component that offers managers programs that respond directly to their problems like (1) team building for all "natural work groups"; (2) problem solving and decision making training to ensure people from different departments are addressing problems using a common language and approach; and (3) training to help people become better able to work in groups.
- One that includes an internal consulting component that provides line managers people who can help them solve problems.

Perhaps the most important principle has to do with what we expect. If we believe in something and expect it to work, it has a much better chance of succeeding than if we do not. This is a Pygmalion at work in American manufacturing. Just as Eliza Doolittle learned to speak the King's English because Henry Higgings believed she could do it, we will overcome the people-related barriers to integrated manufacturing if we believe we can do it. If we believe in our hearts that people can't change and that departments will not cooperate, all the technology in the world will not bring about success.

DEVELOPING NEW COMPETENCIES

Given these principles, let's get back to the five changes that CIM is bringing and discuss what specifically can be done about each one.

One had to do with the changing content in many jobs which requires workers to develop and use new areas of competence. There are at least five steps we can take to deal with this change. The first step is that we must assess the characteristics that people bring to these jobs, not merely define job content. This requires identifying for key jobs the necessary competencies in four categories: knowledge, skills, attitude and behavior. (What it is people need to know, what they need to do, and what they should believe and how they should act.)

The second step is to prioritize these competencies to highlight those that will make the most difference in an integrated manufacturing climate.

Third, there should exist a method for the incumbent to assess where he/she stands in comparison to the needed priority competency.

Fourth, there should be made available to each person ways to move from the present level closer to the desired level.

Fifth, there should be a performance appraisal system which rewards development of the competencies that are deemed most important.

As it is used here, "competencies" means those characteristics (areas of knowledge, skills, attitudes and behavior) which distinguish excellent performers from those who are average performers. These often subtle characteristics mean the difference between doing a job that is "good enough" and breaking new ground, going beyond expectations.

One manufacturing firm we know of went through a reorganization three years ago as it began a long-term CIM effort. The job of the supervisor was changed at that time and since then some supervisors performed very well while others did a passable job. The human resources group was asked to design a new training and development program for the supervisors and they decided on a competency-based approach. Fifty-eight different, specific items were defined and judged to be common among the excellent performers and missing among the average performers. These were prioritized, grouped and used as topic areas for a 32-hour training program for all supervisors; that program's design includes exercises, case studies, style questionnaires and lectures which are all geared to this model of supervisor competence. During the program the supervisor is able to gather data on where he/she stands compared to the model of competence, determine personal improvement goals and a plan to achieve them. This is one way to help ensure that training is focused on the areas that will make the most difference.

IMPROVING COMMUNICATIONS

A second change was that more interpersonal communication will be needed. There are a number of training programs available today that can help in this regard. But the first step must be to pinpoint the barriers to communication between people and between departments, and in that way, to define what the precise training needs are. Having a bunch of training programs to improve communication may make some training and development consulting company happy, but it is unlikely to really solve the problem. Do a training needs analysis of some kind and follow that up with training focused on the major needs in the departments that are of most significance to CIM success. The needs analysis can include at least two components: 1) a way to find out what people think their training needs are and which are most important to them, and 2) a competency model that defines which characteristics seem to make the most difference between excellent and average performance. Also, make sure that along with the training program that is bought, the ability to deliver that training is transferred to the company.

Another way to deal with this change is for top management to stress its importance by modeling the kind of behavior that it expects others to use. If the vice president of manufacturing is constantly at odds with the vice president of engineering, they can hardly expect interpersonal communication breakthroughs among people in their departments.

NEGOTIATING NEW ROLES

A third area of change had to do with changing roles and relationships and the requirement for some different behavior. One step to take is that as job requirements change, incumbents should be trained in new ways to influence and to negotiate so that the influence process is a help and not a hindrance to the introduction of new technology. We can view influence in terms of styles that are learned. For a number of reasons we tend to get locked into using one or two of these styles in all situations. One reason we get what we want in some instances and don't in others is that we're using the same style in all cases. Training can help people to learn new ways to influence and also to be able to be facile enough to adapt learning styles to the needs of different situations.

Another way to deal with changing roles and relationships is to put in place a way for people to make a transition into new relationships smoothly. "Contracting" at the emotional level must take place to ensure that new roles, responsibilities and limits of authority are clear and accepted. One way to do so is something called "responsibility/authority charting." Here's an example of how it works. If four people from two different departments had to work together on a new project and used the responsibility/authority charting method, they would go through these steps:

1. Each person individually would break down the task into clear discrete steps that are specific and realistic and stated in measurable terms.
2. The four would then meet to share each individual list and then come to a consensus on a final list of the steps in the task, again making certain each step is stated in specific, measurable terms and is realistic.
3. For each step, the group would then make a determination as to the person who is responsible for making sure that step happens, the person who has authority or veto power over that step, the person(s) from whom support is needed in order for the step to be implemented and the person(s) who should be informed about progress.

The value of a process like this is much like that of a strategic plan—the process is as important as the end product. While the end product, in this case a responsibility/authority chart, gives something to measure progress by, the process of getting there involved negotiating roles, building a working relationship and clarifying how exactly that relationship will be managed to get the job done.

A fourth change is that decision making will be made at lower levels in the organization. The right kinds of training focused where it is needed can help to ensure that people are ready and able to take on that authority; and responsibility/authority charting will help in the "contracting" process. Another major step that can be taken here is to measure the organization's climate and determine the barriers to pushing down responsibility. Once these barriers have been identified, their presence and makeup should be fed back to all employees, and each manager and supervisor should devise a strategy to eliminate or minimize the barriers faced by his or her unit; the success of that strategy should then be assessed as part of the performance review system. Conditions for an effective climate survey include the following:

1. Flexible software that provides for quick turnaround time so that people do not have to wait a long time to hear results of the data analysis.
2. Powerful analysis—able to take various "cuts" of data so that it can be determined how various groups of people feel about a particular issue.
3. Feedback to everyone who takes part in the survey.
4. Followed by an implementation process to work on issues.
5. Analysis that indicates importance to change as well as the issues to address so there is some form of priority.

DEVELOPING USER ORIENTATION

The fifth change is the need for more involvement on the part of people who are to use new systems in the process of determining how those systems will be designed and used. There is no substitute for a true user orientation. (The user of a new machine or system is the customer of the person who put it there.) One specific step to take is to make sure that the charters of the key service functions in the organization are oriented toward service. If not, change them. Make sure the department head believes in a user orientation. Also, train people from the service departments in the skills of good consulting: to empirically assess causes in a problem situation, help the client to understand those causes, help the client to devise solutions and help to implement those solutions in such a way that the client becomes stronger.

CONCLUSION

There is no way that Computer Integrated Manufacturing will become a reality unless the people side of the scale is addressed. People, not technology, will realize the marvelous, exciting potential of CIM. But unless we become smarter about managing people, CIM will go down in history as nothing more than a good idea whose time never came.

The changes on the people side of the CIM scale are profound. The steps for addressing them are not easy ones. At the base of this integrated approach is the need for managers, supervisors and hourly workers in American manufacturing firms to learn how to work together; how to talk to each other. It has not been the norm in the way we have run our factories, but those who do learn how to get people to work together and to talk to each other will emerge the victors in the CIM area.

INDEX

Access protocols, 97
   CSMA/CD, 97
   Token passing, 99
Analysis, 118
Arithmetic logic unit (ALU), 116
ARMCO, 52
Artificial intelligence (AI), 151, 162
Assembly, 244
Assembly charts, 167
AutoCAD, 118, 119
Automated guided vehicle, 171, 172
Automated storage and retrieval (ASR), 170
Automated transportation, 171
Automatic programming of tools (APT), 133
AXES of motion, 132

Back scheduling, 179
Bandwidth, 94
Baseband, 94
Bill of materials, 180
Bit map, 109, 114
Broadband, 94
Bus topology, 96
Byte, 115

CAD hardware, 109
CAD package, 108
CAD software, 118
CAD system, 108
CAD/CAM, 128
Capacity requirements planning (CRP), 183
Cartesian coordinates, 131
Cathode ray tube (CRT), 111, 112
Central processing unit (CPU), 116
Chain reaction, 240
Change, management of, 201
Common causes, 48, 63
Communications, 277
Computer-aided design (CAD), 1, 107, 108
Computer-aided engineering (CAE), 60

Computer-aided manufacturing (CAM), 60
Computer-aided process planning, 168
Computer-assisted programming, 133, 151
Computer-assisted technologies, 260
Computer-integrated manufacturing (CIM), 1, 236
   Benefits of, 240, 262
   Implementation of, 255, 260
   Management cycle for, 5
Computer numerical control (CNC), 134
Computer vision, 162
Continuous improvements, 43
Control charts, 70
Controller, 133, 151, 154
Coordinates, 131
Cost of quality, 16, 57
CSMA/CD, 97, 98
Customer, 45
Cutter Laboratories, 79

Data bases, 121, 124
Data base management system (DBMS), 124
dBASE IV PLUS, 125
Decisions in process (DIP), 209
Degrees of freedom, 153
Deming, W. Edwards, 17
   Chain reaction, 240
   Fourteen points, 64, 237
   Management, 17
   Production system, 166
   Seven deadly diseases, 65, 239
Departmental analysis, 49
Design, 118
Direct labor, 198
Direct numerical control, 134
Distributed numerical control (DNC), 135
Drafting, 121
Drawing editor, 108
Drive unit, 151, 160

Electric drives, 160
Employee involvement (EI), 26, 31
Employee stock ownership plan (ESOP), 104
Encoder, 114
End effector, 154
Engineering drawings, 109
Exchange rates, 13
Expert systems, 162

Facilities planning, 168
Factory management, 195, 199
Fayol, Henri, 19
Feedback, 46
Fetch cycle, 116
Finite element analysis, 119
Fiscal policy, 12
Flexible manufacturing systems, 173
Flow process charts, 167
Fluoresce, 111
Ford, Henry, 44
Ford Motor Company, 49
Frequency division multiplexing, 94

General Motors (GM), 2
Global Competition, 2, 44
Graphics systems, 109
Group technology, 168
Guaspari, John, 16

Hard copy, 109
Hardware, 154
Hydraulic drives, 160

Implementing CIM, 255
Industrial robot, 152
Input devices, 117
Inspection, 49
Institute of Electrical and Electronic Engineers (IEEE), 61
   802 standards, 61
   802.3, 89, 101
   802.4, 89, 100
Integration, 32, 33
International Standards Organization (ISO), 89

Just-in-time (JIT), 26, 31, 135, 138, 229

Kanban, 146
Kilobyte, 116
Kinematics, 121

Lammi, Ray, 17
Lead through programming, 160
Leadership, 36, 273
Local area network (LAN), 94
   Access protocols, 95
   Bandwidth, 94
   Topology, 95
Los Nietos, 52

Machiavelli, 204
Machine centers, 127, 130
Machine tools, 130
Maintenance, 149
Make or buy, 166
Management, 18, 20
   Deming's way, 20
   Integration, 32, 33
   Of change, 201
   Participative, 79
   Traditional, 18, 20
Management information systems (MIS), 59
Management wave, 221
Manipulator, 151, 154
Manufacturing
   cells, 168, 170
   Computers, 244
   Costs, 174, 196
   Economic impact of, 8
   Growth, 10
   Progress, 9
   Technology, 199
   US, 11
   Wages, 9
Manufacturing automation protocol (MAP), 89, 121
Manufacturing resource planning (MRP), 26
Marketing and sales, 108
Mass production, 29
   Benefits, 29
Master production schedule, 180
Materials, 196
Materials handling, 244
Material requirements planning, 174
Matsushita, Konusuke, 18
MRP systems, 176

Natural language processing, 162
NC programs, 133

Non servo control, 151, 154
nP charts, 75
Numerical control (NC), 127, 129

Office automation, 60
Off-line programming, 160
Open systems interconnection (OSI), 90
  Seven layers, 91, 93
Operation sheets, 168
Operations process charts, 167
Overhead, 197

P charts, 75
Parallel transmission, 116
Participative management, 79
Phosphoresce, 111
Pixels, 112
Plotter, 117
Polar coordinates, 131
Pneumatic drives, 160
Printer, 117
Process flow mapping (PFM), 38
Process planning, 166
Process variability, 48
Product design, 108, 243
Product planning, 108
Production management, 245
Production planning, 108, 165
Production system, 166
Programming, 133, 160
Project teams, 262

"Q" process, 53, 61
Quality, 15, 44
  Cost, 57
  Improvement, 56

R charts, 72
Raster technology, 112
Real time, 109
Registers, 116
Requirements (customers'), 45
Ring topology, 96
Robots, 151, 152
Route sheets, 168
Run charts, 68

Serial transmission, 116
Servo control, 151, 159
Servomechanism, 129
Shift register, 114
Simulated motion, 121
Sketchpad project, 109
Soft copy, 109
Special causes, 48, 63
Standard routings, 181
Star topology, 97
Statistical control, 48, 63
Statistical process control (SPC), 63, 87, 105
Stroke technology, 111
Structural trade policies, 13
Supplier, 45

Teach pendant, 160
Technical and office protocol (TOP), 101, 121
Text editor, 108
Time division multiplexing, 95
Time phasing, 182
Token passing, 99, 100
Topology, 95
  Bus, 96
  Ring, 96
  Star, 97
Total quality control (TQC), 26, 31

US manufacturing, 11

Value added, 45
Variability, 46, 48
Video cassette recorder (VCR) 2, 105
Video controller, 107, 112, 113
Video display, 107, 109

Weirton Steel, 104
Weyerhaeuser, 248
Word, 115
Word length, 115
Word processor, 108
Work center schedules, 190
Work in process (WIP), 208
Work process, 45

$\bar{X}$ charts, 72

A 8
B 9
C 0
D 1
E 2
F 3
G 4
H 5
I 6
J 7